In this new book, Li Qu presents a comprehensive and sensitive interpretation of Barth's understanding on the nature of created time and its relation to divine eternity. As a preparation, Li Qu explores representative theological as well as natural, scientific and philosophical accounts of the nature of time and its relation to divine eternity. In the central thesis he argues cogently that it is only from a specifically Trinitarian perspective that God's eternity and our time can be joined concretely and actually. The study is well documented with an extensive bibliography. There is no question that his exposition and analysis of Barth's text are faithful and readable. This is an up-to-date contribution to Barthian scholarship on a very contemporary topic.

Dr Graham McFarlane
Vice Principal Academic
London School of Theology

Concrete Time and Concrete Eternity: Karl Barth's Doctrine of Time and Eternity and Its Trinitarian Background

Li Qu

MONOGRAPHS

© 2014 by Li Qu

Published 2014 by Langham Monographs,
an imprint of Langham Creative Projects

Langham Partnership
PO Box 296, Carlisle, Cumbria CA3 9WZ, UK
www.langham.org

ISBNs:
978-1-783689-78-1 Print
978-1-783689-76-7 Mobi
978-1-783689-77-4 ePub

Li Qu has asserted his right under the Copyright, Designs and Patents Act, 1988 to be identified as the Author of this work.

All rights reserved. No part of this publication may be reproduced, stored in a retrieval system or transmitted, in any form or by any means, electronic, mechanical, photocopying, recording or otherwise, without the prior written permission of the publisher or the Copyright Licensing Agency.

Unless otherwise stated, Scripture quotations are from the New Revised Standard Version Bible, copyright © 1989 National Council of the Churches of Christ in the United States of America. Used by permission. All rights reserved.

British Library Cataloguing in Publication Data
Qu, Li, author.
   Concrete time and concrete eternity : Karl Barth's doctrine
of time and eternity and its trinitarian background.
   1. Barth, Karl, 1886-1968 2. Time--Religious aspects--
Christianity. 3. Eternity--History of doctrines--20th
century. 4. God (Christianity)--Eternity. 5. Trinity.
   I. Title

231.7-dc23

ISBN-13: 9781783689781

Cover & Book Design: projectluz.com

Langham Partnership actively supports theological dialogue and a scholar's right to publish but does not necessarily endorse the views and opinions set forth, and works referenced within this publication or guarantee its technical and grammatical correctness. Langham Partnership does not accept any responsibility or liability to persons or property as a consequence of the reading, use or interpretation of its published content.

Contents

Acknowledgements ix

Abbreviations xi

Introduction 1
    Section 1:
        Temporal and Atemporal God Debate 1
    Section 2:
        The Development of the Conception of Eternity in Barth 5
    Section 3:
        Structure and Literature Review 8
        3.1 The Structure of the Book 8
        3.2 Literature Review 12

Chapter 1 15
    Preliminary Studies
    Section 1:
        Time and Eternity: Historical Theological Views 15
        1.1 "What is time?" The Augustinian Puzzle 15
        1.2 "What is eternity?" The Boethian Definition 20
        1.3 Saint Anselm: Combination of Transcendent and
            Immanent Eternity 24
        1.4 Duns Scotus: The Temporal Eternity 27
        1.5 Schleiermacher: The Suspicious Timeless Eternity 31
        1.6 Conclusion 35
    Section 2:
        Time and Eternity: Modern Physical Views 36
        2.1 Newtonian Absolute Time 36
        2.2 Einsteinian Relative Time 38
        2.3 Quantum Theory and Time 41
        2.4 Time in Quantum Gravity 44
        2.5 Conclusion 45
    Section 3:
        Time and Eternity: Modern Philosophical Views 46
        3.1 Kant: Time as the Form of Inner Sense 46
        3.2 Kierkegaard: Self as Synthesis of Time and Eternity 53
        3.3 McTaggart: Unreality of Time 61

  3.4 McTaggart's Paradox and Stump & Kretzmann's
    ET-Simultaneity 67
  3.5 Conclusion 70

Chapter 2 73
The Eternal Concrete Father
 Section 1:
  Eternal Trinity and Three One-sidednesses 73
   1.1 The Trinitarian Form of God's Eternal Temporality..............73
   1.2 The First One-sidedness...76
   1.3 The Second One-sidedness...78
   1.4 The Third One-sidedness 80
 Section 2:
  The Eternal Creator Revealed 84
   2.1 The Eternal Creator in the Immanent and Economic Trinity...84
   2.2 Revelation Time..90
   2.3 Conclusion 96
 Section 3:
  The Father's Eternal Preservation 97
   3.1 Time as the Form of Creature 97
   3.2 Eternal Preservation of the Creator 100
   3.3 Conclusion 106
 Section 4:
  The Eschatological Creator 106
   4.1 The Creator in Eschatology...106
   4.2 Pannenberg's Response..115
   4.3 Conclusion 120

Chapter 3 123
The Eternal Concrete Son
 Section 1:
  Eternity before Time – The Preexistence of the Son 123
   1.1 The Preexistence of the Son 123
   1.2 Preexistence and Predestination 131
   1.3 Conclusion 134
 Section 2:
  Eternity in Time – The Incarnation of the Son 134
   2.1 The Incarnation of the Son as the Turning Time 134
   2.2 The Incarnation and the Triune God..............................138
   2.3 Incarnation as the Reconciliation between
     Time and Eternity..145
   2.4 Conclusion 149

> Section 3:
>> Eternity after Time – The Resurrection of the Son......................150
>>> 3.1 Jesus' Resurrection as Historical Event 150
>>> 3.2 Jesus' Resurrection as Eternal Event 158
>>> 3.3 Conclusion 161

Chapter 4..163
The Eternal Concrete Holy Spirit
> Section 1:
>> The Eclipse of the Spirit 163
>>> 1.1 The Eclipse of the Spirit?....................................163
>>> 1.2 Some Further Charges 170
>
> Section 2:
>> Holy Spirit the Eternal Creator 173
>>> 2.1 Eternal Concrete Creator..................................173
>>> 2.2 Conclusion 179
>
> Section 3:
>> Holy Spirit the Reconciler in "Time Between"..............180
>>> 3.1 The Reconciler in the Time of Community 180
>>> 3.2 Conclusion 187
>
> Section 4:
>> Holy Spirit the Eschatological Redeemer.......................187
>>> 4.1 The Promise of the Holy Spirit 187
>>> 4.2 Conclusion 199

Chapter 5 201
Conclusion
> Section 1:
>> A Concrete Trinitarian Understanding of Time and Eternity 201
>>> 1.1 Relational in Ontology 201
>>> 1.2 Trinitarian in Background................................204
>>> 1.3 Concrete in Character......................................205
>
> Section 2:
>> The Significance of Barth's Contribution 207
>>> 2.1 It transcends the Temporal and Atemporal Debate...........207
>>> 2.2 It transcends the A-series and B-series Dilemma 210
>>> 2.3 It transcends the Absolute and Relative Controversy..........212

Bibliography.. 215
> Primary Sources 215
> Secondary Sources...215

Acknowledgements

First of all, I am grateful to the Father, Son and Holy Spirit who are the topic of this thesis and the Lord of my life alike. To our triune God is given my deepest thanks and highest praise.

This book is based on a revised version of my PhD thesis. Without the help of many people, this research project would have been impossible. First, I am indebted to my PhD programme supervisor, Dr. Graham McFarlane, for his enduring patience, intelligent advice and strict criticism. The librarians and other staff of London School of Theology gave invaluable assistance in the search for some material.

My special thanks are due to the Langham Partnership (UK & Hong Kong) for awarding a generous scholarship in order to fund this period of research. Finally, to my wife Miranda, belongs all my gratitude for accompanying me and encouraging me continuously in our first five years of marriage.

Abbreviations

CD   *Church Dogmatics*, 13 part volumes, (eds.), G. W. Bromiley and T. F. Torrance, Edinburgh: T & T Clark, 1956-75.
ER   *The Epistle to the Romans*, trans. Sir Edwyn Hoskyns, London: Oxford University Press, 1980.
SJT   *Scottish Journal of Theology*
IJST   *International Journal of Systematic Theology*

INTRODUCTION

Section 1:
Temporal and Atemporal God Debate

The purpose of this book is to study how Karl Barth's doctrine of time and eternity can contribute to the continuing search for a way of understanding the relationship of divine eternity to time or temporality. Traditional debate on this issue focuses on whether eternity, as an attribute of God, is temporal or atemporal. The atemporal trend approaches God's eternity by transcending or negating time, whereas the temporal trend understands the relationship of eternity and time in an immanent way. However, both trends start from time rather than eternity, i.e. the concept of eternity can only be derived from time and not vice versa. For Barth, those advocators of both sides put the cart before the horse and arrive at abstract conclusions. According to Barth, there is no absolute and independent human time outside of God's eternity. Therefore we must start from the triune God and his eternity before a concrete understanding of time could be achieved. It follows, then, that in order to understand Barth's doctrine of time and eternity fully, we need to review briefly the traditional theological arguments first.

What is time? What is eternity? Is divine eternity temporal or atemporal? It appears that from the inception of western Christian tradition as we know it, such questions have fascinated numerous theological minds. The idea that God should be eternal in the sense of atemporal dominates early Christian doctrine. A timeless approach to divine eternity is offered by Augustine and Boethius. Their classical analysis is partially derived from the characteristic of God being omniscient: if God exists outside of time, then God can observe all parts of time throughout the course of history as if they were simultaneous.

For Augustine time and eternity are essentially different from each other. Eternity is perfect stability and total simultaneity; time, however, is unstable and to some extent unreal. Time, in turn, consists of past, present and future. However, what has passed is no longer, what is coming is not yet, and what is, is time only insofar as it becomes past from future. Thus, time tends to be ideal rather than real. Time exists only as the present: the present of the past, the present of the present, and the present of the future.[1] This Augustinian presentism means that time exists in the soul as present memory (*memoria*), present perception (*contuitus*), and present expectation (*expectatio*).[2] Thus the three dimensions of time should be understood as nothing other than a psychological function, an extension of the mind itself. This is our relation to time. On the other hand, God's relation to time cannot be likened to ours. God, as the eternal Creator of time, must exist outside of time and thus transcends time at all times. From God's eternal point of view, all times are simultaneous before the great Creator.

Giving classic definition to God's eternity, Boethius argues that God has divine life that cannot be the same as ours. We creatures lose life to the past or anticipate its future. However the eternal God possesses his life at once, simultaneously, without loss or anticipation. The expression "simultaneous and perfect possession"[3] derives from its opposite concept, i.e. temporal life. Such a simultaneity of all time is not meant to indicate any moment in time, but the absence of temporality. God's "boundless life" thus does not exist in time; on the contrary, it embraces and transcends all time. Furthermore, Boethius' eternity distinguishes itself not only from temporality, but also from time everlasting. The three parts of time – past, present and future – even in the everlasting life still remain separate, and

---

1. Cf. Augustine, *Confessions* XI. 20, trans. R. S. Pine-Coffin (London: Penguin Books, 1961), p. 269. For detailed discussion of Augustine's teaching on time and eternity, see next *chapter*.
2. Cf. Augustine, *Confessions* XI. 28, p. 277.
3. Boethius, *The Consolation of Philosophy*, trans. S. J. Tester (Cambridge: Harvard University Press, 1973), p. 423.

hence cannot be compared with the perfect situation when they are possessed by the eternal God.

After Augustine and Boethius, many Christian thinkers approach divine eternity in an atemporal or timeless way. However, through the course of the history of theology, the atemporal and transcendent character of their doctrine cannot remain unchanged. In Anselm and Duns Scotus we can already sense a certain temporal understanding of divine eternity.

For Anselm, eternity is transcendent but not totally alien to time. On the one hand, he follows Boethius arguing that the being of God possesses life "as a perfect whole at once."[4] According to Anselm, all time is simultaneously present to God's eternity since it is God's eternity that causes everything in time to exist. On the other hand, transcendent though it is, God's eternity also contains all times without wiping out their temporal distinction. God and temporal things do co-exist at the same time. Of course, Anselm does not equally emphasize these two aspects, for the transcendent one dominates throughout his doctrine of eternity. Nevertheless, since there is some immanent characteristic in Anselm's approach, the purely atemporal eternity can no longer be held absolutely.

In Duns Scotus' works, the temporal characteristic of divine eternity becomes more obvious. Following Augustine, Scotus only accepts present as actual and insists that now, and only now, responds to eternity.[5] Such an Augustinian presentism is incompatible with Boethius' classical definition of eternity, since only the "now" or the "instant" can be present to God's eternity, not past and future. In other words, from eternity God can know the future only if he knows it as future, past as past. Temporal events are bestowed to eternity in an order of temporal succession rather than "all at once."[6] Thus God's eternity is temporal rather than timeless.

The traditional debate resumes in a new way nowadays. Since the Cambridge analytical philosopher John Ellis McTaggart published his

---

4. Anselm, *Monologium*, ch. 24, in *Saint Anselm: Basic Writings* (La Salle: Open Court Publishing Company, 1968), p. 83.
5. Cf. Neil Lewis, "Space and Time," in Thomas Williams eds. *The Cambridge Companion to Duns Scotus* (Cambridge: Cambridge University Press, 2003), p. 85; Pascal Massie, "Time and Contingency in Duns Scotus," *The Saint Anselm Journal* 3: 2 (Spring 2006): p. 25.
6. Cf. Massie, "Time and Contingency," p. 25.

article "The Unreality of Time"[7] in 1908, religious philosophers on the subject of time and eternity issues generally fall into one of two camps: A-series or B-series. The series of positions in the tensed "past, present, and future" is the A-series, and that in the tenseless "earlier" or "later" relation is the B-series.[8] Eternity in the A-series sense presumes a God who exists within time. Such a God lives through history like his creatures. The only difference between God and creatures lies in the assumption that God has no beginning and no end. There are several arguments used to make a case for the idea that God is in time. God in the Bible, for example, is thought to be a living God and anyone who lives must live in some temporal framework. Further, God regrets and changes his mind and any change or development must be rooted in time. If God is an agent of change, then he must be in time or at least enter time at the particular point that the change occurs. This is A-series eternity since God's life and changes distinguish past from present from future. Eternity in the B-series sense can be regarded as the modern version of Boethius' classical definition according to which every event is a point in the static four dimensional space-time continuum; every event is either before, after or simultaneous with every other event in the universe; the eternal God, like always, is simultaneous with every event in a tenseless way. Such a God is immutable to any change since there is no real change at all.

In conclusion, both traditional and modern theological debate on the relationship between time and eternity focus on whether divine eternity is temporal or timeless, i.e. whether God exists in time or outside of time. Theologians usually start from time, meditating on its nature and reflecting over its characteristics, then apply what they learn from time to the divine eternity. However, this is not the case in Barth's doctrine of time and eternity. By insisting on a God-to-human and eternity-to-time approach throughout his enormous theological works, Barth changes our understanding of time and eternity reversely.

---

7. J E McTaggart, "The Unreality of Time," *Mind* 17 (1908): pp. 457-74. The arguments in the article had been advanced by McTaggart in chapter 33 of *The Nature of Existence* (Cambridge: Cambridge University Press, 1927) with the simple title of "Time."
8. McTaggart, "Time," p. 88.

Section 2:
The Development of the Conception of Eternity in Barth

Among Barth's immediate predecessors, two have made a great impact on Barth's doctrine of time and eternity. One is Schleiermacher, with whom Barth wrestles throughout his long theological career. By comparing temporal and finite being, Schleiermacher obtains a timeless understanding of divine eternity.[9] At the same time, Schleiermacher also relates eternity to every moment through his famous "feeling of absolute dependence."[10] Our temporal life totally relies on its relationship with the eternal infinite, as he says: "In the midst of finitude to become one with the infinite, and to be eternal in every instance – this is the immortality of religion."[11] In Barth's opinion, Schleiermacher's proposal leaves no place for human and human temporality at all.[12]

Another important predecessor is Kierkegaard. It is of interest to note that Kierkegaard's doctrine of time and eternity plays such an important role in early Barth that in the preface of the second edition of *ER* Barth confesses that: "If I have a system, it is limited to a recognition of what Kierkegaard called the 'infinite qualitative distinction' between time and eternity."[13]

---

9. Cf. Friedrich Schleiermacher, *The Christian Faith*, eds. H. R. Mackintosh (Edinburgh: T. & T. Clark, 1976), pp. 204-6.
10. Cf. Schleiermacher, *The Christian Faith*, pp. 16-8.
11. Friedrich Schleiermacher, *On Religion*, trans. Terrence N. Tice (Richmond: John Knox Press, 1969), p.157.
12. In Barth's words, "[w]e are sometimes assured that our being in the present is pre-eminently our proper, immediate, absolute being in time. But this is only to make a virtue of necessity. Is it not obvious that in the actual present we have no time? Schleiermacher's contention that we are eternally in every moment would seem to be nearer the mark. All this boasting about being in the present really amounts to Schleiermacher's contention. But this suffers from two disadvantages. First, by speaking of eternal being it abandons the problem of man's being in time; and secondly, by claiming for man what can only be postulated of God, it rules out the problem of human being altogether." See *CD* III/2, p. 528.
13. Karl Barth, *The Epistle to the Romans*, trans. Sir Edwyn Hoskyns (London: Oxford University Press, 1980), p. 10.

Under the influence of Schleiermacher and Kierkegaard, in his early period, especially in *ER*, Barth's teaching on time and eternity is to some extent timeless. After Kierkegaard, Barth stresses the infinite qualitative distinction between time and eternity. In such a dialectical relationship, eternity takes absolute preeminence by the fact that Barth defines time in light of eternity by calling time a "parable" of eternity.[14] Furthermore, three dimensions of time are separated by a Schleiermacherian eternal moment: "Between the past and the future – between the times – there is a 'Moment' that is no moment in time. This 'Moment' is the eternal Moment – the Now – when the past and the future stand still, when the former ceases its going and the latter its coming."[15] We can detect here Barth's Augustinian "presentism" and atemporal approach to understand eternity. Roberts rightly points out that in the *ER,* eternity could only be understood as "the intrusion of a timeless 'Moment' 'between' the successive stages in the temporal order."[16]

In some works between *ER* and the *Church Dogmatics,* especially in *The Resurrection of the Dead,*[17] Barth changes his extremely dialectic approach and "criticizes, the 'annihilation' of time by eternity, for 'real eternity' is that which 'marks' time as infinite. Eternity as the timeless tangential intersection is ontologically inadequate, it provides no 'base', and is merely subversive of time, adding nothing to it at all."[18] As for the doctrine of time and eternity in *CD,* Kooi argues:

> If in Barth's early theology the pregnant confrontation between time and eternity was in the foreground and revelation was only conceivable as a canceling out of time, in the *Kirchliche Dogmatik* the opposition is replaced by something which underlies and connects. Therefore Barth can also say,

---

14. Cf. *ER,* p. 497.
15. *ER,* p. 497.
16. R. H. Roberts, "Barth's Doctrine of Time: Its nature and Implications," in S. W. Sykes eds. *Karl Barth: Studies of His Theological Method* (Oxford: Clarendon Press, 1979), p. 99.
17. Barth, *The Resurrection of the Dead,* trans. H. J. Stenning (London: Hodder & Stoughton, 1933).
18. Roberts, "Barth's Doctrine of Time," p. 100. Cf. Barth, *The Resurrection of the Dead,* pp. 110-2.

'God has time for us'. In God's self-revelation time participates in divine duration, in the abundance of God's time at the moment of the revelation. The analogical form prevails. Thus there also remains a difference between God's time and our time, but human time is not cancelled out, but rather receives a foundation and is brought to perfection.[19]

The real situation is not so simple. In *CD* I/2, Barth's fulfilled time or revelation time is, on one hand, a kind of timeless time like the "eternal now" in *ER*, because it is a time that differentiates itself from all other times. On the other hand, since this revelation time is based on a concrete event – the Easter event in which the risen Christ lives in time concretely for forty days – this time is indeed temporal. In *CD* II/1, Barth discusses eternity as pre-, supra- and post-temporality, i.e. "the temporal quality of eternity."[20] Cullman charges Barth for that "eternity may again be conceived as qualitatively different from time, and so as a result there may again intrude that Platonic conception of timeless eternity which Karl Barth in the *Dogmatik* is nevertheless plainly striving to discard."[21] Cullmann's criticism is similar to Moltmann's on *CD* III/2 which we shall discuss in detail in chapter 2. However Cullmann's charge could be justified but Moltmann's could not, because the temporality of eternity in *CD* II/1 is somewhat abstract but that is not the case of *CD* III/2. On the contrary, in *CD* III/2, the temporality of eternity reaches its climax.

---

19. Cornelis Von Der Kooi, *As in a Mirror: Calvin and Barth on Knowing God: A Diptych*, trans. Donald Mader (Leiden: Brill, 2005), p. 359.
20. Oscar Cullmann, *Christ and Time: The Primitive Christian Conception of Time and History*, trans. Floyd V. Filson (Philadelphia: The Westminster Press, 1950), p. 63.
21. Cullmann, *Christ and Time*, p. 63.

Section 3:
Structure and Literature Review

3.1 The Structure of the Book

In chapter 1, I retrieve the development of the terms "time" and "eternity" in three traditions: theological, modern philosophical and modern scientific. Since Barth rarely reflects on the nature of time and eternity, his use of these concepts is relatively uncritical. Thus, as we study Barth's doctrine, we must make clear what these concepts really mean when a theologian, philosopher or scientist employs them.

In theological tradition, the paradigm[22] of interpreting divine eternity shifts from atemporality to temporality. From Augustine and Boethius onwards, the basic view that God's eternity is timeless dominates the tradition. The Medieval Scholastics, eminently Anselm, Thomas Aquinas and John Duns Scotus, advance divine atemporality along a Augustinian and Boethian way. However, absolute atemporality appears more and more difficult to hold and the temporal understanding of divine eternity emerges in the theological tradition. In Anselm and Scotus we detect that the temporal factor permeates the doctrine irretrievably so that it appears so susceptible when Schleiermacher, the direct predecessor of Karl Barth, tries to revive the traditional atemporal interpretation.

In the modern physical tradition, the paradigm of time understanding shifts from Newtonian absoluteness to Einsteinian relativity. Since 1687, with the publication of *Philosphiae Naturalis Principia Mathematica*,[23]

---

22. Borrowed from Thomas Kuhn's landmark work in philosophy of science *The Structure of Scientific Revolutions* (Chicago: The University of Chicago Press, 1962). However, Kuhn's use of the term "paradigm" is obscure. McGrath sorts out two senses in Kuhn: "1. the word is used in a general sense, to refer to the broad group of common assumptions which unites a particular group of scientists – it is an accepted cluster of generalizations, methods, and models; 2. the term is also used in a more specific and restricted sense to refer to a past scientific explanatory success, which seems to offer a framework which can be treated as normative, and is hence treated as exemplary thereafter – until something finally causes that paradigm to be abandoned." See Alister E. McGrath, *Science & Religion: An Introduction* (Oxford: Blackwell Publishers Ltd, 1999), p. 80. Here I use the term in the second sense.

23. Isaac Newton, *The Principia: Mathematical Principles of Natural Philosophy*, trans. I. Bernard Cohen and Anne Whitman (Berkeley and Los Angeles: University of California Press, 1999).

Newton's notion of absolute time dominated the world of physics for the next two hundred years. Newtonian metaphysical absolute time is so ideal that it may only be realized and actualized by God. In the early 20th century, Einstein makes the paradigm shift fundamentally by his Special Theory of Relativity and General Theory of Relativity. In the Einsteinian paradigm, we are forced to think no longer of space and time but rather to look at a four-dimensional space-time continuum, in which time appears to be more space-like than temporal.

Within the modern, western philosophical tradition there are no obvious paradigm shifts. Kant treats time as the form of human inner sense, which is embedded in our mind as *a priori*. Human consciousness is only able to obtain knowledge of the outer world by the use of categories, which are temporally structured. Time, thus, is a bridge between subjective experience and objective world. Further, Kant argues that the validity of time is confined to the subjective experience of the objective world since the reality of time ought not to be applied to "things-in-themselves."[24] Kierkegaard synthesizes time and eternity in human existence. We must see their opinions on these issues are parallel rather than successive or conflicting because they employ the term "time" in different areas. In the twentieth century, McTaggart sets up two paradigms: temporal A-series and atemporal B-series. Nowadays many philosophical discussions on time and eternity can be described as a competition between these paradigms. It is still an ongoing competition in which no side could claim itself as the "dominant paradigm."

In these three traditions, there is no one single dimensional "paradigm shift." When a new paradigm emerges, the old one still retains its vitality by which it can survive the competition. As far as divine eternity is concerned, the temporal-atemporal understanding is still an open question. What Karl Barth contributes to this issue is that he transcends this dilemma from the temporal side and he achieves this within a Trinitarian frame. Bearing this in mind, at the very beginning of chapter 2, I illustrate Barth's unique approach to God's pre-, supra- and post-temporality in light of the unity of

---

24. Cf. Kant, *Immanuel Kant's Critique of Pure Reason*, trans. Norman Kemp Smith (Houndmills: Macmillan Education LTD, 1933). p. 82.

immanent and economic Trinity.[25] Then in the remaining parts of chapters 2, 3 and 4, I focus on the respective relationship between the three persons of divine Trinity and our time.

Chapter 2 to chapter 4 contain material central to this book. In these three chapters, I study Barth's doctrine of time and eternity in a *systematic Trinitarian way*. First, the Father reveals himself as the eternal Creator. In this mode the Father is coeternal with the Son and the Holy Spirit, for eternal Father, Son and Holy Spirit are witnessed in the Old Testament and New Testament in the time of expectation, fulfillment and recollection. In the beginning, God the Father creates time as the form of creature; in our time, God the Father preserves us before our birth, throughout our lifetime and after our death through his Son and Holy Spirit; in the end, God the Father creates everything anew and begins the eternal life with us in the Son through the Holy Spirit.

Second, the Son reveals himself as the eternal Reconciler. Before the incarnation, the eternal Son preexists concretely for us, for our salvation; in the incarnation, the eternal Son, by reconciling time and eternity, becomes contemporary of all times and thus he reveals his lordship over all times; after the incarnation, the resurrected Son brings God's eschatological salvation to our own time, so that we can live in real expectation rather than in despair.

Third, the Holy Spirit reveals himself as the eternal Redeemer. In the beginning, the Holy Spirit proceeds from the Father and the Son, as the coeternal Creator, presenting himself to us, constituting the twofold existence of humanity as body and soul and changes human life into Christian life; in the time between the first and second *parousia*, the Holy Spirit enlightens church history, links the beginning and the end of our salvation history; in the Holy Spirit, the eschatological future is not the future which lies far from our temporal time, since the Holy Spirit presents the future consummation of God's salvation to us in our time here and now.

Although three persons or modes have their divine work eminently in one aspect – the Father in creation, the Son in reconciliation and the

---

25. As Hunsinger comments, "Barth makes perhaps the first sustained attempt in history to reformulate eternity's mystery in fully Trinitarian terms." See George Hunsinger, "*Mysterium Trinitatis*: Karl Barth's Conception of Eternity," in *Disruptive Grace*, p. 189.

Holy Spirit in redemption – there is no separation in the eternal Trinity. Whenever the Trinitarian three are divided in a sharp and absolute way, we inevitably fall into an abstract trap. The oneness and threeness must be held as the two sides of the same coin. Webster thus reminds us:

> [O]f each divine work we need to say (a) that it is *absolutely* the work of the undivided godhead; (b) that each person of the godhead performs that work in a *distinct* way, following the manner and order of that person's hypostatic existence; and (c) that particular works may be assigned *eminently* to one person, without rescinding absolute attribution to the undivided Trinity and without denying that the other two persons also participate in that work in the distinct mode proper to them. For the definition of the person to whom a work is eminently assigned includes that person's relation to the other persons and to the single divine essence; appropriation is not individuation.[26]

From chapter 2 to chapter 4, I rely mainly on paraphrases and internal analysis. While in chapter 5, *Conclusion*, at first I summarize Barth's Trinitarian approach to time and eternity as: relational in ontology; Trinitarian in background; concrete in character. In his doctrine Barth gives a specifically Trinitarian content to the conceptions of time and eternity and thereby significantly moves forward theological understanding of the relationship between these two. Next I bring Barth's doctrine into a conversation with three traditions, which are sketched out in chapter 1. We can see that in the first two traditions, i.e., theological tradition and modern philosophical tradition, Barth's doctrine transcends 1) the traditional debate of temporal and atemporal God, and 2) the A-series and B-series dilemma. In the third, modern scientific tradition, a Trinitarian understanding of time and eternity might also make a contribution to the absolute and relative controversy on the issue of time.

---

26. John Webster, "Trinity and Creation," *IJST* 12: 1 (Jan 2010): p. 16.

3.2 Literature Review

As far as I know, the only Trinitarian reading on Barth's doctrine of time and eternity among the published works is Hunsinger's 1999 essay, "*Mysterium Trinitatis*: Karl Barth's Conception of Eternity." According to Hunsinger's interpretation of Barth, God posits himself as divine Trinity of self-identical (*ousia*), self-differentiated (*hypostases*) and self-united (*perichoresis*),[27] which roughly correspond to God's eternity as "pure duration," "beginning, middle and end," and "simultaneity."[28] In linking divine eternity to time, Hunsinger identifies three patterns in Barth's exposition: 1) the downward vector, the entry of eternity into time; 2) the upward vector, the elevation of time into eternity; 3) the conjunction of simultaneity and sequence, the union of eternity with time.[29] Unfortunately, in this part Hunsinger's reading is almost totally *Christological* (especially in incarnation) rather than *Trinitarian* as he promises. Perhaps that is because he explores briefly the relationship between the Holy Spirit and time in another essay, "The Mediator of Communion: Karl Barth's Doctrine of the Holy Spirit."[30] However, even if we put these two essays together, we still do not have a complete Trinitarian picture of time and eternity. For example, such important and intrinsic topics as the Father's creation and preservation of human time, the preexistence of the Son, the specific role of the Holy Spirit in "time between,"[31] etc., are not covered in these two essays by Hunsinger.

Of course there are some other approaches to explaining Barth's doctrine of time and eternity. An obvious one is reading this doctrine in the mode of creation-reconciliation-redemption, which is explicit in the whole structure of *CD*. One simple reason I do not take that way is that Volume V of the *CD* – The Doctrine of Redemption, which should have been developed in a pneumatic frame – was never written. This also causes some difficulties in chapter 4, *Eternal Concrete Holy Spirit*, therefore I have to find Barth's insights on this doctrine in other parts of *CD* and his other

---

27. Cf. Hunsinger, "*Mysterium Trinitatis*," p. 190.
28. Cf. Hunsinger, "*Mysterium Trinitatis*," p. 197.
29. Cf. Hunsinger, "*Mysterium Trinitatis*," pp. 203-5.
30. Especially in the part 5 "Eschatological in Form." Cf. Hunsinger, "The Mediator of Communion," pp. 173-9.
31. For details about "time between" see section 2 in chapter 4.

works. Another reason appears a little bit complicated: studying Barth in that mode, I would have to focus on God's work rather than God's person. Although perhaps there is no priority between the two in Barth,[32] I still prefer the latter because as Creator, Covenant-partner and Redeemer, the triune God approaches time from eternity in a very personal way.

R. H. Roberts' reading of Barth in his long essay, "Barth's Doctrine of Time: Its Nature and Implications", also takes a Christological framework. While correctly stating that eternity and time are related in Barth's thought after the union of God and humanity in the election, incarnation and resurrection of Jesus Christ,[33] Roberts fails to appreciate the concrete and historic side of the eternal Son. He disastrously sums up Barth's theology as "a reworking of metaphysical theology, albeit in 'biblical' disguise."[34] However, Roberts himself is at fault for he allows the conceptual *analogia fidei* to dominate his methodology. What he can see through a pair of conceptually stained glasses is only the abstract "inner logic" of Barth's doctrine, without concrete blood and flesh.

On the contrary, Robert Jenson overstresses the historicity of Jesus Christ, making Jesus' life the "central event in the life of eternal God."[35] God's eternal being is to some extent "determined"[36] or "defined"[37] by his engagement with history in Jesus Christ. This one-sidedness of emphasizing God's supra-temporality is also caused by a partial understanding of Barth's concrete Trinitarian approach to present the relationship between time and eternity. In this sense Hunsinger comments Jenson's *God after God: The God of the Past and the God of the Future, Seen in the Work of*

---

32. Because Barth always reminds us that there is no hidden God behind the God revealed, i.e., the immanent Trinity and economic Trinity are one. etailed discussion in section 1 of chapter 2.
33. Cf. Roberts, "Barth's Doctrine of Time," pp. 117 ff.
34. Roberts, "Barth's Doctrine of Time," p. 145.
35. Robert Jenson, *God after God: The God of the Past and the God of the Future, Seen in the Work of Karl Barth* (Indianapolis: Bobbs-Merrill, 1969), p. 72.
36. Jason M. Curtis, *Trinity and Time: An Investigation into God's Being and His Relationship with the Created Order, with Special Reference to Karl Barth and Robert W. Jenson* (Edinburgh: Ph D dissertation, 2007), p. 38.
37. George Hunsinger, *How to Read Karl Barth* (Oxford: Oxford University Press, 1991), p. 17.

Karl Barth as "the most provocative, incisive and wrong-headed reading of Barth available in English."[38]

All in all, a fully concrete Trinitarian interpretation of Barth's doctrine of time and eternity is still waiting to be developed. What Barth's specific doctrine can contribute to our general understanding of time and eternity is also a question needing to be addressed. Such are the very tasks I am trying to undertake in this book.

---

38. Hunsinger, *How to Read Karl Barth*, p. 15.

CHAPTER 1

Preliminary Studies

Section 1:
Time and Eternity: Historical Theological Views

1.1 "What is time?" The Augustinian Puzzle

"What is time?" When a theologian or a philosopher faces this question, Saint Augustine's famous reflection comes to mind: "What, then, is time? I know well enough what it is, provided that nobody asks me; but if I am asked what it is and try to explain, I am baffled."[1] This puzzle is recorded in his *Confessions* Book XI, an article dealing with the thesis of time. The book divides into two parts: in the first, Augustine deals with what he calls "cosmic time" in light of creation and defends his argument that time itself

---

1. Augustine, *Confessions* XI. 14, p. 264. On Augustine's doctrine of time, see Etienne Gilson, *The Christian Philosophy of Saint Augustine*, trans. L. E. M. Lynch (London: Victor Gollancz, 1961), pp. 189-96; Christopher Kirwan, *Augustine* (London & New York: Routledge, 1989), pp. 167-86; Serge Lancel, *St Augustine*, trans. Antonia Nevill (London SCM Press, 2002), pp. 407-10; Robert J. O' Connell, S. J., *St. Augustine's Confessions, the Odyssey of Soul* (New York: Fordham University Press, 1989), pp. 135-44; Richard Sorabji, *Time, Creation and the Continuum* (London: Gerald Duckworth & Co. Ltd., 1983), pp. 29-32; Simo Knuuttila, "Time and Creation in Augustine," in Eleonore Stump and Norman Kretzmann eds. *The Cambridge Companion to Augustine* (Cambridge: Cambridge University Press, 2001), pp. 103-15; Genevieve Lloyd, "Augustine and the 'Problem' of Time," in Gareth B. Matthews eds. *The Augustinian Tradition* (Berkeley and Los Angeles: University of California Press, 1999), pp. 39-60; Wolfhart Pannenberg, "Eternity, Time and Trinitarian God," *Dialog: A Journal of Theology* 39:1 (Spring 2000): pp. 9-14; M. B. Pranger, "Time and Narrative in Augustine's Confessions," *Journal of Religion* 81: 3 (Jul 2001): pp. 377-94; Jonathan Westphal, "The Retrenchability of 'the Present'," *Analysis* 62: 1 (Jan 2002): pp. 4-10; Enno Rudolph, "Gibt es eine Theologie der Zeit?" *Zeitschrift für dialektische Theologie*, 16 (2000): pp. 130-1.

began with creation;² in the second, Augustine studies the nature of time itself, what he describes as "the affection of mind."³

Confessions was written in Augustine's early 40s, when he had been the bishop of Hippo for about five years and converted from Manichaeism to Christianity for twelve years. In Augustine's time, Christianity's encounter with the philosophical critique of ancient religiousness had ranged over several centuries and the doctrine of creation and time⁴ also had been the target of many attempted refutations in the centuries before the composition of *Confessions*. However, "what the philosophers objected to," according to Christopher Kirwan, "was not so much creation itself: they could accept, that is, that the universe came into being, and even that it had a maker or makers who brought it into being, but they jibbed at the idea of there being a first moment of its being, a moment with the property that nothing – except perhaps gods – existed before then."⁵ Since the debate between Augustine and the philosophers⁶ concerned not so much as to *whether* the universe was created by God, but rather *when* it was created by God, such questions can be transformed thus: was there any time (finite or infinite) before the act of creation? Augustine answers unequivocally "no" – time did not exist before creation came into existence. Time was made by God together with the cosmos and thus is part of it.⁷ God, as the eternal Creator of time, must exist outside of it rather than inside of it, i.e., God comes "before" or transcends all time. Consequently we cannot confine the Creator's transcendence over time to our creaturely point of view. Thus

---

2. Augustine, *Confessions* XI. 1-13.
3. Augustine, *Confessions* XI. 13-31.
4. Questions such as: "When did God create heaven and earth?" "Was there an idle time of God before the creation of cosmos?" "Why did God create the universe when he did and not at another time?" "Why did God decide to make heaven and earth then, which he had not made previously?" are typical ones raised by Manichaeism to show the absurdities of Christian doctrine of creation implied in Genesis 1:1. Cf. O' Connell, *St. Augustine's Confessions, the Odyssey of Soul*, p. 138; also Henry Chadwick's note in *Saint Augustine Confessions* (Oxford: Oxford University Press, 1991), p. 227. Referring God's idleness "before" the creation, Sorabji calls these "idleness" arguments. See Sorabji, *Time, Creation and the Continuum*, p. 233; also Augustine's original text, *Confessions* XI. 13, p. 262.
5. Kirwan, *Augustine*, p. 155.
6. Especially the Manichees.
7. Cf. Augustine, *Confessions* XI. 13, 14, p. 262-3.

Augustine's answer inevitably leads to a kind of atemporal or timeless eternity of God. Consequently, Augustine argues:

> Although you are before time, it is not in time that you precede it. If this were so, you would not be before all time. It is in eternity, which is supreme over time because it is a never-ending present that you are at once before all past time and after all future time. For what is now the future, once it comes, will become the past, whereas *you are unchanging, your years can never fail* [Ps 101:28]. Your years neither go nor come, but our years pass and others come after them, so that they all may come in their turn. Your years are complete present to you all at once, because they are at a permanent standstill. They do not move on, forced to give way before the advance of others, because they never pass at all. But our years will all be complete only when they have all moved into the past. Your years are one day, yet your day does not come daily but is always today, because your today does not give place to any tomorrow not does it take the place of any yesterday. Your today is eternity. And this is how the Son, to whom you said I have begotten you this day [Ps 2:7], was begotten coeternal with yourself. You made all time; you are before all time; and the 'time', if such we may call it, when there was no time was not time at all.[8]

God's relation to time, thus, cannot be likened to our relation to time. Humans are temporal creatures whose "inability to perceive things simultaneously and in the unity of an indivisible act is primarily the inability of things to exist simultaneously in a permanent and stable unity."[9] We live *in* time, thus we discern the different parts of time – past, present or future; beginning, middle, or end. We are unable to cognize these parts simultaneously, that is the reason why those kinds of "idleness" questions

---
8. Augustine, *Confessions* XI. 13, p. 263.
9. Gilson, *The Christian Philosophy of Saint Augustine*, p. 195.

have been proposed. On the contrary, all times are simultaneous before God. "Simultaneity of all times" has been regarded as the almost standard interpretation of God's atemporal or timeless eternity since Augustine,[10] although few (if any) make it clear how God could perceive or possess all times "at one time."[11] One thing, however, needs to be mentioned: whilst Augustine employs the Son as an example of God's atemporal eternity the relation of eternity and the second person of the Trinity lacks some inevitability – to explain "this day" as "coeternal" seems too casual to be accepted. However, when Karl Barth bridges time and eternity, as we shall see in the following chapters, the Son acts as the inevitable agent with and through whom time is created from God's eternity.

The second part of *Confessions* Book XI begins with one puzzle mentioned above that baffled Augustine. Admittedly, Augustine is not baffled for long – he arrives at the existence of the three divisions of time by apagoge:

> All the same I can confidently say that I know that if nothing passed, there would be no past time; if nothing were going to happen, there would be no future time; and if nothing were, there would be no present time.[12]

These three categories, however, do not exist on the same level. Since the past is no longer and the future is not yet, neither is as actual as the present. Thus, Augustine places the present in the central part of the structure of time so that the past and the future must be understood in light of the present. "It might be correct," observes Augustine, "to say that there are three times, a present of past things, a present of present things, and a present of future things. Some such different times do exist in the mind, but nowhere else that I can see. The present of past things is the memory; the present

---

10. We shall see it more clearly in Boethius' classical definition in the next section.

11. The difference between these two kinds of relations, i.e., God-time and human-time, is summarized by Lloyd as: "God is envisaged as having a completeness of self-knowledge in which no aspect or element of his being remains absent or opaque. The human mind, in contrast, cannot have it all at once." See Lloyd, "Augustine and the 'Problem' of Time," p. 40.

12. Augustine, *Confessions* XI. 14, p. 264.

of present things is direct perception; and the present of future things is expectation."[13]

We can draw two conclusions from Augustine's discussion. First, the existence of time is dependent upon the human consciousness, a thinking self-being behind the three divisions of time.[14] Along with Slaatte, we can give an existential interpretation of Augustine's meditation: "Time, for Augustine, did not mean objective movement or measurement, as it did for Aristotle, but a mental product of concrete, personal experience."[15] Furthermore, we can tell that here time is not related to the human subject in general, but to the concrete individual, say, Augustine himself – that is, the thinking subject.[16]

Second, as a consequence, the three divisions of time appear to be the direct result of the intuitive observation of the thinking subject. How can I think about time in a different way? I remember the past, feel or think (it depends on whether I am an existentialist or a rationalist) about the present and expect the future. I cannot change the past, e.g. awarding England the championship of the last World Cup instead of Spain. In the future I may have certain influence, e.g. queuing a whole night to get a better seat at the Royal Opera House; but it always seems impossible to make my lottery ticket the winning ticket. At last, fortunately, the present is highly under my control. For example, although I am not sure if the girl I have been

---

13. Augustine, *Confessions* XI. 20, p. 269.
14. As Knuuttila puts it: "Augustine does not offer any philosophical or theological definition of time in Book II of the *Confessions*. He tries to explain how we are aware of time and how its existence could be explained from the psychological point of view." See Knuuttila, "Time and Creation in Augustine," p. 113.
15. Howard Alexander Slaatte, *Time and Its End* (New York: Vantage Press, 1962), p. 40. Genevieve Lloyd also interprets Augustine's treatment of time in an existential way: "In the Confession he attempts to take account of time as it bears on human existence – to engage with the ways in which time makes him 'a problem to himself.' The work tells the story of his gradual coming to understand what it is to be a consciousness in time. If we are to understand fully what he has to say about time, we must take seriously the fact that it occurs in the context of an autobiography." See Lloyd, "Augustine and the 'Problem' of Time," p. 39.
16. "It is in my own mind," says Augustine, "then, I measure time." See Augustine, *Confessions* XI. 27, p. 276.

admiring secretly will say that she also loves me, it is up to me as to whether I give her a bunch of roses or a greeting card.[17]

However, Augustine's teaching about the nature of time is not without problems: when past and future are retrenched into the present, are they (all three divisions of time) simultaneous? If at present, I remember past things; at present, I perceive present things; again at present, I expect future things, does this not mean I am able to perceive things simultaneously like God? And does my temporality look like eternity? Indeed at this point we raise one of the more serious critiques of Augustine's doctrine of time: Augustine's tentative solution of dealing with time as a *distentio animi*, the spreading out of the soul in the region of dissimilitude as the present memory of the past, and the present perception of the present, the expectation of the future, makes time look really like eternity.[18]

Apart from this eternity-like present, we cannot find a coherent Christological and Trinitarian stand in *Confessions* such as we may learn later from Karl Barth's ideas about time and eternity in *CD* II/1, where Barth regards eternity as an attribution of God from the beginning, and the three divisions of time cannot be thought about apart from Jesus Christ the Son – the eternal word of God becomes the temporal human being. Compared with Barth's teaching, Augustine's doctrine is more personal and existential.

1.2 "What is eternity?" The Boethian Definition

Boethius inherited Augustine's main idea about God's eternity, namely, the simultaneity of all time, in his definition of eternity.[19] It was Boethius who

---

17. The interactions of the subject and three divisions of time may vary from one thinker to another. For example, while Augustine relates past, present and future to memory, perception and expectation, Kierkegaard matches them with repentance, anxiety and despair. Although both Augustine's and Kierkegaard's teachings imply some existential and psychological characters, the latter is definitely more emotional than rational. When those interactions are perceived from different perspectives, the difference of the results could be huge. We may see it more clearly when we discuss Kierkegaard in section 3 of this chapter.

18. "His solution," says Sorabji, "that past, present and future can all be available at once as a *distentio* in the mind, has the paradoxical effect of making time more like eternity. Time is frozen for inspection, and available all together." See Sorabji, *Time, Creation and the Continuum*, p. 30.

19. "Two ideas are prominent," says Kirwan, "in Augustine's perplexing account of eternity: God's years stand, and all of them are present simultaneously. Both ideas had been anticipated by Plotinus and recur in the more famous more influential definition

"above all transmitted to the Christian middle ages the Neo-Platonist concept of eternity"[20] and thus, gave God's eternity a classical definition. The definition was recorded in the last book of *The Consolation of Philosophy*, which, among all Boethius' works, is rightly esteemed the climax of his achievement:

> Eternity, then, is the whole, simultaneous and perfect possession (*possessio*) of boundless life, which becomes clearer by comparison with temporal things.[21]

This classical definition has been held as the typical statement of atemporal eternity ever since. The three definitive terms "whole (*tota*)," "simultaneous (*simul*)" and "perfect (*perfecta*)," some scholars believe, exclude the duration of time.[22] Boethius raises a sharp contrast between eternity and temporality. The former is something like a mathematical point and this point, located outside of the temporal line, corresponds to each point of the line. The latter is, even though infinite, merely momentary fragments. Since Boethius derives his concept of eternity by comparison with

---

of eternity by Boethius a century later." see Kirwan, *Augustine*, p. 169. For Boethius' opinions on time and eternity, see Henry Chadwick, *Boethius: The Consolations of Music, Logic, Theology, and Philosophy* (Oxford: Clarendon Press, 1981), pp. 217-8, 244-7; Sorabji, *Time, Creation and the Continuum*, pp. 119-20, 255-6; E. J. Khamara, "Eternity and Omniscience," *Philosophical Quarterly* 24: 96 (Jul 1974): pp. 204-19; Brian Leftow, "Boethius on Eternity," *History of Philosophy Quarterly* 7: 2 (Apr 1990): pp. 123-42; Eleonore Stump and Norman Kretzmann, "Eternity," *The Journal of Philosophy* 78: 8 (August 1981): pp. 429-58.

20. Sorabji, *Time, Creation and the Continuum*, p. 119.
21. Boethius, *The Consolation of Philosophy*, p. 423.
22. Two previous King's College London scholars, Richard Sorabji and Christoph Schwöbel, both argue that Boethius' eternity does not allow duration: "Duration," says Sorabji, "has been read into not only the talk of completeness, of life, and into the talk of staying still. Someone might want to add the point that eternal life cannot end. But it will already be clear how these ideas are to be understood in the context of an eternal life God can possess the *completeness* of life, precisely because his life is not spread out. Staying still is a negative idea excluding change rather than implying duration, and the same goes for unendingness." See Sorabji, *Time, Creation and the Continuum*, p. 121, italic by the original author. "Eternity in this sense," in Christoph Schwöbel's words, "not only implies that God is not subject to the perishing characteristic of finite created being, but also that as an atemporal being God has no location in time and no temporal duration and that temporal indicators cannot be predicated of him." See Christoph Schwöbel, *God: Action and Revelation* (Kampen: Kok Pharos, 1992), p. 52.

its opposite, i.e., time or "temporal things," and since only the latter can be described, imagined or reasoned, all characteristics of God's eternity, actually, can only come from its opposite by comparison. Boethian eternity is no more than the negation of temporal things: no temporal thing can "embrace" whole space and time equally,[23] whereas eternity possesses them perfectly;[24] no temporal thing can "grasp" past and future, whereas eternity holds them in its hands. By this "simultaneous and perfect possession," Boethian eternity differs from Platonic and Aristotelian eternity.

For Aristotle, Boethius argues the time of the world has no beginning or end, hence is infinite. However, the Aristotelian infinite time cannot possess "the whole space of its life" simultaneously because both the past and future are out of its reach. Thus the infinity of time does not deserve to be called eternity.[25] The situation is similar in Plato's case. Boethius claims that the Platonic "coeternal"[26] created world is not eternal either. Even the world is drawn out from the life of the eternal God. As such, it does not automatically share the ability of divine mind, which alone can embrace at once the whole time. Boethius calls this Platonic world "perpetual (*perpetuum*)" and insists that God alone is indeed "eternal (*aeternum*)".[27]

Both the Platonic and Aristotelian concepts of eternity, which are connected with immutability, are also derived from negation: time requires a beginning and an end, so that whatever is without beginning and end is necessarily atemporal, and is in this sense eternal. However, for Boethius, the decisive factor is not the infinity of time, but rather the simultaneity of all time. We may see from Boethius' argument that past, present and future even in the everlasting world still remain separate and incommunicable,

---

23. "For whatever lives in time proceeds in the present from the past into the future, and there is nothing established in time which can embrace the whole space of its life equally, but tomorrow surely it does not yet grasp, while yesterday it has already lost." See Boethius, *The Consolation of Philosophy*, p. 423.

24. "Whatever therefore comprehends and possesses at once the whole fullness of boundless life, and is such that neither is anything future lacking from it, nor has anything past flowed away, that is rightly held to be eternal, and that must necessarily both always be present to itself, possessing itself in the present, and hold as present the infinity of moving time." See Boethius, *The Consolation of Philosophy*, p. 423, 425.

25. Cf. Boethius, *The Consolation of Philosophy*, p. 423.

26. Boethius, *The Consolation of Philosophy*, p. 425.

27. Boethius, *The Consolation of Philosophy*, p. 427.

and hence have nothing in common with the uniform and perfect situation when God embraces them in eternity. The distinction between eternity and perpetuation makes the atemporal characteristic of Boethius' eternity extremely outstanding.[28] An analogy given by Larson can properly illustrate the Boethian distinction between temporality and eternity:

> Perhaps eternity may be likened to a bookcase full of books, all of which are ordered alphabetically, but which are yet equally and simultaneously accessible to an "eternal observer" who stands apart from the books, i.e., is transcendent to the books.[29]

The significance of the distinction rests, however, at an epistemological level rather than an ontological level. "Everything which is known," according to Boethius, "is grasped not according to its own power but rather according to the capability of those who know it."[30] This principle can explain why he employs "possession" as the key word of his classical definition. When the distinction between eternity and temporality transforms into the distinction between God and human, we may understand the term "possession" even better.

In the very last section of *The Consolation of Philosophy*, Boethius discusses the distinction of two thinking subjects – God and human. Here we meet with a further distinction: prevision (*praevidentia*) and providence (*providentia*). Boethius' notion of "possession" does not mean the former but the latter. "The divine perception," Boethius points out, "runs ahead over every future event and turns it back and recalls it to the present of its own knowledge, and does not alternate, as you suggest, foreknowing now this, now that, but itself remaining still anticipates and embraces your change at one stroke. And God possesses this present instant of comprehension and

---

28. The distinction between eternity and perpetuation could be found in Augustine's doctrine as well, but not as sharp as the one which Boethius raises here.
29. Duane H. Larson, *Times of the Trinity* (New York: Peter Lang Publishing Inc., 1995), p. 23. In *The Consolation of Philosophy*, similarly, Boethius has his own analogy in which God's providence is likened to seeing things in prospect from the highest mountain.
30. Boethius, *The Consolation of Philosophy*, p. 411.

sight of all things not from the issuing of future events but from his own simplicity."[31] While the successiveness remains as the limitation of human perception, God transcends it by his simultaneity. Even human life can be endless, but it does so as a series of moving moments and has nothing in common with God's eternal perfection or perfect eternity.

Boethius' definition of eternity, for its succinct expression and abundant content, remains as the starting point of the subsequent theological and philosophical discussion till our age.[32] However, the atemporal and transcendent characteristic of his definition cannot remain unchanged. In the following parts, we may detect how the temporal and immanent factors were developed by the theologians of different periods.

1.3 Saint Anselm: Combination of Transcendent and Immanent Eternity

Anselm of Canterbury is an important successor of Augustine and Boethius. He inherited and developed some key issues concerning time and eternity raised by them.[33] For example, in his definition of eternity, Anselm is indebted to Boethius' classical definition: "if this Being [God] is said to exist always; since for it, it is the same to exist and to live, no better sense can be attached to this statement, than that it exists or lives eternally, that is, it possesses interminable life, as a perfect whole at once. For its eternity apparently is an interminable life, existing at once as a perfect whole."[34] For Anselm, as for Boethius, God's eternity transcends time: "He exists before

---

31. Boethius, *The Consolation of Philosophy*, p. 433.

32. In 1981, Eleonore Stump and Norman Kretzmann published their article "Eternity" in *The Journal of Philosophy* 78: 8 (August 1981) and soon became a modern classic. The article based its argument on Boethius' definition.

33. For Anselm's opinions on time and eternity, see G. R. Evans, *Anselm and Talking about God* (Oxford: Clarendon Press, 1978), pp. 57, 72, 130; Jasper Hopkins, *A Companion to the Study of St. Anselm* (Minneapolis: University of Minnesota Press, 1972), pp. 29, 160-1; Brian Leftow, *Time and Eternity* (Ithaca and London: Cornell University Press, 1991), pp. 183-216; Nelson Pike, *God and Timelessness* (London: Routledge and Kegan Paul, 1970), pp. 130-66; Dennis C. Holt, "Timelessness and the Metaphysics of Temporal Existence," *American Philosophical Quarterly* 18: 2 (Apr 1981): pp. 149-56.

34. Anselm, *Monologium*, in *Saint Anselm: Basic Writings* (La Salle: Open Court Publishing Company, 1968), p. 83.

all things and transcends all things, even the eternal things. The eternity of God is present as a whole with him."³⁵

However, the similarity between Boethius and Anselm stops here. In fact, both discuss the concept of eternity from different contexts. Anselm's prime aim in developing his notion of eternity is to explain how God's independence is possible.³⁶ Thus his motivation is ontological, whereas Boethius' definition is given to answer an altogether different, epistemological problem concerning God's omniscience. It is not surprising, therefore, to find that the Boethian and Anselmian definitions are not quite the same.³⁷ Anselm argues:

> It is also evident that this supreme Substance is without beginning and without end; that it has neither past, nor future, nor the temporal, that is, transient present in which we live; since its age, or eternity, which is nothing else than itself, is immutable and without parts. Is not, therefore, the term which seems to mean *all time* more properly understood, when applied to this Substance, to signify eternity, which is never unlike itself, rather than a changing succession of times, which is ever in some sort unlike itself? ... For, since it has already been shown that this Substance is nothing else than its own life and its own eternity, is in no wise terminable, and does not exist, except as at once and perfectly whole, what else is true eternity, which is consistent with the nature of that Substance

---

35. Anselm, *Proslogium*, chap. 20, in *Saint Anselm: Basic Writings*, p. 26.
36. Cf. Evans, *Anselm and Talking about God*, p. 57.
37. In *A Companion to the Study of St. Anselm*, Hopkins says: "Since Anselm knew the *Consolation of Philosophy*, he is obviously indebted to Boethius for his definitional formulation. In a broad sense, of course, both Anselm and Boethius are drawing upon Augustine's distinction between eternity and perpetual existence in time. Eternity differs from perpetuity because in the former there are no distinction of before and after, earlier and later. That is, eternity is eternity precisely because its dimension is altogether nontemporal. Although Anselm in the *Monologion* is reflecting Augustine's viewpoint, he is doing so exactly in terms of its Boethian articulation" (p. 29). It seems that Hopkins has missed the background difference between Boethius and Anselm due to their literary similarity.

alone, than an interminable life, existing as at once and perfectly whole?"[38]

On the other hand, the Anselmian transcendence is not as absolute as is its Boethian counterpart. An intrinsic relationship of time and eternity is discernible in this paragraph: "Eternity has its own "simultaneity" and encompassed all of the things that occur at the same time and place and that occur at different times and places."[39]

For Anselm, eternity is supra temporal but not totally alien to time. On the contrary, it contains and sustains all times without wiping out their temporal distinction. He argues that without God nothing could anywhere or ever exist. As such, God must exist everywhere and always.[40] Consequently, God and temporal things do exist at once or at the same time. Here we need to compare two scholars' opinions about this question: on which level, according to Anselm, is God intrinsic to time? Firstly, we may discern a weak interpretation in Hopkins:

> Whatever is going to happen, as well as what has already happened, is present to the mind of God without temporal distinction. Accordingly, God views all things as if they were present, so that rather than having *foreknowledge* of the future which we await, he has knowledge of an eternal present. In viewing all human choices from within this eternal present, his knowledge no more interferes with the freedom of these choices than does one human being's awareness of another's (temporally) present choice interfere with that other's freedom.[41]

---

38. Anselm, *Monologium*, pp. 82-3.
39. Anselm, *On the Harmony of the Foreknowledge, the Predestination and Grace of God with Free Choice*, trans. Hopkins and Richardson, in *Anselm of Canterbury*, vol. 2 (London: S. C. M., 1976), p. 162.
40. Cf. Anselm *Monologium* chap. 21, pp. 72-8.
41. Hopkins, *A Companion to the Study of St. Anselm*, p. 160-1, italic by the original author.

Secondly, a strong explanation can be found in Leftow:

> We have seen the *Monologion*'s elaborate dialectic struggle for a way to say that an eternal God is somehow present *in* and located *at* all times, though not contained by any. Finally we have seen Anselm argue that eternity is like a super temporal coordinate, and this allows God to be *with* all times and temporal creatures at once while all these remain temporally discrete.[42]

Hopkins' italic, *foreknowledge,* takes a stand which is even weaker than Boethius', for he only allows God to interfere with time in a Boethian *previsional* sense rather than a *providential* sense. Comparatively, Leftow's italics indicate a much deeper intrinsic relationship between eternity and time, which is, I believe, also desired by Anselm himself.

Since there are some common substances between eternity and time, Leftow says that, "Anselm holds that God is temporally omnipresent."[43] Anselm's teaching may be illustrated well by many concrete and personified analogies employed by Barth. For Barth, as for Anselm, the purely atemporal eternity can no longer be accepted as viable.

1.4 Duns Scotus: The Temporal Eternity

In the late medieval period, from the works of Duns Scotus,[44] we can identify a temporal approach to the understanding of time and eternity. Time, for Scotus as for Aristotle, is primarily the number of motion with respect to before and after, viz., the objective measurement (*mensura*).[45] As a scholastic realist, Scotus' ultimate concern is always the reality of physical

---

42. Leftow, *Time and Eternity*, p. 216, italics by the original author.
43. Leftow, *Time and Eternity*, p. 191.
44. For Duns Scotus' opinions on time and eternity, see Richard Cross, *Duns Scotus on God* (Aldershot: Ashgate Publishing Limited, 2005), pp. 121-3; C. R. S. Harris, *Duns Scotus*, vol. 2 (New York: The Humanities Press, 1959), pp. 129-46; Michael Sylwanowicz, *Contingent Causality & the Foundations of Duns Scotus' Metaphysics* (Leiden: E. J. Brill, 1996), pp. 182-6; Lewis, "Space and Time," pp. 69-99; Massie, "Time and Contingency in Duns Scotus," pp. 17-31.
45. Cf. Harris, *Duns Scotus*, vol. 2, pp. 129-30; Lewis, "Space and Time," pp. 89-90.

objects and their motions. On the one hand, time appears to have only a subjective existence, since it does not add anything substantial to motion. Thus, Harris points out that,

> Just as number adds no substantive determination to the things numbered, so time adds no real characteristic to motion, but is only a subjective mode under which motion is conceived, a conceptual determination applied to motion by the mind. And though the motions of time and motion are formally distinct, the reality to which they are referred is one and the same.[46]

On the other hand, such an Aristotelian notion does not exhaust the essence of time. Scotus also seeks a compromise between the Aristotelian objective view and the Augustinian subjective view.[47] Although, as stated above, time and motion are objectively identical, their conceptual distinction does make a difference. While there can be no motion without time, we can conceive of time without motion, because even in a world where motion had ceased we could still have a notion of before and after. That is to say, subjective time can be independent of objective motion. Such potential time could be the state of an incorporeal creature, whose genuine rest can be measured without motion.[48]

As for eternity, Scotus' doctrine is even more complicated. In addition to the time-eternity double distinction, he proposes a triple distinction: eternity, eon and time.[49] He distinguishes these three types of "measurements" (*mensurae*) according to the respective objects (*mensurata*) they measure: God, as a simple and changeless being, is measured by eternity;[50]

---

46. Harris, *Duns Scotus*, p. 130.
47. As Lewis puts it, "Although many philosophers have been quite prepared to grant, against Aristotle, the possibility of extra-or intracosmic void, very few have been prepared to dispute Aristotle's rejection of the possibility of time without motion. And yet Scotus thinks that it is possible for there to be time in a certain sense in the total absence of motion." See Lewis, "Space and Time," pp. 89-90.
48. Cf. Lewis, "Space and Time," pp. 91-92.
49. Cf. Harris, *Duns Scotus*, p. 141.
50. This is, of course, an Augustinian and Boethian stand.

the creature falls into two kinds – the one, which is actually changeless, but potentially susceptible of change, e.g., abstract conceptions (substances, qualities, etc.), spiritual entities (pure human soul, angels, etc.), is measured by eon; the other, which is both actually and potentially subject to change, e.g., stones, plants and animals, is measured by time. Eternity has neither beginning nor end; eon has beginning but no end; time has both beginning and end.[51]

Even though the "Subtle Doctor" had made such a subtle triple distinction, it is still very controversial whether his eternity is timeless or not. In one place, he appears to accept the Boethian definition:

> Eternity then includes "life" as part of its connotation, because life is the quasi subject of foundation for eternity. Now it is certain that life, like perfect existence, is in God extramentally. But the other three components of the Boethian definition, namely, "endless" (which excludes cessation), "all at once" (which excludes succession), and "possessed perfectly" (which excludes dependence and participation), only add to "life" a positive or negative relation, it seems.[52]

However, it is difficult to maintain an absolutely timeless interpretation of the Boethian definition, for the central part of the definition has been moved to "life" rather than "the other three components", and that reads into the whole definition much existential and subjective inclination. Furthermore, elsewhere Scotus does reject the Boethian *totum simul*:

---

51. Cf. Harris, *Duns Scotus*, pp. 143-4.
52. Duns Scotus, *God and Creatures, The Quodlibetal Questions*, trans. F. Alluntis and A. B. Wolter (Princeton: Princeton University Press, 1975), p. 142. Harris holds that Scotus' eternity is something like Boethian *totum simul*. Cf. Harris, *Duns Scotus*, p. 144, but Cross reminds us: "Boethius' definition might just be a way of asserting that God's life is not a process. He possesses all his parts or intrinsic properties at once. But the same could be true of a completely intrinsically static but everlasting item, and perhaps even of substances in general, provided that we distinguish a substance from its life-story. For a substance may not be a process even if its life-story is. Temporal items do not have to have temporal parts. On many – indeed, most – views of substances, not only ancient and medieval but also modern, a material substance is not a four-dimensional object, but a three-dimensional object that, for any time that it exists, exists as a whole." See Cross, *Duns Scotus on God*, p. 122.

> There is nothing of time but an instant. Therefore, although [time] flows continuously, it will not simultaneously be a whole in respect of eternity... Therefore, nothing is present to eternity but a 'now' of time.[53]

Obviously, such an Augustinian "presentism" is incompatible with Boethius' classical definition of eternity, since only the 'now' or the 'instant' can be present to God's eternity, not the past and the future.[54] Thus eternity is temporal rather than timeless. Cross argues for God's timelessness in Scotus by asserting that there is no temporal gap between God's willing and its effect: God's willing is causally sufficient for its effect and God does not have to wait for the result.[55] Unfortunately, God's will, according to Scotus, is not as "causally sufficient" as it appears. On the contrary, in order to reconcile God's immutability with the truth that something new really happens in the world, Scotus has to introduce "other causes" into the relation of God and world. Hence God's will cannot solely account for the new effect caused.

Retaining God's immutability, Scotus argues, three principles are needed: first, a complete immutable agent cannot produce immediately any new movement or mobile thing; second, an immutable agent cannot cause immediately a new kind of effect; third, and the most important, a completely immutable agent could not immediately cause a new kind of effect *unless* other causes intervened.[56] Considering all these three principles, Scotus confirms both God's immutability and the new effect caused (e.g. human activity) in the world. As Sylwanowicz puts it: "This created effect is a radically new and distinct locus of self-moving activity in its very essence and thus cannot be thought of as person to God's eternity prior to its actual existence in history."[57] The actual person cannot be seen as physically

---

53. Scotus, *lectura* I, d. 39, qq. 1-5, n. 85, cited in Lewis, "Space and Time," p. 85.
54. Lewis argues that: "this leaves open the possibility that the future and past are real, only not present, and thus are fit objects for God's eternal vision, which extends to all that is real. Rather, Scotus means that all that is real of time is an instant – the present instant." See Lewis, "Space and Time," p. 85.
55. Cf. Cross, *Duns Scotus on God*, p. 122-3.
56. Scotus, *God and Creatures, The Quodlibetal Questions*, pp. 482-3.
57. Sylwanowicz, *Contingent Causality & the Foundations of Duns Scotus' Metaphysics*,

present to God's eternity, otherwise Scotus would contradict himself, for he admits above that "nothing is present to eternity but a 'now' of time only is simultaneous with God's eternity." Thus, combining 1) the immutable God does generate something new; and 2) God's eternity is only simultaneous with our actual present; we confirm that for Scotus, 3) God's eternity is temporal rather than timeless.

Furthermore, Scotus' eternity, like time, is also a kind of duration, although these two durations have some substantial differences: eternity, containing no past and future, is a duration without parts or divisions, whereas the duration of time is essentially made up of parts.[58]

In Scotus' doctrine of time and eternity, we may detect that the Augustinian and Boethian purely atemporal views of eternity can no longer be accepted in their original senses. The temporal factor becomes more and more obvious. Scotus, as an outstanding representative of late medieval theology, bridged the ancient doctrine and its modern development. Although some parts of his teaching, e.g., the potential time, the three divisions of eternity, eon and time are quite difficult for modern readers to understand,[59] we are still indebted to him for his subtle analysis of immutability and new effect which has surely deepened our reflection upon this doctrine.

1.5 Schleiermacher: The Suspicious Timeless Eternity

Positively or negatively, Schleiermacher played a unique role in Barth's life-long mental activity.[60] Schleiermacher is both the father of liberal theology and its most talented representative. Much of Barth's early reputation was based on his critique of nineteenth-century liberal Protestantism,[61] and

---

pp. 182.
58. Cf. Harris, *Duns Scotus*, p. 144.
59. Cf. Harris, *Duns Scotus*, p. 146.
60. For the relation of Schleiermacher and Barth, see James O. Duke and Robert F. Streetman eds. *Barth and Schleiermacher: Beyond the Impasse?* (Philadelphia: Fortress Press, 1988); Robert Sherman, *The Shift to Modernity* (New York: T & T Clark, 2005).
61. "What has established itself as the conventional picture of Barth (one with which Barth himself at times agreed) was that his theology changed gear twice: once when he moved away from theological liberalism, and once more when he moved beyond 'dialectical' theology into his mature dogmatic work." See John Webster, "Introducing Barth," in *The Cambridge Companion to Karl Barth*, eds. John Webster (Cambridge:

there is still ongoing debate with Schleiermacher in Barth's late works.[62] However, in spite of many well-known differences, there may be some crucial similarities in their respective thoughts, no more so than where the time-eternity issue is concerned.[63]

Schleiermacher founds his entire dogmatics on the famous "feeling of absolute dependence" and this feeling is fundamentally related to the divine causality.[64] The relationship of time and eternity must be interpreted in light of this feeling. "I trust," says Schleiermacher, "I have just made clear to you in what way any pious person can rightly be said to bear a constant and eternal existence within himself, to have made it his own. If our feeling never attaches itself to mere particulars and if its content is rather our relation to God, in which all that is merely individual and transitory is superseded, then what our feeling contains can only be eternal, not transitory. Thus one can rightly say that the religious life is that in which we have already offered up and disposed of all that is mortal and are already actually enjoying immortality."[65]

That "God is eternal" is Schleiermacher's "first doctrine" on the Divine Attributes. Thus, he argues, "By the Eternity of God we understand the absolutely timeless causality of God, which conditions not only all that is temporal, but time itself."[66] Since only God's eternal power can cause that consciousness, the eternity of God cannot be separated from His omnipotence; otherwise our religious feeling would be empty. Why should the divine causality and eternity have to be timeless? Schleiermacher puts it this way:

Cambridge University Press, 2000), pp. 12-3.

62. "Nor should it be forgotten," Webster reminds us, "that Barth is capable of finely drawn and generous reading of those from whom he is theologically distant, and that the thinker whom he studied most critically and with the greatest disagreement – Schleiermacher – is also the thinker whom he read with the greatest deference and sensitivity." See Webster, "Introducing Barth," pp. 9-10.

63. For Schleiermacher's opinions on time and eternity, see Nelson Pike, *God and Timelessness*, pp. 167-88; Robert R. Williams, *Schleiermacher the Theologian* (Philadelphia: Fortress Press, 1978), pp. 87-9, 183-5.

64. Cf. Schleiermacher, *The Christian Faith*, pp. 16-8.

65. Friedrich Schleiermacher, *On Religion*, trans. Terrence N. Tice (Richmond: John Knox Press, 1969), pp. 154-5.

66. Schleiermacher, *The Christian Faith*, p. 203.

> This is achieved through expressions denoting the temporal, and therefore as it were pictorially, since the temporal oppositions of before and after, older and younger disappear in coincidence when applied to God.[67]

This paragraph resonates with the Boethian comparison between eternity and temporal things. The only difference is that Schleiermacher gets his conclusion much sooner and easier than Boethius does. One cannot help asking him: why "the temporal oppositions of before and after, older and younger disappear in coincidence when applied to God"? Even if the disappearance of those oppositions is true, is it enough to say that God is timeless? Schleiermacher appears to have been aware of the difficulty he caused, for he changes an angle to resolve the problem:

> If eternity were taken as pure timelessness, nothing really is affirmed. But this can only happen if eternity is placed among the inactive attributes, while yet it is also thought that each such attribute by itself alone express the Essence of the Divine Being. On the other hand, it disappears if, as we demand, this conception is combined with that of omnipotence. For, in that a divine activity is posited, something may be posited, unknown indeed and perhaps not clearly conceivable, but by no means simply nothing. Indeed, finite being offers us some real help in conceiving the idea of eternity, since to a great degree time is merely an adjunct to finite being in so far as it is cause. But in so far as finite being produces time-series with their content, thus remaining the same and identical with itself (as, e.g., the Ego, as the enduring ground of all changing spiritual states, especially of resolves, each of which again as a moment of the Ego produces a concrete time-series), then, as the enduring causal ground relatively to the changing caused,

---

67. Schleiermacher, *The Christian Faith*, p. 204.

it is posited as timeless. And with some such kind of analogy we must rest content.[68]

Must we rest content with it? I do not think so. However Schleiermacher's discussion simply stops here, leaving too much to be desired. Indeed, when he introduces the doctrine of redemption and its ethical results, his God can remain timeless no more, since an incarnate God must be, to some extent, subject to time, although not necessarily confined by it.

Schleiermacher is unsatisfied with the traditional self-contained concept of divine immutability. In his opinion, the biblical God is not only a self-sufficient God who transcends the world in his own eternity, but also a self-actualizing God who incarnates himself among us. Thus "the immutability of divine love requires the mutability of divine power."[69]

Inevitably, a God who is both mutable and immutable in his action is incompatible with a God who has an attribute of timelessness. As Nelson Pike points out:

> Schleiermacher seems to have been aware of a logical tension between the idea that God is timeless and the standard interpretation of divine creation.[70] Schleiermacher also seems to have been alert to the internal friction involved in the claim that a timeless being is omnipotent. It is not at all obvious that a timeless individual can be consistently characterized as having any creative power let alone creative power that is unlimited or infinite.[71]

---

68. Schleiermacher, *The Christian Faith*, pp. 205-6.
69. Robert R. Williams, *Schleiermacher the Theologian*, p. 184. In the following paragraph, Williams gives an excellent summary of Schleiermacher's teaching which insists that God is both mutable and immutable: "God must be mutable in order to enter into concrete relation with man, and because sin can be overcome even by divine grace and causality only in a temporal career and time-process. On the other hand, God must be immutable. To be sure, such immutability is not the same as a divine self-actualization in abstraction from or apart from the world. The content and concrete expression of divine immutability is divine love, manifest in redemption" (p. 185).
70. For Schleiermacher, creation has two stages: incomplete creation and its completion – redemption.
71. Nelson Pike, *God and Timelessness*, p. 173. However, Pike's reading of Schleiermacher

Although some important issues remain unresolved in Schleiermacher's doctrine of timeless eternity, and sometimes his arguments are inconsistent, there are still some important approaches which Karl Barth inherits consciously or unconsciously: eternity conditions time and not vice versa; eternal God incarnates into concrete temporal world, etc. These are also theological rules Barth obeys strictly when he develops his comprehensive doctrine on time and eternity.

1.6 Conclusion

In this section we have reviewed the development of the doctrine of time and eternity and focused on two issues. The first concerns whether God's eternity is temporal or timeless. Augustine and Boethius clearly prefer the latter. However, in Anselm and Scotus we detect that the temporal factor permeated into the doctrine irretrievably so that it appears so susceptible when Schleiermacher tries to revive the atemporal interpretation. The second is related to the first and concerns whether past and future are as "real" as present in God's eternity. The answer to the first question entails the answer to the second, viz. a temporal approach leads to presentism, whereas an atemporal approach favors the opposite.

Of course, the distinction between the two sides is not so sharp and obvious that we can simply make our own either-or choice. Usually it is difficult to discern the different inclinations in each author, since great theologians are always too subtle to understand – "Subtle is the Lord,"[72] so are his interpreters. However, the resolution of the difficulties does not depend on how to choose or combine the two poles. On the contrary, by

---

is also criticized by Williams as follows: "(1) Pike is aware that Schleiermacher demands that eternity be combined with omnipotent so that the former not be conceived merely negatively and abstractly. Yet Pike proceeds to discuss both attributes separately, and without taking seriously Schleiermacher's point that each delimits and qualifies the other. ... Schleiermacher does not assert that divine eternity is pure or unqualified timelessness. (2) Pike ignores Schleiermacher's declaration that, owing to the methodological abstraction from historical determinacy and concreteness practiced in the first part of *Glaubenslehre*, the first four divine attributes are indeterminate and cannot serve as an adequate description of God." See Pike, *Schleiermacher the Theologian*, p. 99.

72. This is a title of Einstein's biography. See Abraham Pais, *Subtle Is the Lord: The Science and the Life of Albert Einstein* (New York: Oxford University Press, 2005).

developing the doctrine totally within a Trinitarian frame, as did Barth and Pannenberg, something new may emerge from the ancient issues.

Section 2:
Time and Eternity: Modern Physical Views

2.1 Newtonian Absolute Time

Since the seventeenth century Sir Isaac Newton's views on time, although having been subjected to frequent criticism, dominated the scientific world until the advent of Einstein's theory of relativity in the twentieth century. Prior to Newton's era, many theories of time consider a relative time – the idea that time is defined in terms of a change or motion – occurs somewhere in our universe. For example, the solar day – the amount of time it takes for the sun to return to its zenith – is originally thought to be uniform everywhere. Actually, it varies by as much as 20 minutes over the course of a year. The sidereal day in Ptolemaic astronomy – the period of time it takes a fixed star to return to zenith – is considered to be constant. However, some astronomers, most notably Kepler, call into doubt whether the rate of rotation of the earth (a constant rotation is crucial to the uniformity of the sidereal day) remains constant over the course of a year. These relative times are an Aristotelian notion of time, which cannot be separated from motion for it is measured by the means of motion and, therefore, it is the measure itself.

Unsatisfied with these astronomic definitions of time which presume the constancy of certain celestial motions, Newton, in his Magnum Opus, *Philosphiae Naturalis Principia Mathematica*,[73] known as the *Principia*, tries to set up a new foundation for time by distinguishing two kinds of time, i.e., absolute time and relative time:

> Absolute, true, and mathematical time, in and of itself and of its own nature, without relation to anything external, flows

---

73. Isaac Newton, *The Principia: Mathematical Principles of Natural Philosophy*, trans. I. Bernard Cohen and Anne Whitman (Berkeley and Los Angeles: University of California Press, 1999).

uniformly and by another name is called duration. Relative, apparent, and common time is any sensible and external measure (precise or imprecise) of duration by means of motion; such a measure – for example, an hour, a day, a month, and a year – is commonly used instead of true time.[74]

By definition, Newton's concept of an absolute, mathematical time applies for all observers at all places equivalently: someone standing on the London Bridge on earth would experience time the same way as someone standing on Venus. Time flows constantly and uniformly everywhere in the universe. Its course cannot be affected by any force or motion. If two different observers had two perfect clocks, they would always measure the same time interval for the same procedure.

Then the problem is: how could one get an absolutely accurate clock anyway? Of course Newton is aware that clocks are imperfect and measurement of time is always subject to human error,[75] however he still believes in an absolute time that was similar to the Platonic ideal or Kantian "thing in itself", which are also the result of rational imagination rather than empirical observation. Like the ideal formulates the being of physical objects and the "thing in itself" gives rise to phenomena, the absolute time also regulates the relative time and not vice versa:

> In astronomy, absolute time is distinguished from relative time by the equation of common time. For natural days, which are commonly considered equal for the purpose of measuring time, are actually unequal. Astronomers correct this inequality in order to measure celestial motions on the basis of a truer time. It is possible that there is no uniform motion by which time may have an exact measure. All motions can be

---

74. Newton, *The Principia*, p. 408.
75. In this sense J. R. Lucas says: "time is not what the clocks say, but what they are trying to tell." See Lucas, *A Treatise on Time and Space* (London: Methuen & Co., 1973), p. 64.

accelerated and retarded, but the flow of absolute time cannot be changed.[76]

What price must Newton pay for expelling physical motion and measurement from the concept of absolute time? Once isolated from observable flow and change rate, does this God-like time[77] have any significance for our actual world? Can it flow or change in any sense? If yes, at what rate (one second/second, one day/day)? If not, can we still call it "time"? In fact, we have to admit that by positing absolute time as a mere metaphysical abstraction,[78] Newton empties his absolute time, paradoxically, into a kind of timeless time or atemporal time.

2.2 Einsteinian Relative Time

Newton approaches his absolute time through the distinction between absolute and relative time, claiming that the latter can approximate the former but never achieve its perfection. When Albert Einstein introduces his Special Theory of Relativity (STR or SR) in the early twentieth century, however, he suggests that time is relative, not absolute, as Newton claims.[79] Different from those kinds of relative time, which Newton criticizes for its celestial-motion-dependent nature, Einstein finds something really moves

---

76. Newton, *The Principia*, p. 410.
77. Newton admits that his absolute time can only be realized by God. Cf. *The Principia*, p. 941.
78. Cf. Hodgson, "Relativity and Religion," p. 397.
79. For the philosophical and theological significance of Albert Einstein's Special Theory of Relativity and General Theory of Relativity, see Achtner, Kunz and Walter, *Dimensions of Time*, pp. 124-8; Ian G. Barbour, *Religion and Science* (London: SCM Press LTD, 1998), pp. 177-81; Craig, *Time and Eternity*, pp. 32-66; also his "The Special Theory of Relativity and Theories of Divine Eternity," *Faith and Philosophy* 11: 1(Jan 1994): pp. 19-37; and also his "Relativity and the 'Elimination' of Absolute Time," in *Time, Reality, and Transcendence in Rational Perspective*, eds. Peter Øhrstrøm (Aalborg: Aalborg University Press, 2002), pp. 91-128; Garrett J. DeWeese, *God and the Nature of Time* (Aldershot: Ashgate Publishing Limited, 2004), pp. 65-84; Lawrence W. Fagg, *The Becoming of Time* (Atlanta: Scholars Press, 1995), pp. 29-42; Hodgson, "Relativity and Religion: The Abuse of Einstein's Theory," pp. 393-409; Robert John Russell, "Time in Eternity: Special Relativity & Eschatology," *Dialogue: A Journal of Theology* 39: 1 (Spring 2000): pp. 46-55; Roberto Torretti, "On Relativity, Time Reckoning and the Topology of Time Series," in *The Arguments of Time*, eds. Jeremy Butterfield (New York: Oxford University Press, 1999), pp. 65-82.

at a constant and uniform rate in the universe, i.e., the speed of light. Upon acknowledging the Newtonian declaration that "all motions can be accelerated and retarded," Einstein has to argue: "No Sir! The speed of light is exceptional." STR shows how motion and speed always depend on a person's frame of reference and purports that the velocity of light always remains constant, viz. 299,792,458 metres per second,[80] whereas time varies – the faster an object increases in speed, the more time slows down in that inertial frame. Time varies? Yes, the faster an object is moving, the slower time progresses for that object in relation to a stationary observer. Although the effect appears counterintuitive and goes entirely unnoticed in ordinary circumstances, it has been proven to be true by various experiments. For instance, an atomic clock placed on a jet airplane is shown to "tick" more slowly than an atomic clock at rest. Suppose such a situation: you travel in a very fast spaceship and your brother stays firmly on the earth. The faster you travel, the slower your time will pass relative to your brother. If you were able to travel at the speed of light, your time would cease completely and you would only exist trapped in an atemporal state (you may call it "eternity" if you want).

What Einstein did in STR is to force physicists to think no longer of space and time but rather to look at a four-dimensional space-time.[81] According to Einstein, two persons observing the same event could perceive the singular event occurring at two different times, depending upon their distance from the event in question: the observer from a more distant place will perceive an event as occurring later in time; however, the same event cannot occur at two different moments in time. This temporal difference arises from the time it takes for light to travel through space. Since the light does travel uniformly at a constant speed, it is impossible to distinguish temporal difference from spatial distance. Thus, time and space are inextricably linked and form one single space-time continuum.

---

80. Torretti, "On Relativity, Time Reckoning and the Topology of Time Series," p. 71. Of course, here a "second" is a second within our earthly inertial frame where "one second is no longer defined to be 1/86400 of a day: it is 9,192,631,770 beats of a cesium atom." See Paul Davies, *About Time* (New York: Touchstone, 1996), p. 22. People changed the definition of second with the latter, presumably the cesium atom clock is more accurate, "but accurate relative to what?" Davies asked (p. 22).

81. Cf. Achtner, Kunz and Walter, *Dimensions of Time*, p. 124.

In addition to the STR, the General Theory of Relativity (GTR or GR), which Einstein proposed in 1915, takes into account the effects of acceleration and gravity. In STR, time has been spatialized and absorbed into the three-dimension space as its fourth dimension; in GTR, the spacetime continuum has been further twisted with energetic matter formations. Einstein discovers that spacetime is not flat, but curved or "warped" by the existence of matter and energy. Huge celestial bodies in spacetime, like the sun or the earth, can twist spacetime around them. Imagine an apple resting on a stretched out blanket – the weight of the apple warps the sheet. If the earth is an apple, then we can imagine the earth's blanket as spacetime. If we imagine that space is a two-dimensional sheet, a planet placed on this sheet would cause it to curve. In relation to time, the curvature means that the scale of time is influenced by gravity; in a stronger field of gravity time appears to pass more slowly than in a weaker one.[82] In 1962, scientists place two atomic clocks at the bottom and top of a water tower. The clock at the bottom, the one closer to the massive center of the Earth, was running slower than the clock at the top. Thus, the effect caused by a gravitational field in GTR is exactly the same as that caused by accelerated motion in STR.[83] Einstein called this phenomenon time dilation.

One significant impact caused by STR and GTR is the "downfall of the present"[84]: an event which is present for an observer in one inertial frame may be future or past for another one in another inertial frame. No one can claim that his or her perspective is privileged in which there is an absolute now by which all universal events can be divided into past and future. Einstein believes that in the warped four-dimensional spacetime continuum the past, present, and future all exist simultaneously. His most explicit testimony to this faith is recorded in a letter to the widow shortly after the death of his lifelong friend Micheal Besso, saying that "Now he has gone a little ahead of me in departing from this quaint world. This means nothing. For us faithful physicists, the separation between past, present, and

---

82. Cf. Achtner, Kunz and Walter, *Dimensions of Time*, p. 126; Fagg, *The Becoming of Time*, p. 36.
83. Cf. Barbour, *Religion and Science*, pp. 179.
84. See Russell, "Time in Eternity," p. 50.

future has only the meaning of an illusion, although a persisting one."[85] Thus, similar to Newton's case, Einstein's own Relativity Theories lead him to reject time.

In nature, both Newtonian absolute time and Einsteinian relative time are subject to timeless interpretation. However, there is still a crucial distinction between the two: the former implies that there is an absolute, dominant point from which the universe can be observed, i.e., a God's-eye view; whereas the latter purports the opposite – there can be no vantage perspective, for all observers, confined in their own local reference frames, are equal. Craig argues that: "What Einstein did, in fact, was to shave away Newton's absolute time and space, and along with them the aether, thus leaving behind only their empirical measures. Since these are relativized to inertial frames, one ends up with the relativity of simultaneity and of length."[86]

2.3 Quantum Theory and Time

Another physical theory, which has a great impact on the modern understanding of time, is the Quantum Theory.[87] At the end of the nineteenth century and the beginning of twentieth century, physicists were puzzled by a series of experiments concerning light: in some instances, the way in which light behaves could only be explained if it is made up of waves; in other cases, it could only be explained if light behaves like a stream of

---

85. Albert Einstein, *Albert Einstein-Michele Besso Correspondence: 1903-1955* (Paris: Herman, 1949), pp. 537-538.
86. Craig, *Time and Eternity*, p. 47.
87. "It is frequently maintained," says Hodgson, "that the theory of relativity, along with quantum mechanics, demolished the nineteenth-century picture of the universe and created a new world picture that differs radically from that of Isaac Newton." See Hodgson, "Relativity and Religion: The Abuse of Einstein's Theory," p. 393. For the philosophical and theological significance of Quantum Theory, see Achtner, Kunz and Walter, *Dimensions of Time*, pp. 121-3; DeWeese, *God and the Nature of Time*, pp. 84-8; Fagg, *The Becoming of Time*, pp. 43-61; Luscombe, *Groundwork of Science & Religion*, pp. 134-44; Osborn, "Theology and the New Physics," pp. 129-37; Peter E. Hodgson, "God's Action in the World: The Relevance of Quantum Mechanics," *Zygon* 35:3 (Sep 2000): pp. 505–16; Christopher Norris, "Should Philosophers Take Lessons from Quantum Theory?", *Inquiry* 42: 3 (Oct 1999): pp. 311-42; Paul Teller, "The Ins and Outs of Counterfactual Switching," *Nous* 35: 3 (Sep 2001): pp. 365-93.

particles.[88] More strangely, the result of whether light behaves as particles or waves depends on how we look at the apparatus. That means in a quantum scale world the observer inevitably interferes with the observation, hence influences the result. The interference sets up the limit of physical measurement: for microscopic objects (either particles or waves), the equations of quantum mechanics mean that pairs of properties are related. The most important of these pairs is momentum and position. When we try to pin down the behavior of small-scale particles, the more accurately we determine the one, the less we know about the other. This is the famous Heisenberg Uncertainty Principle (HUP).[89] Since the quantum uncertainty prevents simultaneous knowledge of exact positions and exact velocities, what we can know is nothing other than the *probability*. As Hodgson puts it:

> Quantum mechanics is a very successful theory and describes a wide range of phenomena in great detail and to a high degree of accuracy. In many cases it gives us a good understanding of what is taking place. However, we may be so impressed by the success of quantum mechanics that we overlook its defects. Its results are expressed in terms of probabilities. Thus, we cannot calculate in which direction a particle will scatter or when a particular nucleus will decay. Quantum mechanics is therefore incomplete. The question is whether this incompleteness is irreducible or whether there will eventually be a more fundamental theory that gives a more detailed account of reality.[90]

---

88. The famous Thomas Young's two-slit experiment exposes the wave-particle duality of light. Cf. Paul Davies, *God and the New Physics* (London: J. M. Dent & Sons Ltd, 1983), pp. 108-9.

89. A theory developed in an essay published in 1927 by German Physicist and Nobel Laureate Heisenberg. "It says," according to Davies, "you can't know where an atom, or electron, or whatever, is located *and* know how it is moving, at one and the same time. Not only can you not know it, but the very concept of an atom with a definite location and motion is meaningless." See Davies, *God and the New Physics*, p. 102. Cf. Hawking, *A Brief History of Time*, p. 55; Michael Lockwood, *The Labyrinth of Time: Introducing the Universe* (Oxford: Oxford University Press, 2005), pp. 290-2.

90. Hodgson, "God's Action in the World," p. 507.

The replacement of the certainty by the probability has fundamentally changed our concept of future and past. According to classical physics, if we have detailed and accurate observations of the present state of a system we can predict the future state and calculate the past state of the system with confidence. Yet in quantum physics, what we can predict and describe is only the probability of the future and the past.[91]

Although quantum mechanics changes our knowledge about time fundamentally, it is friendlier to time itself than STR and GTR are. Since quantum mechanics simply employs time as "a part of the fixed, theoretical background structure,"[92] it treats time as *time* rather than anything else.[93] Regarding the significance of time in quantum theory, Achtner, Kunz and Walter give a brief remark:

> *Time* is entitled to a special role in quantum mechanics. It differs conceptually from what is *observable*, the measurable quantities, because it is (only) a parameter of the understanding of quantum mechanics. That presents a special problem in connection with the second law and irreversibility since a pure parameter does not admit any distinctive direction of time.[94]

How can God act in such an irreversible time?[95] Indeed the impact of quantum mechanics on time and eternity is less discussed than on divine

---

91. Cf. Brian Greene, *The Fabric of the Cosmos: Space, Time, and the Texture of Reality* (New York: Alfred A. Knopf, 2004), pp. 178-9.
92. Jeremy Butterfield and Chris Isham, "On the Emergence of Time in Quantum Gravity," in *The Arguments of Time*, eds. Jeremy Butterfield (Oxford: Oxford University Press, 1999), p. 147.
93. As Lucas puts it: "Although the Special Theory made time seem spacelike, and the General Theory made it rather functional, quantum mechanics is kind to time. In quantum mechanics time is mostly an independent variable, not under pressure to be anything else. Much more important, however, is the way quantum mechanics supports a tensed understanding of time, with a distinguished present and inherent directedness." See Lucas, "A Century of Time," in *The Arguments of Time*, p. 11.
94. Achtner, Kunz and Walter, *Dimensions of Time*, p. 121.
95. For contemporary quantum divine action, see Robert John Russell, "Does 'The God who acts' Really Act? New Approaches to Divine Action in the Light of Science," in *Theology Today* 54 (1997): 43-65; Lameter, *Divine Action in the Framework of Scientific Thinking*, pp. 153-97.

knowledge, e.g., determinism vs. indeterminism.[96] However, quantum mechanics, together with Chaos Theory[97] and the second law of thermodynamics, implies a temporal eternity of God. Since time in these theories is irreversible, an eternal God, although allowed to foresee and arrange the future, cannot possibly change the past. As Lucas puts it:

> Quantum mechanics seems to support a modal understanding of time, with time as the passage from the open future through the actuality of the present to the unalterable fixity of the past; and this in turn supports an ontological picture, with the passage of time being marked by the accretion of unalterable truth.[98]

2.4 Time in Quantum Gravity

Whereas GTR deals with the fundamental force in the macroscopic world – gravity – quantum mechanics refines the other three fundamental forces in the microscopic world: the electromagnetic force, the weak nuclear force and the strong nuclear force. Recently, some physicists – Glashow, Salam

---

96. According to the "orthodox" Copenhagen Interpretation, quantum mechanics is indeterministic, but there are still many competing deterministic theories of quantum mechanics. Cf. Hodgson, "God's Action in the World," pp. 511-3.

97. In "God's Action in the World: The Relevance of Quantum Mechanics," Hodgson bridges quantum mechanics and chaos theory as follows: "The uncertainty principle, as it is usually understood, sets very tight limits on the results of measurements, so we can ask whether such minute interventions are adequate to produce the macroscopic effects implied by God's action in the world. We could imagine God making billions of such minute interventions so that eventually they produce macroscopic effects, though whether this is consistent with the omnipotence and dignity of God is another question. This may, however, be unnecessary given the effects studied in chaos theory. It is well known that even in classical systems very small changes in the initial conditions often produce very different subsequent behavior. For example, a minute change in the trajectory of a gas molecule greatly affects the dynamics of a collision, and this is magnified in subsequent collisions. More picturesquely, it is referred to as the "butterfly effect" in climate predictions. Such effects have been studied in recent years because computers provide the means to make the lengthy calculations that are required. If we assume that God could foresee the ultimate effects of divine intervention at the quantum level, then a minute intervention could indeed produce a macroscopic effect. Furthermore, in certain circumstances a single quantum event can produce a macroscopic effect, as in the case of Schrödinger's cat." See Hodgson, "God's Action in the World," p. 506-7.

98. Lucas, "A Century of Time," p. 14.

and Weinberg[99] – showed that electromagnetism and the weak nuclear force are two manifestations of a single force – the electroweak force. For a synthesis of the electroweak force and the strong nuclear force there is even tentative circumstantial evidence.[100] However, gravity is far from tamed in the same framework with those three nongravitational forces. Thus the unified theory of GR and quantum mechanics has been regarded as the "Holy Grail" since Einstein's time.[101] Nowadays there are two most prominent ongoing approaches to seek the "Holy Grail": one approach, represented by loop quantum gravity, starts from a GTR perspective, trying to quantize the canonical formulation of general relativity. This approach follows this strategy: "Model gravity as a quantum field on a space-time manifold in which the spatial curvature remains constant over time."[102] An alternative approach, represented by M-theory (previously called string theory), grows out of the quantum particle physics tradition, seeking to embrace gravity. The Strategy of M-theory is to "replace four-dimensional space-time with a three-dimensional space the geometry of which evolves over time and admits of superposition of geometric states at a given time."[103] Yet both loop quantum gravity and M-theory are researching programs waiting to be attested by experimental results and their impacts on the concept of time are only tentative and theoretical. No decisive conclusions can be drawn from either of them.

2.5 Conclusion

Has modern physics changed our opinions about time and God's eternity? If affirmative, has it changed them substantially? These questions appear far from settled. When we discuss our topic in the light of modern physical theories, the problem we have met is not, what do these theories mean to theology? It is rather this, what do these theories mean to themselves?

---

99. Greene, *The Fabric of the Cosmos*, p. 328.
100. Cf. Greene, *The Fabric of the Cosmos*, p. 526.
101. Cf. Butterfield and Isham, "On the Emergence of Time in Quantum Gravity," p. 111; Greene, *The Fabric of the Cosmos*, pp. 328-9.
102. Lockwood, *The Labyrinth of Time*, p. 333. Cf. also pp. 349-64; Greene, *The Fabric of the Cosmos*, pp. 486-91.
103. Lockwood, *The Labyrinth of Time*, p. 333. For time in M-theory, see Greene, *The Fabric of the Cosmos*, pp. 327-412.

That is to say, we cannot draw some certain conclusions from physics and then apply them to theology. There are two reasons forbidding us to do so. Firstly, physical theories need to be interpreted and there is no easy agreement between physical schools; secondly, to some extent, our approach to the physical theories decides our result. As in quantum mechanics, the way we watch decides what we watch, so, if we see eternity from a Newtonian perspective, we get a temporal and dynamic picture; however, if we see it from a Mach-Einsteinian perspective, we get a timeless and static view. And there is no decisive standard by which we can favor one and discard the other.

Section 3:
Time and Eternity: Modern Philosophical Views

3.1 Kant: Time as the Form of Inner Sense

Immanuel Kant, whose contributions to the modern philosophy of time "brought time out of shadows,"[104] inherited his view of time from Newton. His discussions of time[105] concentrate in his first critique, *Critique of Pure Reason*, the most important work in which his main task was accomplished.

In the opening section of the first *Critique*, Kant discusses in detail two ideas – space and time under the title of "Transcendental Aesthetic."[106]

---

104. Sherover, *Heidegger, Kant and Time* (Lannham: University Press of Amarica, 1988), p. 4.

105. For Kant's opinions of time, see Arthur Melnick, *Space, Time, and Thought in Kant* (Dordrecht: Kluwer Academic Publishers, 1989), pp. 20-6, 344-52; Roger Scruton, *Kant* (Oxford: Oxford University Press, 1982), pp. 28-31; Charles M. Sherover, *Heidegger, Kant and Time*; Charles Parsons, "The Transcendental Aesthetic," in *The Cambridge Companion to Kant*, eds. Paul Guyer (Cambridge: Cambridge University Press, 1992), pp.62-100; Paul Guyer, "The Transcendental Deduction of the Categories," in *The Cambridge Companion to Kant*, pp. 123-60; Lucy Allais, "Kant's One World: Interpreting 'Transcendental Idealism'," *British Journal for the History of Philosophy* 12: 4 (2004): pp. 655-84; Charles S. Peirce, "Hypothesis of Space and Time: A Response to Kant," *Transaction of Charles S. Peirce Society* 29:4 (Fall 1993)::pp. 637-73; Jay F. Rothenberg, "Kant and the Problem of Simultaneous Causation," *International Journal of Philosophical Studies* 6: 2 (1998): pp. 167-88.

106. "The word 'aesthetic' here," Scruton explains, "derives from the Greek for sensation, and indicates that the subject-matter of this section is the faculty of sensibility, considered independently of the understanding." See Scruton, *Kant*, p. 29.

Kant handles time totally as a cognitive idea so that his first step is to point out that time is *a priori* rather than experimental. Time, together with space, is not derived from our experience, but given *a priori*. That is, when we perceive something, it is not that we see it first and then know its spatial and temporal position. On the contrary, anything is represented to us *together* with space and time: either at one time and place (simultaneously) or at different times and places (successively). We cannot remove time and space from the objects which are represented to us. As the "forms of intuition,"[107] they underlie all intuitions.

In his next step, Kant distinguishes time from other categories. According to Kant, categories are "concepts of an object in general, by means of which the intuition of an object is regarded as determined in respect of one of the logical functions of judgment."[108] They are the forms by which the objects of intuition can be judged,[109] so they are derived from our act of judgment. According to the various modes of act of judgment,[110] Kant lists twelve categories in four sets: Categories 1) of Quantity: Unity, Plurality, Totality; 2) of Quality: Reality, Negation, Limitation; 3) of Relation: of Inherence and Subsistence, of Causality and Dependence, of Community; and 4) of Modality: Possibility-Impossibility, Existence-Nonexistence, Necessity-Contingency.[111]

Time and space are two ideas, which are not included in Kant's list of categories, because they are different from the other categories. As the form

---

107. Intuition is nothing else but "the representation which can be given only through a single object." See Kant, *Critique of Pure Reason*, p. 75.

108. Kant, *Critique of Pure Reason*, p. 128.

109. Cf. Howard Caygill, *A Kant Dictionary* (Oxford: Blackwell Publishers Ltd, 1995), p. 102; Guyer, "The Transcendental Deduction of the Categories," p. 129.

110. Concerning the generation of these categories, Roger Scruton gives out a brief summary in his *Kant*: "Kant believed that he had arrived at his list of categories by a process of abstraction. Suppose I describe what I now see: a pen writing. The concept 'pen' is a special 'determination' of the wider concept 'artifact', itself a determination of 'material object', and so on. The limit of this train of abstraction is the *a priori* concept which each stage exemplifies: the concept of substance. Beyond that point we cannot abstract further, without ceasing to think… By these, and similar, thought-experiments, Kant supposed that he had isolated, through his list of the twelve categories, all the forms of judgement, and so given an exposition of the concept of objective truth." See Scruton, *Kant*, pp. 28-9.

111. Kant, *Critique of Pure Reason*, p. 113.

of "inner sense,"[112] time is intrinsic to all states of our mind, whether or not they represent any outer object. According to Kant, there could not be any mental experience apart from time. Such mental activities as reading a book, thinking an idea, and just being in a mood are all *temporal* experiences. Before these acts really happen, time was given together with all our sensations. Only with these time-implanted sensations can we recognize, reflect, or represent the world and ourselves.[113]

Like time, all other categories are also *a priori* and they are also forms of intuition. The difference is located in their relationships to intuition (or intuitions), i.e., they are different forms of intuition: time is the form of whole intuition, whereas other categories are forms of partial intuitions. For Kant, there is only one and the same time, which underlies our one and whole representation. Differently, concepts are only forms of partial representations, which means that they are unable to determine the whole representation but, oppositely, are determined by this representation:

> The original representation, time, must therefore be given as unlimited. But when an object is so given that its parts, and every quantity of it, can be determinately represented only through limitation, the whole representation cannot be given through concepts, since they contain only partial representations; on the contrary, such concepts must themselves rest on immediate intuition.[114]

The relationship of time and other categories is not only whole and part, but also the determiner and the determined. We must keep in mind that categories are forms of different subjective judgments, thus without the object which is given for them, they are useless and meaningless. However, everything given for us must be intuited by our inner sense, viz., in the

---

112. "Time is nothing but the form of inner sense, that is, of the intuition of ourselves and of our inner state" (Kant, *Critique of Pure Reason*, p. 77), whereas space is the form of "outer sense."

113. Cf. Sherover, *Heidegger, Kant and Time*, p. 114.

114. Kant, *Critique of Pure Reason*, p. 75.

form of time. Thus time conditions categories and not vice versa.[115] Kant also uses a concrete example to interpret the relationship between time and concepts:

> Here I may add that the concept of alteration, and with it the concept of motion, as alteration of place, is possible only through and in the representation (inner) intuition; no concept, no matter what it might be, could render comprehensible the possibility of an alteration, that is, of a combination of contradictorily opposed predicates in one and the same object, for instance, the being and not-being of one and the same thing in one and the same place. Only in time can two contradictorily opposed predicates meet in one and the same object, namely, *one after the other*.[116]

Inasmuch as time is none other than the form of our inner sense, its validity only applies to the area of the appearance of the object world and its representation in our mind. In other words, time is only a relatively subjective reality rather than an absolutely objective reality. Since the main task of the first *Critique* is to explore how our subjective knowledge is valid in an objective world, it is not surprising that these terms, namely, "appearance" and "representation," deployed by Kant in this *Critique* locate between two extremes – subject and object.[117] Time, although not originating from our experience, has a certain empirical validity.[118] However, such validity must be confined in the scope of our "pure reason." Outside this scope, i.e., in the scope of "things-in-themselves," time no longer counts as a valid property. Thus, Kant argues,

---

115. Cf. Kant, *Critique of Pure Reason*, pp. 181-2.
116. Kant, *Critique of Pure Reason*, p. 76.
117. Charles S. Peirce reproaches Kant for the fact that, in his opinion, Kant's space and time are mere "hypothesis" (Cf. "Hypothesis of Space and Time: A Response to Kant," pp. 49-50). By no means is this a fair accusation for Peirce gets his conclusion only from Kant's subjective address and neglects Kant's objective appeal.
118. "It is only if we ascribe *objective reality* to these forms of representation, that it becomes impossible for us to prevent everything being thereby transformed into mere *illusion*." See Kant, *Critique of Pure Reason*, p. 89.

Empirical reality has to be allowed to time, as the condition of all our experience; on our theory, it is only its absolute reality that has to be denied. It is nothing but the form of our inner intuition. If we take from our inner intuition the peculiar condition of our sensibility, the concept of time likewise vanishes; it does not inhere in the objects, but merely in the subject that intuits them.

What we have meant to say is that all our intuition is nothing but the representation of appearance; that the things which we intuit are not in themselves what we intuit them as being, nor their relations so constituted in themselves as they appear to us, and that if the subject, or even only the subjective constitution of the sense in general, be removed, the whole constitution and all the relations of objects in space and time, nay space and time themselves would vanish. As appearances, they cannot exist in themselves, but only in us. What objects may be in themselves, and apart from all this receptivity of our sensibility, remains completely unknown to us.[119]

That is, the validity of time is confined to the subjective experience of the objective world. Once we exit the realm of pure reason, say, beyond the empirical kingdom, our so-called "transcendental" knowledge must be ideal[120] rather than real. If our reason attempts to achieve real knowledge outside of our experience, antinomies will be unavoidably caused. Kant illustrates four antinomies and the very first one refers to time and space:

Thesis

The world has a beginning in time, and is also limited as regards space.

---

119. Kant, *Critique of Pure Reason*, p. 79, 82.
120. "By the ideal I understand the idea, not merely *in concreto*, but *in individuo*, that is, as an individual thing, determinable or even determined by the idea alone." See Kant, *Critique of Pure Reason*, p. 485.

Antithesis

> The world has no beginning, and no limits in space; it is infinite as regards both time and space.[121]

Kant's argument for the thesis is based on the impossibility of the completion of an infinite series. If the world has no beginning, preceding any given time there is a past infinite series and this infinite series is complete because no beginning point breaks its completion, say, if there is a beginning point the infinite series could not be complete. Kant refuses to accept such a complete infinity:

> If we assume that the world has no beginning in time, then up to every given moment an eternity has elapsed, and there has passed away in the world an infinite series of successive states of things. Now the infinity of a series consists in the fact that it can never be completed through successive synthesis. It thus follows that it is impossible for an infinite world-series to have passed away, and that a beginning of the world is therefore a necessary condition of the world's existence.[122]

The argument for the antithesis appeals to the principle of "sufficient reason." Firstly, Kant deduces the existence of an "empty time": if the world has a beginning, there must be an "empty time" before the beginning.[123] Secondly, the existence of things at any given time must have a sufficient reason, and there is no sufficient reason for the world to come into existence at any time in this empty time.[124] In other words, the world has no

---

121. Kant, *Critique of Pure Reason*, p. 396. For the discussions on the first antinomy, see Paul Guyer, *Kant and the Claims of Knowledge* (Cambridge: Cambridge University Press, 1987), pp. 385-7; Michelle Grier, *Kant's Doctrine of Transcendental Illusion* (Cambridge: Cambridge University Press, 2001), pp. 182-214.
122. Kant, *Critique of Pure Reason*, p. 397.
123. Kant, *Critique of Pure Reason*, p. 397.
124. Kant, *Critique of Pure Reason*, p. 397.

preference to take any point of the empty time as the beginning time. Kant argues thus:

> Since the beginning is an existence, which is preceded by a time in which the thing is not, there must have been a preceding time in which the world was not, *i.e.* an empty time. Now no coming to be of a thing is possible in an empty time, because no part of such a time possesses, as compared with any other, a distinguishing condition of existence rather than of non-existence; and this applies whether the thing is supposed to arise of itself or through some other cause. In the world many series of things can, indeed, begin; but the world itself cannot have a beginning, and is therefore infinite in respect of past time.[125]

Actually, Kant's "empty time" is based on Newtonian absolute time. Anti-Newtonians refute such a kind of time. One of the most famous, Leibniz, argues that, "instants, considered without the things, are nothing at all… they consist only in the successive order of things."[126] The Leibnizian material-related time does not need a sufficient reason to come into being at a certain moment: it must begin with the very moment of the material universe.[127]

Kant's arguments about his antinomies are criticized for "appearing to be question begging."[128] In the first antinomy, what he wants to prove is

---

125. Kant, *Critique of Pure Reason*, p. 397.
126. G. W. Leibniz, *The Leibniz-Clarke Correspondence*, eds. H. G. Alexander (Manchester: Manchester University Press, 1956), 3rd paper, sect. 6.
127. As Robin Le Poidevin puts it: "For Leibniz, one of the chief merits of this view is that it disposed of a puzzle concerning creation, namely, why did God create the universe at the time he did, rather than at an earlier or a later time? Leibniz's answer is that, if times are just successive changes, then necessarily the beginning of the universe coincides with the first moment of time. Since, however, the puzzle depends in large part upon our unwillingness to attribute random choices to God, the corresponding secular question 'Why did the universe come into existence at the moment it did?' had rather less bite." See Robin Le Poidevin, "Relationism and Temporal Topology: Physics or Metaphysics?" in *The Philosophy of Time*, eds. Robin Le Poidevin and Murray MacBeath (Oxford: Oxford University Press, 1993), pp. 151-2.
128. Karl Ameriks, "The Critique of Metaphysics: Kant and Traditional Ontology," in

nothing but that time and space are phenomenal rather than substantial. If we apply the forms of our intuition to things of themselves, such antinomies are unavoidable.[129] However, as Guyer points out, the antinomies "may simply be set aside by recognizing that space and time are, again, nothing but the forms of our intuitions, and that things as they are in themselves, which reason takes itself to know, are thus neither spatially nor temporally finite nor infinite"[130]

From Kant's argument for the thesis, we have a glimpse into his idea about eternity. Actually, he treats "eternity as free from conditions of time"[131] as an attribute of "transcendental theology" which is, of course, beyond our reason. Like any other non-pure-reason idea, it remains ideal rather than real. "Eternity itself," Kant argues, "is far from making the same overwhelming impression on the mind; for it only *measures* the duration of things, it does not *support* them. ...All support here fails us; and the *greatest* perfection, no less than the *least* perfection, is unsubstantial and baseless for the merely speculative reason."[132] Barth, or at least later Barth, perhaps can agree with Kant on the belief that eternity is ideal. However, the Barthian ideal could definitely be more "substantial" than the Kantian reality.

3.2 Kierkegaard: Self as Synthesis of Time and Eternity

Unlike most theologians mentioned in section 1, who emphasize the distinction and division of time and eternity rather than the similarity and unity, Kierkegaard[133] confirms the possibility of attaining the eternity in

---

The Cambridge Companion to Kant, p. 260; Cf. also Sally Sedgwick, "Hegel on Kant's Antinomies and Distinction between General and Transcendental Logic," *Monist* 74: 3 (Jul 91): pp. 403-21.
129. Cf. Caygill, *A Kant Dictionary*, p. 77.
130. Paul Guyer, "Introduction," in *The Cambridge Companion to Kant*, p. 15.
131. Kant, *Critique of Pure Reason*, p. 531.
132. Kant, *Critique of Pure Reason*, pp. 513-4.
133. For Kierkegaard's doctrine of time and eternity, see Edward John Carnell, *The Burden of Kierkegaard* (Exeter: The Paternoster Press, 1965); Melville Chaning-Pearce, *The Terrible Crystal* (New York: Oxford University Press, 1941); C. Stephen Evans, *Kierkegard's Fragments and Postscript: The Religious Philosophy of Johannes Climacus* (Atlantic Highlands: Humanities Press International, 1983); Gregor Malantschuk, *Kierkegaard's Thought* (Princeton: Princeton University Press, 1971); George Pattison, *Kierkegaard and the Crisis of Faith* (London: SPCK, 1997); Howard A. Slaatte, *A Re-Appraisal of Kierkegaard* (Lanham: University Press of America, 1995), pp. 117-34; Steven Shakespeare

humans themselves without hesitation.[134] His approach to understanding time is also totally different from Newton's and Kant's absolute way. Whereas Newton and Kant start from a pure and abstract concept, Kierkegaard bases his argument on the concrete individual: "Man, then, is a synthesis of psyche and body, but he is also a synthesis of the temporal and the eternal."[135]

Our concern here is the second synthesis. However, the second synthesis has a baffling character because, according to Kierkegaard, a synthesis needs a third term to relate the two factors synthesized. As for the first synthesis, the "spirit" counts for the third term to bond body and psyche together; but there is no such term in the second synthesis.[136] Then, why does he abandon the logical consistency? The answer lies in his totally subjective and spiritual approach of existential analysis of humans. From this perspective, the two syntheses are essentially one:

> The synthesis of the temporal and the eternal is not another synthesis but is the expression for the first synthesis, according to which man is a synthesis of psyche and body that is sustained by spirit. As soon as the spirit is posited, the moment is present.[137]

As a synthesis of time and the eternal, our existence is unavoidably temporal. In developing his analysis of existential temporality of selfhood, he

---

Kierkegaard, Language and the Reality of God (Aldershot: Ashgate, 2001); Mark Taylor, *Kierkegaard's Pseudonymous Authorship, a Study of Time and the Self* (Princeton: Princeton University Press, 1975); Julia Watkin, *Kierkegaard* (London: Geoffrey Chapman, 1997); Michael Wyschogrod, *Kierkegaard and Heidegger, The Ontology of Existence* (London: Routledge & Kegan Paul Ltd, 1954); Lious Dupre, "Of Time and Eternity in Kierkegaard's *Concept of Anxiety*," *Faith and Philosophy* 1: 2 (April 1984): pp. 160-76.

134. Cf. Malantschuk, *Kierkegaard's Thought*, pp. 83-5.

135. Søren Kierkegaard, *The Concept of Anxiety*, trans. Reidar Thomte (Princeton: Princeton University Press, 1980), p. 85. See also Kierkegaard, *The Sickness unto Death*, trans. Howard V. Hong and Edna H. Hong (Princeton: Princeton University Press, 1980), p. 13.

136. Cf. Kierkegaard, *The Concept of Anxiety*, p. 85.

137. Kierkegaard, *The Concept of Anxiety*, p. 88.

defines three stages of existence: 1) the aesthetic, 2) the ethical, and 3) the religious.[138]

The aesthetic stage can be understood as either a stage in which the individual is governed by sensuous inclination, or, a stage in which a person is merely an observer of life rather than a moral doer or religious devotee.[139] The person in this stage – the aesthete – is characterized by the "immediate."[140] He is never bothered with existential decision[141] and personal commitment to eternity. For Kierkegaard, the aesthetic stage ranks lowest on the scale of the three because it acknowledges no connection with his own authenticity.[142]

As far as temporality is concerned, an aesthete cannot properly be called an individual.[143] He stays in one of three divisions of time and never tries to actualize the synthesis of his fragmental time and eternity. By trapping himself within the finite time, he is merely a being; he never is becoming.[144] Taylor has an excellent analysis of the aesthete's temporality:

---

138. Time definitely has the crucial role for the different stages of existence. Kierkegaard writes: "The significance attached to time is in general decisive for every standpoint up to that of the paradox, which paradoxically accentuates time. In the same degree that time is accentuated, in the same degree we go forward from the aesthetic, the metaphysical, to the ethical, the religious and the Christian-religious." See Kierkegaard, *The Concluding Unscientific Postscript*, trans. David F. Swenson (Princeton: Princeton University Press, 1941), p. 265.

139. Cf. Taylor, *Kierkegaard's Pseudonymous Authorship*, p. 127.

140. According to Kierkegaard, "immediacy is fortune, for in the immediate consciousness there is no contradiction; the immediate individual is essentially seen as a fortunate individual, and the view of life natural to immediacy is one based on fortune." See Kierkegaard, *The Concluding Unscientific Postscript*, p. 388.

141. Such a question as "To be? Or not to be?" is not a problem for him.

142. If an aesthete were asked the aim of life he would answer: "I do not myself understand it." See Kierkegaard *The Concluding Unscientific Postscript*, p. 388.

143. For such an "individual," "lacking the possibility of divine forgiveness and grace, since, on Kierkegaard's view of the individual's need to develop the eternal of spiritual self ethical-religiously, that eternal self cannot be so developed or completed." See Julia Watkin, *Kierkegaard*, p. 80.

144. This is the difference between aesthetic stage and ethical stage: "the aesthetical in a man is that by which he is immediately what he is; the ethical is that whereby he becomes what he becomes." See Kierkegaard, *Either/Or* Part II, trans. Walter Lowrie (Garden City: Anchor Books, 1959), p. 182.

> The aesthete's experience of time is characterized by an emphasis on any one of the three tenses of time to the exclusion of the other two. One can, therefore, be immersed in the sensual pleasure of the present moment, oblivious to the past and to the future; one can be wrapped up in reflection on the past, forgetful of the present and the future; or one can be so occupied with anticipation of the future that one has no regard for the present and the past.[145]

The ethical stage is a higher existential stage of personal commitment. The ethical sphere of existence applies to those who sense the claims of duty to the eternal.[146] The synthesis of the temporal and the eternal in no way should be taken for granted.[147] It exists in an individual as a possibility or a potentiality, which needs to be actualized in life.[148] When an aesthete stays in his own inward being and refuses any universal obligation, he despairs.[149] Contrary to the aesthete, an ethicist, rather than a consumer or observer of life, is forced to actualize himself by becoming involved in something beyond himself. "A person enters the ethical stage," Carnell points out, "the moment he perceives a serious relation between 1) the essence of the self, 2) the necessity of moment-by-moment choice, and 3) a sense of duty which is nourished by the eternal."[150] By synthesizing the self with the eternal, the individual does not become somebody else and destroy his own temporality; instead he becomes, maybe for the very first time, his authentic self.[151]

---

145. Taylor, *Kierkegaard's Pseudonymous Authorship*, p. 8.
146. Cf. Carnell, *The Burden of Kierkegaard*, p. 67.
147. Cf. Taylor, *Kierkegaard's Pseudonymous Authorship*, p. 7.
148. "The individual is also equipped with the potentiality for spiritual and eternal life, and it is to the extent that an individual chooses to actualize this possibility that there ought to, and can, arise a second synthesis, one between the temporal and eternal, the finite and infinite, necessity and freedom." See Julia Watkin, *Kierkegaard*, p. 28.
149. "Inwardness means that a person turns toward his inner center: he discovers the eternal within himself, but by excluding this inwardness he ends in despair." See Malantschuk, *Kierkegaard's Thought*, p. 340.
150. Carnell, *The Burden of Kierkegaard*, p. 67.
151. Cf. Kierkegaard, *Either/Or* Part II, p. 149. Pattison puts it this way: "To be concerned with eternity is not therefore to seek to escape from time. On the contrary, the more we accept our essential temporality and face up to the sheer impermanence of all human (and of all finite, creaturely) life, the closer we draw to eternity." See Pattison,

It is personal decision and commitment that distinguishes the aesthetic and ethical stages. Also this decision makes the synthesis of time and eternity possible, since "to be in time is to be faced with the either-or decision."[152] Time, for Kierkegaard, is an infinite succession and he has a negative attitude to the three divisions of time.[153] The self cannot escape from the temporal reality, however, by committing himself to ethical ideals.[154] He establishes the continuity between time and eternity and in this sense time becomes the "expression" of the eternal.

However, the ethical obligation, which the self tries to realize, is too ideal and too high for him. He has assumed responsibility beyond his ability; hence he is always frustrated by his continuous failures. Not only an ideal is needed, but also the power is required to realize the authenticity of the self. Thus we come to the next stage – the religious stage. As Dupre points out:

> Active striving alone never comes to terms with its own ultimacy. It never confronts the absolute which it constantly assumes. Only in the religious attitude does the self achieve a conscious relation to that absolute, which at once is the source of free self-realization and transcends it.[155]

Kierkegaard and the Crisis of Faith, p. 100. Watkin argues that: "Within ethics 'eternity' means that one eternalizes or continues in ('repeats') the relationship despite changes of mood and external situation." See Watkin, *Kierkegaard*, p. 66.

152. Taylor, *Kierkegaard's Pseudonymous Authorship*, p. 185.

153. "If time is correctly defined as an infinite succession, it most likely is also defined as the present, the past, and the future. This distinction, however, is incorrect if it is considered to be implicit in time itself, because the distinction appears only through the relation of time to eternity and through the reflection of eternity in time. If in the infinite succession of time a foothold could be found, i.e., a present, which was the dividing point, the division would be quite correct. However, precisely because every moment, as well as the sum of the moments, is a process (a passing by), no moment is a present, and accordingly there is in time neither present, nor past, nor future." See Kierkegaard, *The Concept of Anxiety*, p. 85.

154. "Ethics is still an ideal science, and not only in the sense that every science is ideal. Ethics proposes to bring ideality into actuality. On the other hand, it is not the nature of its movement to raise actuality up into ideality. Ethics points to ideality as a task and assumes that every man possesses the requisite conditions." See Kierkegaard, *The Concept of Anxiety*, p. 16.

155. Dupre, "Of Time and Eternity in Kierkegaard's *Concept of Anxiety*," p. 167.

The religious sphere, for Kierkegaard, is divided into religiousness A and B. "Religiousness A," in Kierkegaard's words, "is the dialectic of inward transformation; it is the relation to an eternal happiness which is not conditioned by anything but is conditioned only by the inwardness of the appropriation and its dialectic."[156] Despite ambiguity of Kierkegaard's treatment of religiousness A,[157] we can be sure of one point: religiousness A is characterized by "immanence," i.e., a Schleiermacherian feeling of dependence,[158] whereas religiousness B – Christianity – is transcendental in nature.[159] Only in this stage, the incarnated eternity – Jesus Christ – meets the temporal man, but it is God seeks man rather than man seeks God.[160] When the encounter happens, that specific time becomes the "moment"[161] at which the Christian is allowed to be simultaneous with his Lord, namely, his temporal existence is confronted by eternity. The "moment" is a crucial concept for Kierkegaard's teaching on time and eternity.[162] Such a Kierkegaardian

---

156. Kierkegaard, *The Concluding Unscientific Postscript*, p. 494.

157. Cf. Carnell, *The Burden of Kierkegaard*, p. 67; Taylor, *Kierkegaard's Pseudonymous Authorship*, p. 241.

158. Cf. Shakespeare, *Kierkegaard, Language and the Reality of God*, p. 204; more interestingly, Taylor gives a semi-Barthian, semi-Schleiermacherian interpretation: "Religion A expresses the awareness of the absolute difference between God and man, and the ontological dependence of the self upon God, by believing that God is the Creator and man is creature." See Taylor, *Kierkegaard's Pseudonymous Authorship*, p. 242.

159. "In religiousness B the edifying is a something outside the individual, the individual does not find edification by finding the God-relationship within himself, but relates himself to something outside himself to find edification." See Kierkegaard, *The Concluding Unscientific Postscript*, p. 498.

160. As Watkin puts it, "Instead of the essentiality for humans to actualize their eternal, ethical-religious selves through repetition or continuity of ethical-religious life, God makes good human deficiency through the coming of Christ to the world." See Watkin, *Kierkegaard*, p. 81.

161. "The moment," says Malantschuk, "asserts the coming of the eternal into the temporal, for the moment is verily a synthesis of time and eternity." See Malantschuk, *Kierkegaard's Thought*, p. 247.

162. "To become conscious in one's eternal validity is a moment that is more significant than everything else in the world. It is as if you were captivated and entangled and could never escape either in time or in eternity; it is as if you lost yourself, as if you ceased to be; it is as if you would repent of it the next moment and yet it cannot be undone. It is an earnest and significant moment when a person links himself to an eternal power for an eternity, when he accepts himself as the one whose remembrance time will never erase, when in an eternal and unerring sense he becomes conscious of himself as the person he is." See Kierkegaard, *Either/Or* Part I, trans. David F. Swenson and Lillian Marvin Swenson (Garden City: Anchor Books, 1959), p. 206.

moment must be taken as "timeless," as an inward event rather than an objective happening, since it does not possess any physical duration.[163] When the Christian and the Christ meet in faith, on one hand, the temporal self becomes united with the eternal God, hence transcends his temporality; on the other hand, the incarnate God enters time without ceasing to be eternal. Within this synthesis, God's eternity does not cancel our temporal life but fulfills it. Such an encounter appears paradoxical. However in essence, it is even more concrete than time itself.[164] Of course this moment is neither a state which any person can attain nor a state which a person can keep all the time, for the sinful man may resist righteousness and such a moment may pass away.

Not only can the individual meet eternity at any moment, but also an age may become a "moment" in the mind of thinkers of a subsequent age. Beyond the personal horizon, Kierkegaard even sketches out a "momentary" picture of a period or an age:

> The time in which the philosopher lives is not absolute time; it is itself a moment. It is always a dubious circumstance when a philosopher is barren; indeed, it must be regarded as a disgrace for him, just as in the Orient barrenness is regarded as a dishonor. Therefore time itself becomes a moment, and the philosopher himself becomes a moment in time. Then in turn our age will appear to a later age as a discursive moment, and in turn a philosopher of a later age will mediate our age, and so on.[165]

---

163. "In that instance," says Chaning-Pearce, " the inward and the eternal meet in a timeless here and now reached through and within, yet ever beyond, our space-time continuum. There is the point of intersection where the longitudinal line of human life, love (eros) thought and time meet the vertical line of eternity and the down-pouring love (agape) of God." See Melville Chaning-Pearce, *The Terrible Crystal*, p. 51. Shakespeare puts it this way: "The presence of the Eternal cannot be present in time in any straitforward way." See Shakespeare *Kierkegaard, Language and the Reality of God*, p. 118.

164. "The concrete eternity is realized in time, whereas the eternity which remains beyond time is altogether abstract and indeterminate." See Shakespeare, *Kierkegaard, Language and the Reality of God*, p. 176.

165. Kierkegaard, *Either/Or* Part II, p. 173.

In the long run, the dichotomy of time and eternity are synthesized inwardly at the moment. In the aesthetic stage, they contradict each other for the individual traps himself in time and neglects the eternal; in the ethical stage, time seeks to realize the eternal but is unable to achieve it; in the religiousness A stage, time relies on eternity immanently; in the religiousness B stage, eternity comes into time and fulfills it. Kierkegaard summarizes all stages this way:

> Immediacy, the aesthetic, finds no contradiction in the fact of existing: to exist is one thing, and the contradiction is something else, which comes from without. The ethical finds the contradiction, but within self-assertion. The religiousness A comprehends the contradiction as suffering in self-annihilation, although within immanence, but by ethically accentuating the fact of existing it prevents the exister from becoming abstract in immanence. The paradoxical religiousness [religiousness B] breaks with immanence and makes the fact of existing the absolute contradiction, not within immanence, but against immanence. There is no longer any immanent fundamental kinship between the temporal and the eternal, because the eternal itself has entered time and would constitute there the kinship.[166]

As mentioned in *Introduction,* Kierkegaard's doctrine of time and eternity plays such an important role in early Barth that in the second *ER*, Barth also stresses the "greedy dialectic of time and eternity"[167] and even uses this absolute distinction as his "system."[168] In this so-called "dialectical theology", Barth "emphasizes the Kierkegaardian infinite qualitative distinction between time and eternity, the gap between God and humans."[169] Interestingly, even for later Barth, in *CD* II, there are still many similarities

---

166. Kierkegaard, *The Concluding Unscientific Postscript*, pp. 507-8.
167. *ER*, p. 530.
168. Cf. *ER*, p. 10.
169. Watkin, *Kierkegaard*, p. 99.

between his approach and that one used by Kierkegaard in religiousness B.[170]

3.3 McTaggart: Unreality of Time

Previous sections in this chapter show that for traditional theology, the main "paradigm"[171] which confines the discussions concerning time-issues can be described as "God's temporality vs God's timelessness." In classical physics and continental classical philosophy, the paradigm shifts into "absolute time vs relative time." The latest paradigm shift, at least in the tradition of analytic philosophy occurs in the early twentieth century. In 1908 the Cambridge analytical philosopher John Ellis McTaggart published a monumental article in the journal *Mind* entitled "The Unreality of Time."[172] From then on, scholars on time-issues generally fall into either of the two camps: A-series or B-series.[173]

Of course, McTaggart's concern in that article is not in supplying a new paradigm for the following discussions. Rather, he argues for the non-existence of time and believes firmly that he has done so successfully by the conclusion of the article. McTaggart's argument consists of two parts. The first part aims to show that the A-series is more essential than the B-series for time.

What are the A-series and B-series? There are two different ways in which we think about time: one is a dynamic or tensed way in which we locate events relative to past, present and future. In McTaggart's words, "For the sake of brevity I shall give the name of the *A* series to that series of positions which runs from the far past through the near past to the present, and then

---

170. See next chapter.
171. Cf. the section about the methodology in *Introduction*.
172. McTaggart, "The Unreality of Time," pp. 457-74. The following quotations are drawn from that chapter reprinted in *The Philosophy of Time*, eds. Richard M Gale (London: Macmillan, 1968).
173. "McTaggart's discussion is a key to the views of time held by twentieth-century analytic philosophers, for one can detect in their writings a common underlying concern: almost all are attempting to answer McTaggart's paradox." See Gale, "Introduction," in *The Philosophy of Time*, p. 65. A-series and B-series can be also described as "Dynamic Theory" and "Static Theory." See William Lane Craig, *Time and Eternity* (Wheaton: Crossway Books, 2001); Garrett J. DeWeese, *God and the Nature of Time* (Aldershot: Ashgate, 2004).

from the present through the near future to the far future, or conversely."[174] The other is a static or tenseless manner in which we locate events relative to earlier or later events. "The series of positions," says McTaggart, "which runs from earlier to later, or conversely, I shall call the *B* series."[175]

Of these two ways of conceiving time, McTaggart argues that A-series is more essential or fundamental. In the first step of this argument he attributes the reality of time to change: no change, no time. However, in a B-series, each event is permanent: no event can begin to be, or cease to be. If we take an event N that is earlier than O and later than M, it is always thus. The position of event N in B-series could never change.[176] Thus, "Queen Victoria's death is later than Newton's and earlier than McTaggart's" is an ever-true statement in B-series. McTaggart discusses the unchangeableness of B-series events in detail with a concrete example:

> If my poker, for example, is hot on a particular Monday, and never before or since, the event of the poker being hot does not change. But the poker changes, because there is a time when this event is happening to it, and a time when it is not happening to it.
>
> But this makes no change in the qualities of the poker. It is always a quality of that poker that it is one which is hot on that particular Monday. And it is always a quality of that poker that it is one which is not hot at any other time. Both these qualities are true of it at any time—the time when it is hot and the time when it is cold. And therefore it seems to be erroneous to say that there is any change in the poker. The fact that it is hot at one point in a series and cold at other points cannot give change, if neither of these facts change—and neither of them does. Nor does any other fact about the poker change, unless its presentness, pastness, or futurity change.[177]

---

174. McTaggart, "Time," p. 87.
175. McTaggart, "Time," p. 88.
176. McTaggart, "Time," pp. 89-90. Cf. William Lane Craig, *The Tensed Theory of Time: A Critical Examination* (Dordrecht: Kluwer Academic Publishers, 2000), pp. 169-217.
177. McTaggart, "Time," p. 92.

According to McTaggart, in B-series without A-series, "the poker is hot on Monday" and "the poker is cold on Tuesday" must be seen as two independent events. Each event is true for its own context. If we say that, "the hot poker on Monday becomes cold on Tuesday," we have already invited an A-series conclusion.

Each event itself is unchangeable, yet change must be possible with such an event, otherwise time would not be real. If we do not want to give up the change in time, there remains only one possibility; namely, change is due to the A-series because only this series allows genuine change. If N, in B-series, is earlier than O and later than M, it is always so. But the event N, in A-series, which is now present, once was future and will be past. Since (1) change is essential to time, and (2) change is identical with A-series rather than B-series, McTaggart concludes that (3) A-series is more basic than B-series.[178]

Then we come to the second part of McTaggart's argument: neither time is real in the A-series. This part contains two arguments with the same conclusion. The first argument begins with a claim that (4) past, present, and future are "incompatible determinations" of an event, e.g., if any event is present, it cannot be past, nor be future. On the other hand, (5) every event does have them all: "if M is past, it has been present and future. If it is future, it has been present and past. Thus all the three characteristics belong to each event."[179] Obviously, (4) and (5) are incompatible, namely, the reality of the A-series as a mode of conceiving time is contradicted by the fact that it requires incompatible characteristics of events to be simultaneous with each other, therefore A-series leads to a contradiction and must be rejected. Thus, together with (3), we must say that (6) time is unreal. Our experience of events as taking place in time is illusory. This is the so-called "McTaggart's Paradox."[180]

---

178. Cf. Gale, "Introduction," in *The Philosophy of Time*, p. 67; Judith Jarvis Thomson, "McTaggart on Time," *Philosophical Perspectives* 15 (2001): pp. 231-2.
179. McTaggart, "Time," p. 95.
180. Cf. William Lane Craig, "McTaggart's Paradox and the Temporal Solipsism," *Australasian Journal of Philosophy* 79: 1 (March 2003): p. 32.

It appears that McTaggart's arguments are far more controversial than the compatibility of (4) and (5). Craig points out that (5) is actually a B-series statement:

> But given McTaggart's tenselessly existing series of temporal events, every event does have all three! Take an event tenselessly located at t1. At t1 that event is obviously present. But because all events are equally real, that same event also has pastness and futurity because at t2 it is past and at t0 it is future. The moment t1 is not any more real or privileged than t0 or t2, and so the event in question must be characterized by the tenses it has at all these times, which is impossible... If someone should say, "But t1 is present relative to t1 and past relative to t2, which is not contradictory," the advocate of tenseless time will say that such relational properties reduce to the tenseless time relation is *simultaneous with* and is *earlier than*, which vindicates the tenseless theory."[181]

Craig calls such a union of dynamic and static theories as "a B-theoretic ontology wedded with A-theoretic temporal becoming."[182] Only when both (4) and (5) belong to A-series, can McTaggart get (6). If (4) belongs to A-series and (5) belongs to B-series, there is no contradiction in A-series, therefore no paradox exists. Then the problem is whether Craig is right when he argues that (5) belongs to B-series. In my opinion, the answer is yes. Even pastness and futurity could be deduced to "earlier than" and "later than" and are, therefore, compatible with the definition of B-series; presentness is definitely not. Had a B-series been allowed to contain an event "simultaneous with" itself, e.g., presentness, there would be no distinction between B-series and A-series.

---

181. Craig, "McTaggart's Paradox and Temporal Solipsism," p. 44. Cf. also Craig, *The Tensed Theory of Time*, pp. 169-71.
182. Craig, "McTaggart's Paradox and Temporal Solipsism," p. 44. For a comment from the tenseless or B-Theory of time point of view, see L. Nathan Oaklander, *The Ontology of Time* (Amherst: Prometheus Books, 2004), pp. 102-5.

G E Moore claims a simple refutation of McTaggart's "notorious hard to understand" argument that if time is unreal then there are no temporal events: no past, present, or future; and nothing is earlier or later than anything else. He states that surely this sentence is being written *presently*, and the writer's breakfast *precedes* his lunch everyday.[183] Gale argues that such an answer to the paradox is not "serious,"[184] yet despite Gale's criticism, the primary concern of post-McTaggart scholars is no longer whether time is real, but whether A-series or B-series is real, or, whether tense is real.

According to Gale, most B-theorists would agree the following four tenets:
(1) The A-series is reducible to the B-series since A-determinations can be analyzed in terms of B-relations between events;
(2) Temporal becoming is psychological since A-determinations involve a B-relation to a perceiver;
(3) The B-series is objective, all events being equally real; and
(4) Change is analyzable solely in terms of B-relations between qualitatively different states of a single thing.[185]

On the other hand, A-theorists would share these common articles:
(1) The B-series is reducible to the A-series since B-relations can be analyzed in terms of A-determinations;
(2) Temporal becoming is intrinsic to all events;
(3) There are important ontological differences between the past and the future; and
(4) Change requires the A-series.[186]

These (3) of both A-theorists and B-theorists, and these (1) of A-theorists still rely on McTaggart's definitions and arguments. The settlement of (1) depends on the resolution of these (2) and (4), namely, are temporal becoming and change real? According to the foregoing argument, it appears that the B-theory cannot allow the real temporal becoming. "But the reality of temporal becoming," argues the A-theorist Craig, "is even more evident

---

183. Cf. Gale, "Introduction," p. 69; Thomson, "McTaggart on Time," p. 249.
184. Gale, "Introduction," p. 69.
185. Gale, "Introduction," p. 70.
186. Gale, "Introduction," p. 77.

to us than the reality of the external world."[187] Even the B-theorist Mellor admits that "tense is so striking an aspect of reality that only the most compelling argument justifies denying it: namely, that the tensed view of time is self-contradictory and so cannot be true."[188] Of course, he believes that McTaggart's Paradox exists in A-series.

However, the B-theory also has its merits. "The popularity of the B-theory of time," Richard Bauckham and Trevor Hart observe, "in recent decades in both analytic philosophy and philosophy of science coincides with the unprecedented importance of the B-series in the social life of the modern period. The representation of time in purely quantitative and homogeneous terms as clock-time and calendar-time, time as it can be represented in the static spatial image of the time line, the time chart or the appointments diary, is characteristic of modern Western culture."[189]

On the other hand, "something of the qualitatively new future, with its hopes and surprises,"[190] should be attributed to A-series time. Yet there are some discrepancies within the A-theorists camp as well. One compelling instance, surprisingly, is something like the ancient Augustinian question: are the three tenses equally real? Or is only the present real? Gale, Schlesinger, Craig and William Seager prefer the latter. They, for those present is like a moving spotlight, which successively illuminates different moments along the series of time,[191] can be described as presentists.[192] The presentists avoid McTaggart's Paradox easily: since only the present is real, an event which is present certainly could not be past and future at the same time, then there is no paradox in the A-series. Arthur N. Prior and Josh Parsons support the former, namely, the realism of past and future.[193] They do not treat the

---

187. Craig, *Time and Eternity*, p. 139.
188. D. H. Mellor, *Real Time* (Cambridge: Cambridge University Press, 1981), pp. 4-5.
189. Richard Bauckham and Trevor Hart, "The Shape of Time," in *The Future as God's Gift*, eds. David Fergusson and Marcel Sarot (Edinburgh: T & T Clark, 2000), p. 43.
190. Bauckham and Hart, "The Shape of Time," p. 44.
191. Cf. G. N. Schlesinger, *Aspects of Time* (Indianapolis: Hakett, 1980), p. 132.
192. Cf. Gale, *The Language of Time* (London: Routledge, 1968); Craig, "Oaklander on McTaggart and Intrinsic Change," *Analysis* 59: 4 (October 1999): pp. 319-20; William Seager, "The reality of Now," *International Studies in Philosophy of Science* 13: 1 (1999): pp. 69-82.
193. Cf. Arthur N. Prior, *Papers on Time and Tense* (Oxford: Clarendon Press, 1968), pp.10-1; Josh Parsons, "A-Theory for B-Theorists," *The Philosophical Quarterly* 52: 206

present as a property which an event must take when the "spotlight" shines on it, thus the flow of time is metaphorical rather than substantial and the change in A-series is no longer so "genuine."

Obviously, A-series and B-series are similar to the traditional temporal and timeless perspectives. Gale regards the A-series as the "temporalistic view of man," whereas the B-series is the "God-like manner."[194] If we see God and ourselves from our own perspective, A-series or B-series appear to be a real dilemma. However, in the following chapters we will find that when we see time and eternity from a Barthian Trinitarian perspective both series may be embraced and transcended.

3.4 McTaggart's Paradox and Stump & Kretzmann's ET-Simultaneity

In 1982, two American philosophers, Eleonore Stump and Norman Kretzmann, published a now well-known paper entitled simply, "Eternity," combining Boethius' classical definition, Newton's and Einstein's theories of time, sketching out a new proposal of the simultaneity of time and eternity. The article can also be accounted as a philosophical and theological response to McTaggart's Paradox.

Firstly, Stump and Kretzmann draw from Boethius' classical definition of eternity four ingredients: (1) Anything that is eternal has life; (2) the life of an eternal being cannot be limited; (3) illimitable life entails duration of a special sort, then every life must involve duration; (4) a phrase in the definition: "the complete possession all at once."[195] Eternity, here, is a mode of existence that is, in Boethius' view, neither reducible to time nor incompatible with the reality of time.[196]

Within a Newtonian absolute frame, they discern three kinds of simultaneity:

(T) T-simultaneity = existence or occurrence at one and the same time;

(January 2002): pp. 1-20.
194. Gale, "Introduction," p. 66.
195. Eleonore Stump and Norman Kretzmann, "Eternity," *The Journal of Philosophy* 78: 8 (August 1981): pp. 431-3.
196. Stump and Kretzmann, "Eternity," p. 434.

(E) E-simultaneity = existence or occurrence at one and the same eternal present;

(G) G-simultaneity = existence or occurrence at once (i.e., together).[197]

According to their explanation of Boethius' definition of eternity, T and E could be simultaneous, which is called ET-simultaneity. The situation would be complicated when the special theory of relativity is taken into account, because Einstein warns us that the concept of simultaneity depends on which reference frame we choose and there is no privileged reference frame. Keeping this warning in mind, they lay out the fourth simultaneity:

(RT) RT-simultaneity = existence or occurrence at the same time within the reference frame of a given observer.[198]

Considering all above, they turn to discuss what ET-simultaneity means:

Let "x" and "y" range over entities and events. Then:

(ET) for every x and for every y, x and y are ET-simultaneous if
either x is eternal and y is temporal, or vice versa; and
(i) for some observer, A, in the unique eternal reference frame, x and y are both present – i.e., either x is eternally present and y is observed as temporally present, or vice versa; and
(ii) for some observer, B, in one of the infinitely many temporal reference frames, x and y are both present – i.e., either x is observed as eternally present and y is temporally present, or vice versa.[199]

Stump and Kretzmann employ an example to illustrate this kind of simultaneity. They suppose they are in 1974 and Richard Nixon will die

---

197. Stump and Kretzmann, "Eternity," p. 435.
198. Stump and Kretzmann, "Eternity," p. 438.
199. Stump and Kretzmann, "Eternity," p. 439.

in 1990. It is true that an eternal entity *is* ET-simultaneous with Nixon in 1974, when he is alive; and with him in 1990, when he is dead. Since the eternal entity is *at once* simultaneous with all events, Nixon's future death in 1990 does not mean that it pre-exists in 1974 somehow. However, epistemologically ET-simultaneity indeed seems incoherent: "We know that Nixon is now alive. An omniscient eternal entity *knows* Nixon is now dead. Still worse, an omniscient eternal entity also *knows* that Nixon is now alive, and so Nixon is apparently both alive and dead at once in the eternal present."[200] Poor Nixon, becomes a Schrödinger's cat[201] in McTaggart's paradox: when the microscopic indeterminacy is transformed into macroscopic world, Schrödinger's cat is both alive and dead, which is obviously absurd from our conventional perspective; similarly, when the temporary events (Nixon's life and death) are observed from an eternal point of view, Nixon is both alive and dead at the same time (or should we say "at the same eternity"?).

They resolve the apparent paradox in a manner similar to Craig. The problems caused here are due to the ambiguity of the terms "now" and "at once". We know that: (1) Nixon is alive in the temporal present – the eternal entity knows that; and (2) Nixon is dead in the eternal present. (1) and (2) are not incompatible. Even (2) is not incompatible with (3) Nixon is alive in the eternal present. Since "Nixon is temporal, not eternal, and so are his life and death,"[202] both his life and death could be ET-simultaneous with the eternal entity.

---

200. Stump and Kretzmann, "Eternity," p. 439.
201. The so-called "Schrödinger's cat experiment" is: A cat is placed in a sealed box. In this box there is a system containing a flask of lethal gas which can be diffused if a radioactive substance decays. The decay is described by a wave function and if we do not observe the cat, its wave function is a superposition of two states: "the cat alive" and "the cat dead". When we open the box, the collapse of the wave function occurs and this superposition disappears: we have only one of the two states mentioned above. The consequence of the experiment is that "indeterminacy originally restricted to the atomic domain becomes transformed into macroscopic indeterminacy." See Erwin Schrödinger, "The Present Situation in Quantum Mechanics: A Translation of Schrödinger's 'Cat Paradox' Paper," trans. John D. Trimmer, in John Archibald Wheeler and Kenneth Zurek eds. *Quantum Theory and Measurement* (Princeton: Princeton University Press, 1983), p. 157. Cf. also Lockwood, *The Labyrinth of Time*, pp. 302-13.
202. Stump and Kretzmann, "Eternity," p. 443.

That is to say, (1) is an A-series statement and (2) is a B-series statement. The apparent paradox is caused by the confusion of the two ways we conceive and talk of time, namely, "a hybrid A-B-theory."[203]

The power of Stump and Kretzmann's proposal consists in the possibility of ET-simultaneity, whereas its weakness, similar to the B-theory, is the lack of God's will. As such, God's eternity at most can synchronize with our temporality. Yet why do I need to mind whether an observer outside my time is simultaneous with me? Why does God need to mind it?[204] The isolation of God's B-series like eternity and human A-series like temporality calls for a Trinitarian understanding of both time and eternity, because the second and third persons of the eternal triune God have entered our actual time, our concrete history. The God is not an abstract existence outside of human domain; on the contrary, he is the God once incarnated among us for some 30 years and his spirit is being with us right here and now.

3.5 Conclusion

Time for Kant, is a bridge between subject and object. The external world can only be represented to the internal consciousness in the temporal form, thus time is and only is the form of inner sense which is forbidden to be applied to the things in themselves, otherwise the antinomies will inescapably be caused. Kierkegaard also started his study inwardly. The temporal self seeks to actualize himself by synthesizing with eternity, thus he needs to be open to his own future. However, in the last stage of life – death – the ultimate synthesis cannot be realized by the psychological subject. Therefore, the eternal God comes to temporal man and man meets God in faith at the "moment".

As for McTaggart, although few accept his argument of the unreality of time, two terms he used in his analysis – A-series and B-series – for their simplicity and evidence, have earned him many followers. So far, the

---

203. Craig, "McTaggart's Paradox and Temporal Solipsism," p. 44.
204. As Christopher A. Franks observes: "Now, the notion of God as an "observer" may be just a figure of speech. But it is a misleading one, especially since our authors do not point out the crucial difference – that is causing the created realities that God "sees." So they liken God to the temporal observer, noting that God must discern whether events are present to God eternally or temporally." See Christopher A. Franks, "The Simplicity of Living God," *Modern Theology* 21:2 (April 2005): p. 290.

connection of the main issues discussed in this chapter can be established: on the one hand, temporal eternity-absolute and dynamic time-A-series; on the other hand, atemporal eternity-relative and static time-B-series.

CHAPTER 2

The Eternal Concrete Father

Section 1:
Eternal Trinity and Three One-sidednesses

1.1 The Trinitarian Form of God's Eternal Temporality

In the previous chapter, we retrieved the history of the concepts of time and eternity in three traditions: theological, philosophical and scientific. Inevitably, such a historical purview raises more questions than it resolves. Of course the topic itself is complicated and at least within the scientific tradition people do not need to worry about the problem of eternity, therefore they may concentrate on the nature of time itself. However the relationship between time and eternity is a primary concern to many philosophers and theologians. It might be to one's surprise that when we survey the problem in philosophical and theological traditions, as a general rule, scholars also start from time rather than eternity. From this vantage point, eternity is defined in light of time and not vice versa, in philosophy and theology alike. However, it must be said that if we start from a wrong point it is not at all certain that we shall arrive at the right place at the end. According to Barth, neither time nor eternity could be understood properly this way, a way only leading to abstraction and nothingness. For him, rather, the relationship between time and eternity will not be approached rightly as long as we start from the perspective of time, that is, studying the nature of time first, then approaching eternity through negating, possessing or extending time.

When we move to Barth's doctrine of time and eternity, however, we see a different picture. For Barth, one can never talk about time without referring its relation to the triune God, its Creator, Reconciler and Redeemer in three modes of the Father, Son and Holy Spirit. Otherwise we result in nothing other than abstract and empty theories. Thus Barth reminds us:

> The many philosophical theories of time which deny its reality and regard it as a mere form or abstraction or figment of the imagination can only be finally abandoned when we consider that God Himself once took time and thus treated it as something real. But it also means critically that there is no such thing as absolute time, no immutable law of time.[1]

Certainly this applies not only to philosophical theories, but also to theological concerns. Theological understandings of the relationship between time and eternity could easily lead to abstraction if we merely focus on an omni-something God[2] rather than the Father, Son and Holy Spirit, the God of Abraham, Isaac and Jacob. For Barth, there is no isolated and hence absolute time – time without eternity. Thus at the beginning of the section "Man in His Time" in *CD* III/2, Barth summarizes the relation between time and eternity: "Man lives in the allotted span of his present, past and future life. He who was before him and will be after him, and who therefore fixes the boundaries of his being, is the eternal God, his Creator and Covenant-partner. He is the hope in which man may live in his time."[3] As Creator, God is pre-time in his eternity; as Covenant-partner, God is supra-time by entering time from his eternity; as eschatological Redeemer on whom human hopes lie, God is post-time in his eternity. Only in this triple relationship does our human time[4] stand, otherwise it inevitably

---

1. *CD*, III/2, pp. 455-6.
2. Barth also employs "omnipresence," and "omnipotence" when he studies "The Perfections of Divine Freedom" in *CD* II/1. However his discussions never result in abstract conclusions. His God is always a personal and concrete God – the God in Jesus Christ and the God for us.
3. *CD* III/2, p. 437.
4. When Barth uses the term "time," he almost always means "human time." Rarely does he care about the time of other creatures or the time of the universe. The reason is clear: "Indeed, we do not know what it means for beings in the earthly cosmos to be in time. We have no means of observing or conceiving their temporality. But we can observe and conceive our own." See *CD* III/2, p. 521, cf. also p. 523.

collapses into abstraction and nothingness. The relationship between human temporality and divine eternity derives from the relationship of creature and its Creator, Reconciler and Redeemer. In this triple relationship between time and eternity, Father, Son and Holy Spirit are Co-Creator in pre-temporality, Co-Reconciler in supra-temporality and Co-Redeemer in post-temporality.

Such is Barth's Trinitarian way of interpreting God's relationship with time: time is human's creaturely form which is embraced by God's eternity; God's eternity is temporal rather than timeless. From an eternal point of view, God's temporality has a threefold structure. First, God is pre-temporal. Barth does not shy away from the question of "What was God doing before he created the world?" and he answers that question positively: "God decided to call into being the world and man by his Word."[5] For Barth, God's Word has always been Jesus Christ. Even before the creation, Jesus the Son was with God the Father. The Holy Spirit is also the eternal Creator who creates time for us with the Father and the Son.

Second, God is supra-temporal. "Supra" here does not mean separation or transcendence, on the contrary, it has an immanent sense: the eternal God preserves our temporality as our Covenant-partner in our time. From our point of view, time is separated from its own beginning and end, but time cannot be separated from eternity.[6] The touching point here, once again, is Jesus Christ. Among the three persons in eternal Trinity only the second person comes into our time *personally*.[7] In the Son, eternity and temporality become one in its ultimate form. However, even in his incarnation, the Son never separates himself from the Father and the Holy Spirit.

The third dimension of God's time is God's post-temporality. God the Father is the final goal of the creation. All our roads must lead to his eternity, otherwise they can only lead to nothingness and thus they are not the

---

5. Barth, *CD* II 1, p.622.

6. For Barth, eternity is always real duration, there is no difference among beginning, middle and end. When time is related to eternity, it is not separated from its beginning and end.

7. As Hunsinger puts it: "When God humbles himself in Jesus Christ by entering time, he becomes one of us, like us in all things." See Hunsinger, "*Mysterium Trinitatis*," p. 203.

real roads at all.[8] Beyond eternity there is nothing: God alone will exist after all things. God will look back and judge everything that has happened in the universe. According to his will, everything in time will be decided finally without any appeal, but at the same time, everything will be fulfilled as well by the Son and the Holy Spirit.

These three dimensions of divine temporality must be seen as one inseparable continuum, for Barth always emphasizes the harmony of God's pre-temporality, supra-temporality and post-temporality in light of Trinitarian eternity. By no way should we break the coherence of the three dimensions of God's temporality. Unfortunately, theologians easily stress one of the three dimensions and neglect or trivialize the other two. Thus Barth has to remind us of the three one-sidednesses in history.

1.2 The First One-sidedness

By a brief reflection on the history of Protestant theology Barth identifies three kinds of one-sidedness in understanding the three-fold structure. The first one refers to the sixteenth century Reformers[9] who put much emphasis on God's pre-temporality to the extent that God's supra-temporality and post-temporality have become a kind of appendix. Barth criticizes this position thus:

> It is true, of course, that in that eternity there can be an "earlier" as there can be a "now" and a "later," for eternity is certainly not the negation but the boundary of time as such. But for this very reason "then" cannot mean only "earlier." When we speak of God's eternity we must recognise and accept what is "earlier" as something also present and future, God's predestination is a completed work of God, but for this very reason it is not an exhausted work, a work which is behind us.[10]

---

8. Cf. *CD* II/1, pp. 629, also R. Dale Dawson, *The Resurrection in Karl Barth* (Aldershot: Ashgate, 2007), p. 38.
9. Cf. *CD* II/1, pp. 631-2.
10. *CD* II/2, p. 181.

In the doctrine of election and divine providence of Reformation theology, everything in time had been predestined by God, therefore there is no room left for human co-operation and merit. On the other hand, although Barth is fully aware of his predecessors' and contemporaries' one-sidednesses, his own teaching is also criticized as tilting to what he lists as the first one-sidedness. Gunton and Berkouwer are two representatives of this charge. In Gunton's opinion, the reason why Barth cannot avoid the mistake he himself identifies and criticizes is the dominant position in his system of his doctrine of election.[11] Thus, Gunton argues, "Because in his inner being God is an electing God, both creation and redemption are embraced within the concept of election."[12] According to Berkouwer, it is also "the triumph of election" that overpowers all so that human temporality never actually has a chance.[13]

However, Hunsinger reminds us that Barth's conceptions of time and eternity need to be clarified, for they are not fully explicit in his argument. Thus Hunsinger puts it: "Veiled behind Barth's appeal to the particularity of Jesus (veiled perhaps even partially to himself) is the extent to which all dimensions of 'temporality' are subjected to radical reinterpretation according to christological and Trinitarian modes of thought."[14] This "radical reinterpretation" is exactly what he does in his aforementioned essays "*Mysterium Trinitatis*: Karl Barth's Conception of Eternity" and "The Mediator of Communion: Karl Barth's Doctrine of the Holy Spirit." In these essays, Hunsinger tries to counterbalance this charge of one-sidedness caused by "the triumph of election" with his christological and Trinitarian reading of Barth's conceptions of time and eternity. He is at least partially

---

11. Cf. Gunton, *Christ and Creation*, pp. 94-5.
12. Gunton, *Christ and Creation*, p. 95.
13. Cf. G. C. Berkouwer, *The Triumph of Grace in the Theology of Karl Barth* (Grand Rapids: Wm. B. Eerdmans, 1956), pp. 89-122. Hunsinger comments on Berkouwer's argument as such: "Because the divine decree of election presented by Barth as *a priori* and eternal, and because it elects all humanity to salvation, "monism" is the inevitable result. The act of election – eternal, *a priori*, and sovereign – overpowers all. The triumph of grace is secured, but only at the expense of genuine human decision and the decisive significance of history. Humanity and history are effectively and monistically absorbed into the triumphant eternity of God and thereby virtually evacuated of all but illustrative significance." See Hunsinger, *How to Read Karl Barth*, p. 13.
14. Hunsinger, *How to Read Karl Barth*, p. 15.

successful in achieving his aims by making explicit that human temporality is concretely touched and redeemed in the Son's incarnation and the Holy Spirit's communion.[15] Besides Hunsinger's explanations, the counterbalance of the first one-sidedness in Barth's doctrine may become more explicit in Jesus' resurrection (chapter 3) and the Holy Spirit's work in "time between" (chapter 4).

1.3 The Second One-sidedness

The second one-sidedness in understanding God's temporality lies in eighteenth- and nineteenth-century theology. Opposed to the theology which was held by sixteenth-century Reformers, eighteenth- and nineteenth-century theology focuses on what Barth has called God's supra-temporality.[16] "The actual relationship of God to time in its duration, his presence and government in the world and the soul and in the religious experience of the individual, now became central to an understanding of his eternity."[17] Obviously, Barth has mainly Schleiermacher in his mind when he is saying this. Due to the predominant position of God's supra-temporality, God's pre-temporality becomes only an introduction and God's post-temporality is paid even less attention in this period than in the sixteenth century.

A helpful example of this one-sidedness in the early twentieth century is found in H. R. Mackintosh who by stressing Jesus' personality and humanity too much, makes Christ's preexistence only understandable in light of the incarnation and not vice versa:

> We cannot think eternity crudely as equivalent to time without beginning and without end; and the chronological quality of preexistence is therefore fatal to its adequacy as a final or coherent representation of what, *ex hypothesi*, is above time. Christ cannot after all be pre-existent in any sense except that in which God Himself is so relatively to the incarnation.[18]

---

15. Cf. Hunsinger, "*Mysterium Trinitatis*," pp. 203-5; "The Mediator of Communion," pp. 173-9.
16. Cf. *CD* II 1, p.632.
17. *CD* II/1, p. 632.
18. H. R. Mackintosh, *The Doctrine of the Person of Jesus Christ* (Edinburgh: T & T

While the supra-temporal dimension in incarnation is important,[19] it cannot be separated from the pre- and post-temporal dimension. Out of God's divine freedom, he has not chosen to be an eternal Father who only loves, judges and redeems us on high. On the contrary, he humbles himself to be one of us. That means he has taken the form of our contemporary time on his own divine time – eternity. The specific history of the incarnate Son is given from eternity for all human beings and all times. As Hunsinger puts it:

> The historicity of his life is fully real, and he cannot be known without it, for he never lives without it. Yet he is not encapsulated in this historicity in an unqualified way. For his historicity is indissolubly connected with his eternity. It is therefore at once affirmed, negated, and reconstituted on a higher plane. Its mere historicity is transcended and overcome. Its distinctive particularity is at once preserved and yet overcome by being integrated into the perichoresis of eternity. It is made integral to the eternal life of Jesus Christ and therefore acquires a differentiated presence and distinctive power in relation to all other historical moments and historical beings. In all its concrete particularity and uniqueness, it becomes the Word of God that is ultimately addressed to each and every human creature.[20]

Clark, 1913), p. 457.

19. "It is the incarnation," Torrance argues, "the concrete reality of God in space and time, that enables Barth to think out the ontic as well as the cognitive basis for theological activity." See T. F. Torrance, *Karl Barth: An Introduction to his Early Theology, 1910-1930* (London: S. C. M., 1962), p. 193.

20. Hunsinger, *How to Read Karl Barth*, p. 242. On this issue, Pannenberg also rightly points out the significance of the incarnation to the doctrine of time and eternity: "The incarnation of the Son sets aside the antithesis of eternity time as the present of the Father and his kingdom is present to us through the Son. This present not only contains all the past within it, as the idea of Christ's descent into Hades shows, but it also invades our present in such a way that this becomes the past and needs to be made present and glorified by the work of the Spirit. The removal of the antithesis of eternity and time in the economy of God's saving action according to the wisdom of his love is the reconciliation between Creator and creature." See Pannenberg, *Systematic Theology*, volume 1, trans. Geoffrey W. Bromiley (Grand Rapids: William B. Eerdmans Publishing Co., 1991), pp. 445-6.

When eternity comes into time, God "re-creates it and heals its wounds, the fleetingness of the present, and the separation of past and the future from one another and from present."[21] Since the Son's presence in time is a decision made from eternity and returned to eternity, it cannot be separated, either logically or ontologically, from his preexistence and his future.[22]

Yet even under the form of our contemporary time, God still retains his complete lordship over the time: He is still before the beginning, above the duration and after the end of time. Barth calls this the "concrete form of eternity as readiness for time."[23]

1.4 The Third One-sidedness

Barth points out that at the end of nineteenth century and the beginning of twentieth there is a one-sided reaction to the third side that had been neglected till then.[24] He refers to two Blumhardts and those who think that the discovery of the message of the kingdom of God and the scientific exegesis, especially of the New Testament, attain a previously unknown exactness in both secular and religious history.[25] They give a central position to the prayer: "Thy kingdom come."[26] The younger Blumhardt even links the fight for the kingdom of God to eschatology and the hope of the Socialist Labour movement.[27] In their works, eschatology, and therefore

---

21. *CD* II/1, p.617.
22. "Therefore, insofar as the life of Jesus Christ is eternal," Hunsinger points out, "the interconnection of the various temporal forms of this life (past, present, future) is one of mutual coinherence. These forms are the temporal forms of his one life action. In eternity the totality of this action is present in an ever-living, dynamic, and differentiated unity. …In the eternity of his one life action, the differences we know between past, present, and future are not extinguished, but integrated and to that extent overcome. The pattern of their integration is the dynamic, perichoretic pattern of mutual coinherence." See Hunsinger, *How to Read Karl Barth*, p. 241.
23. *CD* II/1, p.619.
24. Cf. *CD* II/1, p.633.
25. Cf. *CD* II/1, p.634.
26. For J.C. Blumhardt's and C. F. Blumhardt's prayers about "Thy kingdom come," Cf. Vernard Eller eds. *Thy Kingdom Come: A Blumhardt Reader* (Farmington: Plough Publishing House, 2007).
27. Cf. Bruce L. McCormack, *Karl Barth's Critically Realistic Dialectical Theology* (Oxford: Clarendon Press, 1995), pp. 123-4.

God's post-temporality is re-discovered, but the problem is that the kingdom of God is too easily confused with any secular social movements.[28]

As aforementioned, Gunton thinks the first one-sidedness exists in Barth's thought, that is, Barth's doctrine is too "protological"[29] and "eschatology is lost."[30] On one hand, he agrees with Barth's charge for the third one-sidedness by saying that "the future is a much overrated realm."[31] Indeed, there might be good reasons that the resurrection should receive more attention than the notion of preexistence, as Jenson points out:

> Indeed, the logic of what one might call a founding "postexistence" of Christ is more central in the New Testament than is the notion of "preexistence." Here is another place at which the eschatological character of the biblical narrative has been slighted and must be newly observed.[32]

However, if we separate the preexistence and resurrection, or stress the latter to such an extent that the preexistence is marginalized from God's temporality, we may go too far from the truth. Pannenberg's theology evidences an extreme example.

---

28. Barth criticizes that the younger Blumhardt, Kutter and Ragaz "combined the Christian expectation of the kingdom of God and the Socialist expectation for the future." See *CD* II/1, p.634.

29. Gunton, *The One, The Three and The Many*, p. 160.

30. "Real eschatology is lost, or at least suggests only the playing out of that which has already been decided in advance in a way that endangers the freedom at once of the Spirit and of the creation." See Gunton, *Christ and Creation*, p. 95.

31. Gunton, *The One, The Three and The Many*, p. 93. When saying this, Gunton keeps Moltmann and Pannenberg in mind. Cf. Colin E. Gunton, *The One, The Three and The Many*, pp. 92-3, 160; Gunton, "Foreword," in John Colwell, *Actuality and Provisionality: Eternity and Election in the Theology of Karl Barth* (Edinburgh: Rutherford House Books, 1989).

32. Jenson, *Systematic Theology* Volume 1, p. 142. In Jenson's opinion, Barth prefers the preexistence to the postexistence: "When Barth refers to God's own eternity, to the eternity of the choice that he is, he regularly and decisively qualifies this as "before all time." Why is it never "after all time"? It must be said: The eschatological character of God's reality and work, so clear in Scripture, does not determine the structure of Barth's vision as it should." See Jenson, "Karl Barth," p. 34. Cf. also Simon Gathercole, "Preexistence, and the Freedom of the Son in Creation and Redemption: An Exposition in Dialogue with Robert Jenson," *IJST* 7: 1 (2005).

Firstly, Pannenberg argues for an ideal preexistence which can only be understood in light of the resurrection and not vice versa:

> The idea of preexistence, however, is not required always and everywhere to express this relation to the eternal essence of God. Thus we may speak of an ideal preexistence of divine thoughts of creation prior to their execution in history. Like all creaturely reality, this preexistence in the purpose of God would be on the condition of the divine freedom and would not be constitutive for the identity of the divine essence."[33]

Secondly, Pannenberg argues that the content of God's election is also something ideal and thus not constitutive of the identity of divine essence:

> He [Barth] made the connection between the eternal deity of the Son and the historical existence of the man Jesus by means of the doctrine of predestination. The first "object" of predestination is the Son of God as destined to be the Son of man, the preexistent God-man Jesus Christ, who as such is the eternal basis of the divine election (*CD* II/2, §33. 1; cf. III/1, 50f.). Along these lines Barth distinctively doubled the concept of preexistence, referring to the deity of Jesus Christ, the eternal Son, in I/1, 414, and to the human reality of Jesus in II/2, 110. But by doing this, and relating the two aspects by means of the concept of election, he did not manage to define conceptually the connection between the preexistence of the eternal Son as such and the historical filial relation of Jesus to the father. For the act of the election is part and parcel of the freedom of God's relation to the world, so that its content cannot be constitutive for the eternal identity of his divine

---

33. Pannenberg, *Systematic Theology*, volume 2 (Edinburgh: T&T Clark, 1991), p. 370. For Pannenberg, the preexistence of the Son, compared with the resurrection, carries very little weight in Christology. Perhaps the only reason why Pannenberg needs the preexistence of the son is merely to avoid the charge of adoptionism: "The starting point of Jesus Christ in preexistence has the function of ruling out an adoptionist understanding of the exaltation." See Pannenberg, *Systematic Theology*, volume 2, p. 377.

essence. If it were, the world itself would be the correlate of this essence.[34]

If the act of election and preexistence of the Son cannot be constitutive for the divine essence, then which event, if any, in history is essential to the eternal deity? Pannenberg's answer is "resurrection." Everything related to Jesus Christ must be understood in light of the resurrection.[35] Not only do the sonship and divinity of Jesus depend on the resurrection, also in addition human salvation has no other basis apart from the resurrection. In this sense Pannenberg contends that "[o]nly in connection with the end of the world that still remains to come can what has happened in Jesus through his resurrection from the dead possess and retain the character of revelation for us also."[36] Thus, by over-emphasizing both the eschatological dimension and salvation history, and at the same time, as well as idealizing and marginalizing the notion of preexistence, Pannenberg unavoidably falls into the third one-sidedness warned by Barth.[37]

Thus far we have outlined Barth's Trinitarian frame of understanding time and eternity and its general challenge and criticism. In what follows we now enter this frame and look more closely at the relationship of human temporality with each person of the eternal Trinity. We start from the first mode (or person) in the Holy Trinity – the eternal Father.

---

34. Pannenberg, *Systematic Theology*, volume 2, p. 368.
35. "That God is revealed in Jesus can only be asserted on the basis of his resurrection from the dead." See Wolfhart Pannenberg, *Jesus – God and Man*, trans. Lewis L. Wilkins and Duane A. Priebe, (Philadelphia: The Westminster Press, 1977), p. 141.
36. Pannenberg, *Jesus – God and Man*, p. 107.
37. This one-sidedness in Pannenberg is implicit in Molnar's comment on Pannenberg. According to Molnar, the separation of the incarnation and resurrection, the earthly Jesus and "exalted Lord" in Pannenberg leads to a "two-stage Christology." Cf. Paul D. Molnar, *Incarnation and Resurrection: Toward a Contemporary Understanding* (Grand Rapids: Wm. B. Eerdmans, 2007), pp. 282-8.

Section 2:
The Eternal Creator Revealed

2.1 The Eternal Creator in the Immanent and Economic Trinity

According to Barth, God reveals himself in a triune mode. The first eternal mode is God the Father who is the fount of the Son and the Holy Spirit: "God's Trinitarian name of Father, God's eternal fatherhood, denotes the mode of being of God in which he is the Author of his other modes of being."[38] The Father is the source of the deity, however this does not mean there is priority or subordination within the Trinitarian relationship.[39] The Son and the Holy Spirit are of one divine essence (*homoousia*) with the Father and they are coeternal as the Creator. The relationship between the Father, Son and Holy Spirit should not be understood as the relationship between the Creator and the creature, although there are some similarities and analogies of these two kinds of relationship:

> As the Father, God is in himself the origin which has no other (not even an eternal and divine) origin, the source of the other eternal modes of existence of the divine essence and as the Creator, in virtue of his originative activity *ad extra*, he is the absolutely sovereign Lord of all that exists and is distinct from himself. As the Father, God procreates himself from eternity in his Son, and with his Son He is also from eternity the origin of himself in the Holy Spirit; and as the Creator he posits the reality to all the things that are distinct from himself. The two things are not identical. Neither the Son nor the Holy Spirit is the world; each is God as the Father himself is God. But between the two, i.e., between the relationship in God himself and God's relationship to the world, there is an obvious proportion.[40]

---

38. *CD* I/1, p. 393.

39. Cf. *CD* I/1, p. 393; Geoffrey W. Bromiley, *An Introduction to the Theology of Karl Barth* (Grand Rapids: William B. Eerdmans Publishing Co., 1979), p. 18.

40. *CD* III/1, p. 49. In another place, Barth also says that "[c]reation is the temporal

From the eternity of the relation of the Father, the Son and the Holy Spirit, it follows that not only God the Father is to be claimed as the Creator. Son the Reconciler and Spirit the Redeemer are also the eternal Creator, whereas Father the Creator is the eternal Reconciler and Redeemer too.[41] In this communion, the Father eternally renews, protects and saves his creature. For Barth, there is an analogy between the relationship of Creator-creature and the relationship within the eternal Trinity. Whitehouse confirms the analogy of relations in Barth by saying that creation "has some analogy to the eternal begetting of the Son by the Father while differing from this in its contingency and history."[42]

To bridge the *ad intra* Trinity and *ad extra* Trinity, there are two movements within the divine union. Firstly the Father eternally begets the Son. The Son is eternally begotten by the Father and there is no ontological distinction between the members of the Godhead with respect to their immanent relations. The second person of the Trinity does not only become the Son of God in his incarnation since apart from the incarnation he is eternally God the Son. The eternal sonship means that there is no ontological subordination. Barth thus argues:

> God is the eternal Father inasmuch as from eternity and in eternity he is the Father of the Son who from eternity and in eternity participates in the same essence with him. In this relation and not in any other way God is God – the God who reveals himself in the Son as the Creator and as our Father.[43]

---

analogue, taking place outside God, of that event in God Himself by which God is the Father of the Son." See Barth, *Dogmatics in Outline*, trans. G. T. Thomson (London: S. C. M. Press, 1949), p. 43.

41. Cf. *CD* I/1, p. 395.

42. Walter A. Whitehouse, "Karl Barth on 'The Work of Creation': A Reading of *Church Dogmatics*, III/1," in Niger Biggar eds. *Reckoning with Barth: Essays in Commemoration of the Centenary of Karl Barth's Birth* (London: Mowbrays, 1988), pp. 46-47. Cf. also Andrew K. Gabriel, "A Trinitarian Doctrine of Creation?: Considering Barth as a Guide," *McMaster Journal of Theology and Ministry* 6 (2003-2005): p. 43.

43. *CD* I/1, p. 394.

For Barth, the coeternal Father and Son reject any kind of subordinationism. However, Zizioulas advocates the priority of the Father in the Trinity. The Father, for Zizioulas, is the "ground" or "cause" of the personhood of the Son and the Spirit in an asymmetrical way. The Son and Spirit can only derive their personhood from the Father.[44] Zizioulas declares that "[i]n making the Father the 'ground' of God's being – or the ultimate reason for existence – theology accepted a kind of subordination of the Son to the Father without being obliged to downgrade the Logos into something created."[45] Alan Torrance questions Zizioulas' position on the ground that it suggests the causal and derivative act of the Father and may threaten the "primordial reality" of the Holy Trinity, thus he asks: "If the Trinity derives from a causal act of the Father, is the 'concept' of the 'Holy Trinity' really being conceived as ontologically primordial? Does *the* exclusively primordial reality not actually become the person of the Father?"[46] Gunton also rejects the Father as the single "cause" of the Trinity by saying: "Whatever the priority of the Father, it must be conceived in such a way as to detract from the fact that all three persons are together the cause of the communion in which they exist in mutual and reciprocal constitution."[47]

Secondly the Holy Spirit eternally proceeds from the Father and the Son.[48] This is the unchangeable relationship between the Holy Spirit and the other persons of the Godhead. Eternally the Holy Spirit is the Spirit of the Father and the Son. The Holy Spirit is the intra-power of the divine communion which unites and distinguishes the three modes of Trinity in eternity. In Barth's words, the Holy Spirit is "the communion and self-impartation realized and consisting between both from all eternity; the principle of their mutual love proceeding from both and equal in essence;

---

44. Cf. John D. Zizioulas, *Being as Communion: Studies in Personhood and the Church* (Crestwood: St. Vladimir's Seminary Press, 1985), pp. 40-1; Douglas H. Knight, *The Theology of John Zizioulas: Personhood and the Church* (Aldershot and Burlington: Ashgate Publishing House, 2007), pp. 81-3; Colin Gunton, *The Promise of Trinitarian Theology* (London and New York: T & T Clark, 1991), p. 197; Kevin Giles, *The Trinity & Subordinationism* (Downers Grove: InterVarsity Press, 2002), pp. 99-100.
45. Zizioulas, *Being as Communion*, p. 89.
46. Alan J. Torrance, *Persons in Communion: An Essay on Trinitarian Description and Human Participation* (Edinburgh: T & T Clark, 1996), p. 292.
47. Gunton, *The Promise of Trinitarian Theology*, p. 196.
48. Barth always emphasizes the western *Filioque*. Cf. *CD* I/1, p. 395, 483.

the eternal reality of their separateness, mutuality and convolution, of their distinctness and interconnection."[49] In salvation history, the Holy Spirit sustains the Christian community in the time between the first and second *parousia* of Jesus Christ and makes the eschatological redemption present to us in our time. As Barth puts it:

> The work of the Holy Spirit, however, is to bring and to hold together that which is different and therefore, as it would seem, necessarily and irresistibly disruptive in the relationship of Jesus Christ to His community, namely, the divine working, being and action on the one side and the human on the other, the creative freedom and act on the one side and the creaturely on the other, the eternal reality and possibility on the one side and the temporal on the other.[50]

While Barth stresses the unity of the Trinity, he also distinguishes the three modes in the Godhead. There are not three modes changing alternatively in time: rather all three modes exist simultaneously in eternity. In this sense Barth states that "[t]he eternity of the fatherhood of God does not mean only the eternity of the fellowship of the Father with the Son and the Spirit. It also protects the Father against fusion with the Son and the Spirit."[51]

From the eternal triune relationship it follows also that the knowledge of revelation will not lead us beyond the revelation itself. God's revelation is fully disclosed to us in the Son through the Holy Spirit. There is no further "hidden God" other than the God revealed in his son Jesus Christ through the Holy Spirit. So there is no separation between the economic and immanent Trinity. As Barth puts it:

> All our statements concerning what is called the immanent Trinity have been reached simply as confirmations or

---

49. *CD* III/1, p. 56.
50. *CD* IV/3, p. 761. Cf. also Timothy Bradshaw, "Karl Barth on the Trinity: A Family Resemblance," *SJT* 39: 2 (1986): pp. 149-52. We shall discuss the work of the Holy Spirit in detail in *Chapter Four*.
51. *CD* I/1, p. 397.

> under-linings or, materially, as the indispensable premises of the economic Trinity. They neither could nor would say anything other than that we must abide by the distinction and unity of the modes of being in God as they encounter us according to the witness of Scripture in the reality of God in His revelation.[52]

Barth argues thus because any distinction between the immanent and economic Trinity would separate God himself from his revelation and open the door to the possibility of natural theology. However, that does not mean there is no difference at all between the economic and immanent Trinity. For Barth also emphasizes the significance of making "a deliberate and sharp distinction between the Trinity of God as we may know it in the Word of God revealed, written and proclaimed, and God's immanent Trinity, i.e., between 'God in Himself' and 'God for us,' between the 'eternal history of God' and His temporal acts."[53] Barth makes such a distinction in order to defend divine freedom, i.e., God addressing himself to us not out of a necessity, but out of his free choice. Based on Barth's statement that "the content of the doctrine of the Trinity…is not that God in his relation to man is Creator, Mediator and Redeemer, but that God in himself is eternally God the Father, Son and Holy Spirit…[God acting as Emmanuel] cannot be dissolved into his work and activity,"[54] Molnar argues that although for Barth the immanent Trinity is identical in content with the economic Trinity, there is also a need to make a sharp distinction between the two "in order to underscore God's freedom *in se* and *ad extra*."[55] To make a proper distinction between the immanent and economic Trinity, may help us to approach the relation of time and eternity more rightly. Thus Molnar points out:

---

52. *CD* I/1, p. 479.
53. *CD* I/1, p. 172.
54. *CD* I/2, pp. 878-9.
55. Paul Molnar, "The Trinity and the Freedom of God," *Journal for Christian Theological Research* 8 (2003): p. 60.

If, however, a proper distinction between the immanent and economic Trinity had been made, then we could say that God's time is uniquely his and so is above and prior to our time and that when God suffered in Jesus Christ it was indeed a miraculous condescension that cannot be explained in terms of consciousness.[56]

If we simply follow the famous "Rahner's Rule" – "the economic Trinity is the immanent Trinity, and the immanent Trinity is the economic Trinity,"[57] – then the fusion of the Creator and the creature is inevitable, even making the Creator eternally dependent on his creature to be what or who he is. Thus Shults comments: "This axiom did not answer the question of *how* to speak of the distinction *and* unity of the economic and immanent Trinity."[58] Obviously, what matters here is "how" to make a proper distinction between the two kinds of Trinity. To do that we must distinguish the immanent and economic Trinity concretely rather than abstractly. We are inclined to think abstractly about God's Trinity with a simple dilemma, i.e., an eternal imminent Trinity and a temporal economic Trinity. As Kiauka observes:

> When the immanent Trinity has been reassigned to eternity, whereas the divine economy to time, God's eternity is either against temporality, or to be understood as united or integrated with temporality.[59]

---

56. Paul Molnar, *Divine Freedom and the Doctrine of the Immanent Trinity* (London and New York: T & T Clark, 2002), p. 80.
57. Karl Rahner, *The Trinity*, trans. J. Donceel (New York: Crossroad, 1997), p. 22.
58. F. LeRon Shults, *Reforming the Doctrine of God* (Grand Rapids: William B. Eerdmans Publishing Co., 2005), p. 158.
59. [Wenn die immanente Trinität der Ewigkeit, die heilsökonomische hingegen der Zeit zugeordnet werden soll, dann steht entweder die Ewigkeit Gottes seiner Zeitlichkeit entgegen, oder aber wird die Ewigkeit Gottes als eine die Zeitlichkeit übergreifende bzw. tintegrierende verstanden.] Tomas Kiauka, *Zeit und Theologie: Philosophisch-theologische Studien zum Problem "Zeit" Untersucht an Wolfhart Pannenbergs Theologie* (Heidelberg: Ph. D. Dissertation, 2005), p. 118. "tintegrierende" should be "integrierende."

However, to distinguish the immanent and economic Trinity concretely means that we must study closely the relation of time and each mode of the divine Trinity. As Gutenson reminds us:

> [T]he doctrine of the Trinity allows us to conceive the Father as the transcendent one; specifically, the Father holds all the times of creatures in actual presence. However, by virtue of the fact that the three persons are but one God, we can say that "God" holds all times before him in undivided unity. The Son and the Spirit are sent into salvation history for the purpose of reconciling the world to God. Thus, they take up temporal location alongside the creatures, being immanent to them in all their places. Again, we can say that "God" is immanent to the creation. Consequently, the doctrine of the Trinity provides resources for moving beyond an abstract affirmation of the transcendence and immanence of God.[60]

If we separate transcendence and immanence sharply, neglecting the mediating work of the Son and the Holy Spirit between the two spheres, we would inevitably lead both time and eternity into abstraction. Thus Gunton affirms: "the problem with all views of creation as an eternal act, rather than the act of the eternal God both towards and in time, is that they threaten to undermine the goodness of the intrinsic temporality of creation."[61]

2.2 Revelation Time

In early Barth, especially in *ER*, the transcendence of God is given significant position in order to avoid the confusion God and the human caused by natural theology. Thus eternity means only a timeless moment in our

---

60. Charles E. Gutenson, "Time, Eternity, and Personal Identity," in Joel B. Green eds. *What about the Soul? Neuroscience and Christian Anthropology* (Nashville: Abingdon Press, 2004), p. 120. Gunton has a briefer statement: "God's action in time is Jesus Christ; his freedom is as the Father; and the historical actuality of God is the Holy Spirit." See Colin Gunton, *The Barth Lectures* (London and New York: T & T Clark, 2007), p. 108.

61. Colin Gunton, *Father, Son & Holy Spirit* (London and New York: T & T Clark, 2003), p. 141.

time. However, in *CD*, the later Barth approaches God's eternity in a more and more temporal way. As Gunton rightly points out:

> In *Der Römerbrief* we have a highly timeless God: the idea of a timeless God breaking into time. By now he wants to say eternity means God's time. Not that God is temporal but that God is open to human time. Revelation shows us, for Barth, that God has time for us. God created time, therefore it is not intrisically alien to him. It is Greek way to define eternity as timeless; eternity for Barth is a kind of divine time, a kind of super-time.[62]

In Gunton's opinion, Barth's concept of eternity in *CD* II/1 still remains as timeless, although it comes into our time and embraces time. On the other hand, since eternity is not totally outside of time, this timelessness could not be "absolute," so Gunton admits that Barth's divine eternity here is "not clear."[63] Michael Welker states that Barth's approach is "paradoxical metaphysical."[64] Indeed here Barth's concept of eternity appears a little abstract and metaphysical. However we should keep in mind that Barth has not yet fully developed his doctrine of election and Christology and in *CD* II/1, he still treats this concept as one of God's attributes in a traditional way, though he replaces the term "attributes" with "perfections."[65] In *CD* III/1, Barth points out without ambiguity that God's eternity is temporal:

> That it is not in time is something which can be said only of God's eternal being as such, i.e., God in his pure, divine form of existence. Even in this sense God is not non-historical and therefore non-temporal. He is not non-historical because as

---

62. Gunton, *The Barth Lectures*, p. 108.
63. Gunton, *The Barth Lectures*, p. 108.
64. "On the one hand," Welker argues, "Barth identifies God and eternity with an infinite self-surpassing of time; on the other, he opposes God and eternity to totalized time. Thus, he offers a paradoxical metaphysical construct." See Michael Welker, "God's Eternity, God's Temporality, and Trinitarian Theology," *Theology Today* 55:3 (1998): p. 318.
65. Cf. *CD* II/1, pp. 608–78.

the Triune he is in his inner life the basic type and ground of all history. And he is not non-temporal because his eternity is not merely the negation of time, but an inner readiness to create time, because it is supreme and absolute time, and therefore the source of our time, relative time. But it is true that in this sense, in his pure, divine form of existence, God is not in time but before, above and after all time, so that time is really in him.[66]

Therefore, there is also a development from timeless to temporal understanding of divine eternity in Barth. Here, we may pay attention to a middle stage of that development; a stage concerning the eternal Father. In *CD* I/2, Barth identifies three kinds of time: God-created time, i.e., the time originally created by God; our time, i.e., the fallen time; and the "third time," i.e., the revelation time.[67] Barth's concern here is the third time, which is based on the event of Jesus Christ and thus is God's time for us, the only real time:

> God had time for us, his own time for us – time, in the most positive sense, i.e. present with past and future, fulfilled time with expectation and recollection of its fulfillment, revelation time and the time of the Old Testament and New Testament witness to revelation – but withal, his own time, God's time and therefore real time.[68]

It is impossible to find *our time* other than God's time for us and *God's time* other than the time revealed to us.[69] For Barth, "our time" alone could not be an independent concept for our time cannot sustain itself from flowing

---

66. *CD* III/1, p. 68. In another place, Barth also says: "The God thus addressed is, of course, the eternal God, but not the timeless God of the Greeks; he is the covenant God of Israel, revealing himself in time. Not in the sight of God the Timeless, but in the sight of him, the very temporally revealed, are a thousand years as a day." See *CD* I/2, p. 66. Cf. also Gunton, *The Barth Lectures*, p. 150.
67. Cf. *CD* I/2, pp. 45-50.
68. *CD* I/2, p. 49.
69. Cf. *CD* I/2, p. 45.

away. Both created time and fallen time are time past. What is real in our life is our hope and expectation for the fulfillment of our time. "The old," Barth explains, "will have passed away in the incarnate Word of God. The history of Israel runs to meet this Word and so this passing away. It only runs to meet it. Yet it does run to meet it. It signifies the proclamation of world judgment in fulfilled time. It is the time for expecting it. However, because it is the time for expecting it, it is itself revelation-time."[70] Barth even calls the third time the "eternal time": "Therefore eternity is not apart from time. So the time God has for us, as distinguished from our time that comes into being and passes away, is to be regarded as eternal time."[71] Obviously, the most significant difference between our fallen time and this eternal time lies in that there is no absolute separation between the past, present and future in God's eternal time. Due to our fallen state, time has lost its original coherence. Had God left us in our isolated time alone, we would have lived in temporal regret and desperation. However, God's revelation time has a positive, even creative function for our time:

> Revelation in the sense of Holy Scripture is an eternal, but not therefore a timeless reality. It is also a temporal reality. So it is not a sort of ideal, yet in itself timeless content of all or some times. It does not remain transcendent over time, it does not merely meet it at a point, but it enters time; nay, it assumes time; nay, it creates time for itself.[72]

However, from a human perspective, how would one respond to God's revelation time? Do we resist it severely or run away from it out of our sinful nature? Or, are we overwhelmed by God's creative time so that we totally lose our own? Welker takes the former stand in a weak sense when he argues that,

---

70. *CD* I/2, p. 86
71. *CD* I/2, p. 50.
72. *CD* I/2, p. 50.

> [s]ince not all the times and all the coordinations of times correspond to God's will and God's intentions and will perhaps not even correspond to them in any possible future, and since many coordinations of times are mediated by creatures and thus do not automatically correspond to God's good will, it would be wrong to understand God's eternity as *a priori* related to all times.[73]

Barth might agree with Welker on his observation. We do always try to flee from God's spirit and presence (Ps 139:7), saving our time for our own. Thus our time indeed does not "correspond to God's will and God's intention." However Welker comes to his point too quickly by cutting apart the relation between our time and God's time for us. According to Barth, our fallen humanity cannot stop God's good will for us in Jesus Christ, nor can our limited time set any boundary on God's eternity, as Torrance points out: "Barth's position rests upon an immense stress on the concrete activity of God in space and time, in creation as in redemption, and upon his refusal to accept that God's power is limited by the weakness of human capacity or that the so-called natural reason can set any limits to God's self-revelation to mankind."[74]

If this relation could be lacerated, we might talk about an independent existential state without Jesus Christ. For Barth, such a state is untrue and abstract. There is no human time outside of God's revelation, i.e., the event of Jesus Christ. Thus Barth argues:

> It regards revelation as necessary against the background of God's and not a human *a priori* in time and history. It therefore regards "fulfilled time" from the standpoint of the fulfillment, not of the time. Time in fulfilled time is what it is entirely and altogether in virtue of its fulfillment. In other

---

73. Welker, "God's Eternity, God's Temporality, and Trinitarian Theology," p. 321.
74. T F Torrance, "The Ground and Grammar of Theology," in Alister McGrath eds. *The Christian Theology Reader* (Oxford: Blackwell, 1995), p. 86. Cf. also *CD* III/2, p. 527.

words, history is what it is, entirely and altogether in virtue of the Subject who acts here.[75]

The fulfilled time means concretely the forty days in the Easter event. It is a time at which the eternal God presents and reveals himself to his creature directly. The fulfilled time is the present time in the three dimensions of revelation time. Three dimensions of time in Barth's doctrine of the Word of God are presented as the time of expectation, the revelation time, and the time of recollection. Here revelation time means "God is present to man as the coming God,"[76] i.e., the fulfilled time or Easter time of present time. The time of expectation is the time of the Old Testament. Since the Old Testament "is the witness to the genuine expectation of revelation," its time is "high above the other times in the time area *ante Christum natum*."[77] The authenticity of the time of expectation lies in its relationship with the revelation time, i.e., it is expectation of revelation and this expectation can only be asserted from the side of revelation.[78] The time of recollection is the time of the New Testament. "The New Testament," Barth points out, "like the Old Testament, is the witness to a togetherness of God and man, based on and consisting in a free self-relating of God to man. What in the Old Testament, in the expectation, was God's covenant with man, is here, in the fulfillment, God's becoming man."[79] However, the time of recollection is not the fulfilled time.[80] Even the time of recollection is the time "after" the fulfilled time. The fulfilled time is the time touched directly by the Creator's eternity, thus a kind of eternal time which differentiates itself from all times before and after it. On the other hand, although the time of expectation and time of recollection are not fulfilled

---

75. *CD* I/2, p. 60.
76. *CD* I/2, p. 60.
77. *CD* I/2, p. 70.
78. Cf. *CD* I/2, p. 71.
79. *CD* I/2, p. 105.
80. Barth thinks so because "[t]he forty days and the apostolic age, fulfilled time and the time of recollection, are two different things. There is no word of the apostles and their communities after Pentecost thinking that they were living directly in the eternal presence of God in the days of Easter. Revelation remains revelation and does not become a revealed state." See *CD* I/2, p. 118.

time, they are "genuine" times because both are directed to the fulfilled time and thus penetrated by the fulfilled time. Barth stresses the coherence of the three dimensions of revelation time:

> We cannot speak of the time of revelation without also speaking of its pre-time. It, too, is revelation-time, although in the sense of the time of expecting revelation. Genuine expectation of revelation does not exist without the latter; as expected, revelation is also present to it. Where expectation is genuine, "previously" does not mean "not yet"; just as, where recollection is genuine, "subsequently" does not mean "no longer." Genuine expectation and genuine recollection are testimonies to revelation, mutually as different as expectation and recollection are different, but one in their content, in their object, in the thing attested, and also one in that for them this thing attested is neither merely future nor merely past; as "future" and as "past" it is present.[81]

To sum up, Barth's fulfilled time in revelation is, more or less, a kind of "eternal time," i.e., timeless time like the "eternal now" in *ER*, because it is a time that differentiates itself from all other times. However, since this time is based on a concrete event – the Easter event in which the risen Christ lives in time concretely for forty days, thus fulfilling time once and for all, reconciling all times witnessed in the Old Testament and New Testament into this fulfilled time – this revelation time is indeed temporal.

2.3 Conclusion

First, the Father reveals himself as the eternal triune God. The Father is coeternal with the Son and the Holy Spirit. The eternal immanent Trinity acts concretely as the temporal economic Trinity, thus the triune God is both transcendental and immanent to us. There is no subordination in Trinity at all, either ontologically or economically.

---

81. *CD* I/2, p. 70.

Second, the eternal Father, Son and Holy Spirit are witnessed in the Old Testament and New Testament in the time of expectation and recollection. Between these times is the fulfilled time at which the eternal God reveals himself directly in time, thus this time becomes the time that is present to all time. The fulfilled time differentiates itself from other times and penetrates the time before and after the Easter event.

Section 3: The Father's Eternal Preservation

3.1 Time as the Form of Creature

We creatures live in discrete times. Our past, present and future have never been a continuum. In *CD* III/2, Barth analyzes human temporality in detail. On the past and the future, Barth takes an Augustinian psychological stand: the past exists in our memory, the future in anticipation; both memory and anticipation are incomplete and unreliable, hence are to some extent "unreal."[82]

Once we possess the past, we live in a time which has its actuality, but now it has gone and its memory is a mere subjective conjecture. What we experienced as reality now "[w]e can recall only a few scraps of the vanished and forgotten past and its contents, its life and history. And even what we recall sinks back to oblivion. And in its limited sphere memory is not the present reality."[83] Since the past has ceased to belong to us, there is a huge ditch between our past and our present and future, because our memory cannot guarantee the identity of ourselves in different passages of time. Barth illustrates this in a Heraclitian way: "We are no longer the people we were years ago, yesterday, or even this morning. Of course we should like to cling to what was, but the present and the future are already beckoning us."[84]

---

82. Cf. *CD* III/2, pp. 512-5.
83. *CD* III/2, p. 513.
84. *CD* III/2, p. 513.

Similarly, uncertainty also threatens the future. We can never say for sure that the future belongs to us. We have all kinds of plans and intentions about what is coming to us, however what really comes to us is always out of control. Even our dreams will come true some time later, they are not true yet, not true at the moment. In this sense Barth says:

> Anticipation is no substitute for the reality anticipated. And the future when it comes may partially or totally confound our expectations. It is almost a law of nature that this should be the case. We are always poor prophets even of what is to happen within the next hour or so, to say nothing of a year or two hence, or centuries to come. The future – if we have one at all, and in whatever form we have it – is even more obscure than the past. In relation to it, even our identity with ourselves is only a guess, and a doubtful one at that.[85]

If the past and the future are not real, then how about the present? We still remember two points in Augustinian presentism: first, only the present is real – neither the past nor the future could be understood apart from the present, for the past is no other than the present in memory, the future is no other than the present in expectation. Second, the reality of the present is dependent upon the human consciousness, a thinking self. Compared with memory and expectation, the present is our direct perception. Barth differs from Augustine at both points.

Firstly, Barth denies the reality of the present. Augustine derives the past and the future from the present. On the contrary, Barth defines the present as the shifting boundary of the past and the future.[86] The present is, like a point without length, merely "time between times."[87] Both the past and the future have duration, whereas the present possesses no duration. In this sense, the present does not deserve to be called "time" at all. Secondly, Barth denies our direct perception of the now or present. The

---

85. *CD* III/2, p. 513.
86. Cf. *CD* III/2, p. 514.
87. *CD* III/2, p. 514.

way we experience the present determines that it is less real than the past and future. For Augustine, the past and the future can only be experienced as the present memory and present expectation. Oppositely, Barth argues that the present can only be experienced in the form of memory or expectation since "[w]e are and live out only what we were in a partly forgotten, partly remembered past and will be (perhaps) in an unknown future, i.e., in all the questionableness of our being in past and future time. In the present in which we think we have it most securely we have no time."[88]

The unreality and discontinuity of our time lead to emptiness and abstraction. Since the beginning of our life we are threatened by nothingness; we are created as a kind of being which is able to move forward to nothingness.[89] Neither in present nor in past and future can we actually hold or possess even a single moment. In the stream of our time, we realize that "vanity of vanities! All is vanity" (Eccl 1:1). Time as the form of creature, like Newtonian absolute time, is nothing more than an empty container. The container, empty and discontinuous in itself, is always waiting for its fulfillment. The content which can fill the empty vessel can be found nowhere else other than in the eternal Creator himself. Barth thus describes our creaturely time, the empty time expecting its fulfillment and redemption:

> But behind the application of the concept of time fulfilment to that of time in Gal 4, Eph 1 and Mark 1 there lies a definite view of time, it is pictured as an empty vessel, not yet filled, but waiting to be filled up at a particular time. As all the commandments, promises and Prophecies of the prophets and righteous men of the Old Testament, as all its sayings and types, are without content apart from the coming of the kingdom in the man Jesus, and therefore defective in themselves, yet, being related to this event, and destined all along for this content, they are not for nothing, so too it is with

---

88. *CD* III/2, p. 514.
89. Cf. Timothy J. Gorringe, *Karl Barth: Against Hegemony* (Oxford: Oxford University Press, 1999), p. 182.

time in itself and as such. It, too, is empty in both the negative and positive sense: empty of this content and empty for this content.[90]

In our empty time we expect this content, so when the time comes, God fills this empty container with his abundant grace and love. Since there is God's good will in creation, the Creator will never leave his creatures in their empty time alone. From eternity God the Father preserves and sustains our time in the Son and the Holy Spirit.

3.2 Eternal Preservation of the Creator

God the Father as described in the Bible, is not a being of the kind to which the creature belongs and therefore he might equally be the same with the creature; nor is he a self-contained being which has nothing to do with his own creature. He creates and reveals time as the form of his creature in his eternal covenant. With Augustine and Heidegger in mind, Barth criticizes two errors which derive the concept of time merely from the existential condition of human beings: first, "Augustine, like Heidegger, regards time definitively and unequivocally as a self-determination of man's existence as a creature";[91] second, "Augustine, like Heidegger, regards time definitively and conclusively as a conditioned reality."[92] For Barth, our time is never merely ours; it is always "the time God has for us."[93] Our time, as the form of creature, has its own lifespan. Our time is one dimensional from birth to death. We live within the limits imposed by the fact that no one can cross the border of this span. Whatever happens in our life between birth and death is such that the time's disposing effect on us becomes more and more obvious. Thus Barth describes our existential situation under the power of time:

---

90. *CD*, III/2, p. 461.
91. *CD* I/2, p. 46.
92. *CD* I/2, p. 46.
93. This means, "(1) that we have no other time than the time God has for us, and (2) that God has no other time for us than the time of his revelation." See *CD* I/2, p. 45.

We are still moving towards the time when it will be destroyed as it deserves and we shall live in righteousness and true holiness. It still afflicts our being in time as such. Hence, whether we are Christians or non-Christians, we have our time only as a time which continually passes. It is given us from morning to evening, from youth to age, as a time for truly reconciled being. But it steadily escapes us, and therefore, however long, it is always dreadfully short, far too short, in relation to what its fulfillment should be and never is. Hence the being of all creatures in the time allotted them is not merely passing but actually passes. Its goal is its end. It is a being which moves towards death. From its very commencement as life it is a dying.[94]

Yes, we are dying since our birth. Death ends everything in our life and its threatening power affects each moment in our life. By ourselves we are powerless to resist its threatening. What we can do is only to move hopelessly toward it in our lifetime. "Who will rescue me from this body of death?" (Rom 7:24). However, the Father wills not only our death at the end of our lifespan, but also eternal life afterwards. The hope of eternal life protects us from the fearing of death, thus preserves our lifetime in an eschatological way:

> The One whom Jesus reveals as the Father is known absolutely on the death of man, at the end of his existence. His will enters the life of man, not identically with death, nor merely in the same way as death, but really with death, executing death on man, impressing the signs of death upon man. Only in the sharply drawn boundary line of the cross, which is to be drawn again and again, is His will revealed as the will to quicken, bless, and benefit. The life that His will creates will be a life

---

94. *CD* IV/3, p. 337.

that has passed through death, that is risen from death; it will be eternal life, truly a new birth.[95]

God the Father creates time as the form of our existence and reveals it to us. This is a totally divine work which cannot be accomplished by creatures themselves since we have no power to control our life or death at all. Only the Lord of our existence has lordship over both life and death. "To be or not to be?" has never been a question up to us creatures; on the contrary, the entire span of our being is sustained by God and God alone above the abyss of nothingness.[96] Thus Barth argues:

> God alone is above death and after it. He alone has immortality (1 Tim 6:16). If a creature is to have immortal life, i.e., the life which defies and overcomes death, which leaves it behind, which is no longer threatened by it, then in no circumstances can this be simply its autonomous continuation in life. It can be only its new life from God and with God. It can be only the eternal life which is given it by God after the manner of His own life.[97]

God, who prepares eternal life for us before we were created, and stands to receive us in his eternity when we die, also protects us in our earthly life. The fact that physical death is still our mortal boundary is not crucial any more. God's good will in his creatures triumphs over death, which is a great comfort in our otherwise empty time, for the Father's promise of life after death fulfills our emptiness. Such a promise is not a mere idea, but the concrete truth in history, since the co-temporality of God becomes a reality in Jesus Christ and is manifested to us by His resurrection.[98] In this

---

95. *CD* I/1, pp. 387-8.
96. Cf. *CD* I/1, pp. 388-9.
97. *CD* IV/3, pp. 310-1.
98. As Willis observes: "The general co-temporality of God's concurrence with the creature in the divine preservation and governance of the world displays the full dimension of God's specific co-temporality with the creature in the history of the covenant, which centers in the eternal election of all men in Jesus Christ." See Robert E. Willis, *The Ethics of Karl Barth* (Leiden: E. J. Brill, 1971), p. 125.

important paragraph, Barth describes in detail what Jesus Christ achieves for the creatures at the end of time:

> In the final act of salvation history, i.e., in the revelation of Jesus Christ as the Foundation and Deliverer and Head of the whole of creation, the history of creation will also reach its goal and end. It will not need to progress any further, it will have fulfilled its purpose. Everything that happened in the course of that history will then take place together as a recapitulation of all individual events. It will be made definitive as the temporal end of the creature beyond which it cannot exist any more.[99]

We may identify some characteristics in Barth's teaching of the Father's preservation. First, the Father's preservation is eternal. The Father's preservation is pre-, supra-, and post-temporality. Before we were born, God's grace is already there in his creation. After our death, at the end-time, God's preservation continues. Our time, even before its beginning and after its end, is embraced by God's eternity like a baby embraced by its mother. The Father's preservation extends out of our lifespan and breaks the boundaries of our earthly time. That is the reason why this preservation is eternal:

> [I]nasmuch as the faithfulness of God is an eternal faithfulness, this preservation is an eternal preservation. It does not end with the ending of the existence of the creature, just as it did not begin with that existence and is not limited by its limitations. In the eternal counsel of God it was applied and assured to the creature before creation itself. Similarly it is still applied and assured to it even when the creature has completed its appointed course, even when it does not exist any longer. It lays hold of the creature as it were in and with its

---

99. *CD* III/3, p. 88.

limitations; even in and with the limitations of its temporal duration. This is how God willed and created the creature.[100]

Second, the Father's preservation is temporal. The eternal preservation fulfills our time rather than makes it nothingness for the time is given by the Father "in reality and not in appearance."[101] Since there is no separation of these time dimensions in God's eternity, our past, present and future are open to God. Thus our temporality is preserved eternally in God. As Jenson observes:

> According to Barth, God in himself is not atemporal, but temporal. The time which he, in his eternal life, has is the possibility and model of created time. There exists however this fundamental difference between God's time and created time as such: In God past, present and future are not separated; in merely creaturely time they fall apart into a succession of separate "times". In God the past is that which is present as the eternally past, as, so to speak, the qualitatively past. For man, it is that which is "no more." With God therefore, that which in his eternal self-discrimination is rejected is, so to speak, always past, qualitatively past. But when this is carried out in time for the creature, this past achieves a time of its own.[102]

When Barth says that "[e]ternal preservation does not mean a continuation of the existence of the creature,"[103] he means God's preservation is not true in an everlasting sense.[104] When Jesus Christ accomplishes the consummation of the salvation after our time and history, thus the creation reaches

---

100. *CD* III/3, pp. 87-8.
101. *CD* III/1, p. 89.
102. Robert W. Jenson, *Cur Deus Homo? The Election of Jesus Christ in the Theology of Karl Barth* (Heidelberg: Th. D. dissertation, 1959), p. 53.
103. *CD* III/1, p. 89.
104. About God's Eternity in the sense of everlasting, Pannenberg has a clear explanation: "From everlasting to everlasting means from the unimaginable past to the remotest future. Hebrew has no other term for eternity than unlimited duration, whether past or future." See Pannenberg, *Systematic Theology*, volume 1, p. 401.

its goal, there will be no need for the continuation of the creature, because everything in creation has already been achieved. On the other hand, when he says that "[h]e will not be alone in eternity, but with the creature. He will allow it to partake of his own eternal life. And in this way the creature will continue to be, in its limitation, even in its limited temporal duration,"[105] he means the preservation is true in an eternal sense. The Father's preservation does not end with the end of the creature and time, for the temporal duration could even be saved in its "original" form in God's eternity.

Last but not least, the Father not only preserves the creation in a transcendental way, but also in an immanent way. A merely transcendental God is a pagan, an abstract God for Barth. From eternity, the Father relates himself to us as our Covenant-partner. Human time is willed and intended concretely by the Father in our own history and thus corresponds to his eternity.[106] Without the Father's gracious preservation, our time inevitably collapses into fragments and becomes nothing. In this sense Barth argues:

> God's covenant with man is not just an idea, but a connected history in a continuum of time in which individuals share in its initiation and execution, its grace and judgment, having their own particular part in it with their own history in their own time. Hence this covenant can be proclaimed and believed only as the meaning and secret of all human history and time, and all individual histories and times.[107]

On the other hand, this immanent and concrete preservation does not make God's eternity less eternal. Preserved and sustained in God's eternal covenant, the nature of our time has been changed ontologically, i.e., from discrete to continuous, from abstract to concrete. However, the Creator's eternity remains the same for it cannot be changed by time, although it appears to be temporal rather than timeless. Thus Barth argues: "the eternity in which he himself is true time and the Creator of all time is revealed in

---

105. *CD* III/1, p. 90.
106. Cf. *CD* III/2, pp. 525-6.
107. *CD* III/2, p. 524.

the fact that, although our time is that of sin and death, he can enter it and himself be temporal in it, yet without ceasing to be eternal, able rather to be the Eternal in time."[108]

3.3 Conclusion

First, human beings live under the power of time, which is the existential form of the creature. Everyone has his or her lifespan which cannot be surpassed by himself or herself. Time, as the form of creature, is empty and discontinuous in itself, waiting for its fufilment and redemption from the eternal Creator.

Second, our lifespan is enclosed by God's preservation on all sides. God preserves us before our birth, throughout our lifetime and after our death. Nothing is lost in this eternal preservation and only in the time allotted to us we confront God concretely.

Third, the eternal Father preserves his creature in both transcendental and immanent ways. Transcendentally, God alone is above death and gives life to his creature. Immanently, the Father relates himself to us as our Covenant-partner. This relationship with time shows that God's eternity is temporal rather than timeless. Further, this temporal preservation does not make God's eternity less eternal at all.

Section 4:
The Eschatological Creator

4.1 The Creator in Eschatology

Our given time is always coming to an end. It is in a state of transition from the past to the future. "It has its present in this transition, but in no present can it find satisfaction."[109] Though we still are, we shall be no longer and everyone will die sooner or later. Death is the end of everything in our lives. However, if the end and death only mean the negation and curse of time, it

---

108. *CD* IV/1, pp. 187-8.
109. *CD* III/2, p. 587.

is contrary to God's good creation. Barth resolves this problem of theodicy by an insightful analogic deduction:

> The fact that at a particular moment, at the beginning of our time, we emerged from non-being to being is not intrinsically negative or necessarily evil. It is, indeed, the very opposite. It signifies something supremely positive if it is the case, as we have seen, that we come from God. It can be negative and evil only if our end means passing not only into non-being but into the negation of being. If this is what is meant by the death which is the end of our time, it follows as a consequence that we have also emerged from negation. We are then forced to conclude that our beginning is also negative and evil. At first sight there seems to be no reason why we should draw this conclusion about our beginning.[110]

"Death," Barth confesses, "as it meets us, can be understood only as a sign of God's judgment."[111] That is a "universal truth" rather than "just a religious opinion."[112] Nevertheless, "our standing under this sign is not something intrinsic to our human nature. For God did not create us to exist under this impending threat of being hewn down and cast into the fire."[113] There is a way out. At the end of our time we are confronted not only with death itself but also with our Creator, then we still know that all our time line is embraced by God's eternity in Jesus Christ.[114] At the end time we do

---

110. *CD* III/2, p. 595. In brief, "[d]eath is man's step from existence into non-existence, as birth is his step from non-existence into existence." See *CD* III/2, p. 632.
111. *CD* III/2, p. 597.
112. *CD* III/2, p. 607.
113. *CD* III/2, p. 597.
114. In Jenson's words: "of the many images with which Barth evokes the relation of time and eternity, one is clearest. Time is touched by eternity, Barth said, as a circle is touched by a tangent line. The line does touch the circle, yet there is no part of the circle that belongs to the line or part of the line that belongs to the circle. Beings who lived on the circle and moved around it would be stopped when they came to the point of tangency, but could not experience or grasp their impediment itself. Just so are we stopped at "the line of death" where eternity touches time. Christ is Savior in that he occupies that line perfectly." See R. W. Jenson, "Karl Barth," in D. F. Ford eds. *The Modern Theologians* (Oxford: Blackwell Publishers Ltd, 1997), p. 34.

not meet with the God of death, rather the living Creator himself. Neither do we die for the first time, for the Son of the Creator died for us on the cross and was resurrected three days later. Our natural death is our second death.[115] The grace and love of our Creator have been revealed concretely in the death of his only Son, as Barth puts it: "the God who awaits us in death and as the Lord of death is the gracious God. He is the God who is for man. Other gods who are not gracious and are not for man are idols. They are not the true and living God, the One who speaks to us in His eternal Word incarnate in Jesus Christ and crucified and put to death for us."[116] We exist only in the sense that our existence is sustained by the Father in his Son. Our God reigns over us not only as the Lord of life, but also as the Lord of death. His love and grace are present with us even in our death. "We die," Barth writes, "but he lives for us. Even in death we are not lost to him, and therefore we are not really lost. One day we shall cease to be, but even then he will be for us. Hence our future non-existence cannot be our complete negation."[117]

For Barth, there is a time when we were not yet – just as there is also a time when we will not be any more. Human beings exist between these two temporal boundaries: before "to be" and after "not to be". It is the latter one that bears on eschatology. After this "not to be" or "being no more", is there any beyond or future? The answer is "no" in a human by himself or herself – there is no beyond or future after one's death. His or her future can only be created and granted by the eternal Creator. As the Lord, God reveals himself as the end of our death and the beyond and future of us. In this sense Barth argues:

> Man's beyond is that God as his Creator, Covenant-partner, Judge and Savior, was and is and will be his true Counterpart in life, and finally and exclusively and totally in death. Man as such, however, belongs to this world. He is thus finite and mortal. One day he will only have been, as once he was not.

---

115. Cf. *CD* III/2, p. 628.
116. *CD* III/2, p. 609.
117. *CD* III/2, pp. 610-1.

> His divinely given promise and hope and confidence in this confrontation with God is that even as this one who has been he will share the eternal life of God himself. Its content is not, therefore, his liberation from his this-sidedness, from his end and dying, but positively the glorification by the eternal God of his natural and lawful this-sided, finite and mortal being. He does not look and move towards the fact that this being of his in his time will one day be forgotten and extinguished and left behind, and in some degree replaced by a new, other-sided, infinite and immortal being after his time.[118]

The Creator gave his only Son for us, let him die on the cross and raised him from the dead, as the first fruit of the death. He rose and came again "in the manifestation or revelation of his prior human life as it had fallen victim to death as such, but had been delivered from death, invested with divine glory, and caused to shine in this glory, in virtue of its participation in the life of God."[119] If we are not to be guilty of Docetism in our exposition of the resurrected Jesus, we must accept the fact that the glory of God is here present in the "visible, audible and even tangible"[120] return of this very man. Upon what Jesus means to our time, Trowitzsch argues thus:

> Jesus is in charge of the being and time. He establishes and creates them new, breaks them open, breaks their specific despotism and deathly nature, heals their ailments, modifies the movement of time, which made the new fall back every time immediately into what once was and into what is not. He is the place where one gains perspective and all the being concurs.[121]

---

118. *CD* III/2, pp. 632-3.
119. *CD* IV/3, p. 312.
120. *CD* IV/3, p. 312.
121. [Er [Jesus] meistert Sein und Zeit, er erbringt und schafft sie neu, er bricht sie auf, bricht ihre spezifische Despotie und Todesförmigkeit, heilt ihr Gebrechen, verändert die Zeitbewegung, die das Neue noch jedesmal unverzüglich ins Gewesene und Nichtige zurückfallen ließ. Er ist der perspektivische Ort, an dem sich alles Sein trifft.] Michael Trowitzsch, *Karl Barth heute* (Göttingen: Vandenhoeck & Ruprecht, 2007), p. 381.

In order to complete his narration of the history of Jesus' reconciled work, Barth describes the transition from Jesus' sphere to ours. At first we know the accomplished reconciliation through Jesus' death and resurrection. Without the Easter event "which destroys his death, he could not be the One who comes to us as he who has lived and died for us, but only the One who in his death has gone infinitely far from us like anyone else who dies. He would then be a past and dead Mediator and High-priest and King and Lord, etc., unknown and therefore without significance to us as such."[122] By virtue of his resurrection, Jesus himself is liberated from being trapped in history. Thus our time is opened by him in the Holy Spirit and our time is his because he has become a part of it. In Jesus Christ, eternal God's "there and then" becomes our "here and now."[123] In Jesus Christ resurrected from the dead, "the eternal God himself has really turned to us, and acted for us, and indeed become our own. In him the promise of eternal life – not just an extension of this life in a continuation of time, but a life in communion with the eternal life of God himself – is really given."[124] Thus in Jesus Christ alone rests our future and hope. As Barth puts it:

> He is "Jesus Christ today," in all his being and action of yesterday, and its whole power for the world, new in the fact that today, his death and the empty tomb behind him, he moves out from the latency of his being and action of yesterday and from the inoperativeness of his power, appearing to his disciples and in them potentially to all men and the whole cosmos, declaring himself, making known his presence and what has been accomplished in him for all men and for the whole created order, putting it into effect. With its manifestation and

---

122. *CD* IV/3, p. 283.

123. In Barth's words: "He himself is not merely there in his own place, but as he is there in his own place he is also here in ours. He is the One who is on the way from there to here. Hence, as he is for himself, he is also among and for and in and through us. He is and acts on his way from his own particular sphere to our surrounding, anthropological sphere." See *CD* IV/3, p. 279.

124. *CD* III/2, p. 614.

self-declaration, the fact of there and yesterday now becomes the factor of here and today.[125]

How are we included in this history? What does this history have to do with us? How do we get from here and now to Jesus there and then? Or, in Barth's terms, how does Jesus get from there and then to us here and now? How do we leap Lessing's "ugly ditch" between history and faith?[126] It is the work of the Holy Spirit who reconciles us to God himself after the death and resurrection of Jesus Christ, in time between the first and second *parousia*.[127] As Molnar argues: "Barth was suggesting that the Holy Spirit is first the third person of the Trinity and then the Spirit of the raising of the dead; thus God's sovereignty and the certainty of our hope could never become dependent on historical events but would be disclosed in and through them."[128]

The work of the Holy Spirit in the created order is based on the first *parousia* and directed to the second. At the end of Jesus' first *parousia*, "in the Easter event as the commencement of the new coming of Jesus Christ in revelation of what took place in his life and death, it is also revealed that the time which is still left to the world and human history and all men can only be the last time, i.e., time running towards its appointed end."[129] The first *parousia* is thus eschatological throughout its course. The time in the death of Jesus Christ is imparted to us by the power of the Holy Spirit and the end time is given to all the time which remains.[130] As Barth puts it:

> As he lives in relationship to us in our time, we live in relationship to him together with all the men of our own and all times, there being no separation between them and us nor us and them. The day of his revelation in its final form will concretely reveal this. But since our day is a day of his revelation

---

125. *CD* IV/3, p. 291. Cf. also pp. 106-7.
126. Cf. *CD* IV/3, p. 286.
127. Details are given in *Chapter Four*.
128. Molnar, *Divine Freedom and the Doctrine of the Immanent Trinity*, p. 131.
129. *CD* IV/3, p. 295.
130. Cf. *CD* IV/3, p. 296.

as the hope of us all, a day of the promise of the Spirit, it is already true and actual in this day of ours, and thus to be reckoned with in all seriousness and with all joy.[131]

The Holy Spirit, eternally proceeding from the Father and the Son, makes Jesus present to the faithful by giving them the pledge about the Son, that is, moving them toward the Creator's original good will at the end time. Through the work of the Son and the Holy Spirit, our final end would be as complete and perfect as the Father intends in his creation. Thus Barth writes:

> The promise, intimation and guarantee of his coming as Redeemer and Perfecter, of the new cosmic form to be inaugurated by him as the future of the world and their own ultimate future; and the promise, intimation and guarantee of his presence and assistance in their temporal future, in the world which has not yet reached its goal but is only moving towards it, on their own way within the world-occurrence moving to this end.[132]

We receive what Jesus accomplished for us and what the Holy Spirit imparted to us by faith. For the faithful, the promise of the eternal kingdom-life, is already here and now. They already exist as such here and now in a distinctive way, as humans who are determined by this promise and move towards the consummation of the salvation here and now "as they pass from every temporal present to the temporal future still allotted to them."[133] All the way, the Holy Spirit leads and accompanies them. On the contrary, for non-believers, since they lack the Spirit and reject the Son, they "have no promise of the ultimate future, the eternal kingdom and eternal life, they cannot have the enclosed promise in respect of their own existence in time

---

131. *CD* IV/3, p. 364.
132. *CD* IV/3, p. 351.
133. *CD* IV/3, p. 352.

as their immediate future."[134] Thus Barth sums up the role of the Holy Spirit in linking time and eternity:

> If we do not honour the little, penultimate pledge as seriously given to us *hic et nunc* by the present and living Christ, we cannot appreciate or make much of the great and ultimate pledge for the eternal *illic et tunc*. In these circumstances, have we really received the Spirit and his twofold pledge, the temporal as well as the eternal, the eternal as well as the temporal? If we have, how can we help being merry even here and today? It is no contradiction to us that in the one hope in Jesus Christ our time is given us only for eternity and eternity only for our time.[135]

However, Barth's eschatology bridges the faithful and non-believers because "[e]schatologically, all men are under the same future. It is thus impossible for Christian community ever to break away from the wider context in which it finds itself, and forfeit community with its neighbor."[136] Before the beginning, God the Father creates time as the form of his creature. He sends the Son and the Spirit from eternity to our temporality, reconciling and redeeming the fallen time back to his eternity. At the end of the salvation history, what happens is not that we meet a God of death and die to him forever, instead the eschatological Creator makes us anew and starts the eternal life together with us. Through the Son's reconciliation and the Holy Spirit's redemption, we shall meet the eternal Father face to face in an eschatological sense, as Oh puts it: "As Barth repeatedly points out, God's will toward human beings does not end with the fact that God created them and reconciled the sinful to him in Jesus Christ, but with their redemption in the Holy Spirit as divine children to whom God becomes the eternal Father."[137] It is God's eternity that gives meaning to time and

---

134. *CD* IV/3, p. 353.
135. *CD* IV/3, p. 360.
136. Willis, *The Ethics of Karl Barth*, p. 270.
137. Peter S. Oh, *Karl Barth's Trinitarian Theology: A Study in Karl Barth's Analogical Use of the Trinitarian Relation* (London and New York: T & T Clark, 2006), p. 161.

history, and God's eternity promises that the creatures will be reunited with their Creator at the end. In this sense Tanner writes:

> The consummation of the world will be as extensive as its beginnings in creation and providence. The world is for the glorification of God, the self-manifestation of God in what is not God. That process begins with creation, continues in a historical fellowship of God with a particular people, Israel, and ends with Jesus as the one through whom the whole world will show forth God in unity with God.[138]

Barth's eschatology is significant in two dimensions. First is the future cosmic dimension. At the end of the human history, the Father creates new heavens and new earth together with the Son and the Holy Spirit, and with us as well.[139] What Jesus reconciled and the Holy Spirit promised becomes the reality and the beginning of our eternal life. In this sense Gunton says:

> Some late nineteenth- and early twentieth-century biblical scholars and church historians took the discovery of Jesus' essentially eschatological message as Christianity's death-warrant. Jesus saw himself, they held, as the prophet of the end; but the end did not come, and so he was mistaken. The genius of Barth is that he took the very same discoveries to be life-warrant.[140]

Second is the human existential dimension. In eschatological hope, God is coming to us here and now. The future penetrates our present in an eschatological way. However, not every theologian agrees upon this issue.

---

138. Kathryn Tanner, "Creation and Providence," in John Webster eds. *The Cambridge Companion to Karl Barth* (Cambridge: Cambridge University Press, 2000), p. 125.

139. For Barth's eschatological new creation, Cf. Gotthard Oblau, *Gotteszeit und Menschenzeit: Eschatologie in der Kirchlichen Dogmatik von Karl Barth* (Düsseldorf: Neukircher Verlag, 1988), pp. 263-77.

140. Gunton, *Father, Son & Holy Spirit*, p. 216.

Moltmann, from his futurist point of view, charges Barth's eschatology with lacking the hope which should have had an impact on human time:

> No eschatological tension as yet enters time just because God's "post-temporality" is added to his "supra-temporality"; nor does this lend any precedence to the future over against present and past. Even in his own self-criticism of 1948, Barth did not rediscover that access to the eschatological hope which he had encountered early on in the two Blumhardts. His time-eternity dialectic remained stuck fast in the Platonic thinking about origins pursued by his brother, Heinrich Barth.[141]

Here Barth's "self-criticism of 1948" refers to *CD* III/2 which contains "Man in His Time," "*ein Buch im Buche*"[142] which deals with God's act in human history. Moltmann's charge of "Platonic thinking" may apply to Barth's "eternal now" in *ER*, but definitely not to *CD* III/2. In "Man in His Time," Barth has surpassed both the eternal moment in *ER* and the eternity-like fulfilled revelation time in *CD* I/2. Thus "Time is the condition for God's self-realization in human life, which God himself has given through the creation of human beings."[143] Contrary to Moltmann's judgement, the "eschatological tension" is already there in creation in Barth.

4.2 Pannenberg's Response

When we turn to Pannenberg's interpretation of Barth, we see a different image. On the issue of God's eternity, Pannenberg, along with Barth, takes

---

141. Jürgen Moltmann, *The Coming of God: Christian Eschatology*, trans. Margaret Kohl (Minneapolis: Fortress Press, 1996), p. 18. Horton echoes Molitman's charge by saying that "[a]lthough he highlighted the importance of eschatology, Kierkegaard's concept of the 'eternal moment' penetrating history in punctiliar events with no extension in time could not provide sufficient resources for relating eschatology to history." See Michael S. Horton, "A Stony Jar: The Legacy of Karl Barth for Evangelical Theology," in *Engaging with Barth*, p. 351.
142. Ingolf U. Dalferth, "Der Mensch in seiner Zeit," *Zeitschrift für dialektische Theologie* 16 (2000): p. 152.
143. [Zeit ist die von Gott selbst mit der Geschöpflichkeit des Menschen gesetzte Bedingung seiner Selbstvergegenwärtigung in menschlichen Leben.] Dalferth, "Der Mensch in seiner Zeit," p. 178.

a Boethian stand: "Barth rightly applauded this description of eternity as the perfect possession of life, since in it eternity is authentic duration and not just a negation of time. He bewailed the fact that in the theological tradition the definition 'was never properly exploited.'"[144]

In order to avoid the dilemma of an undifferentiated eternal God and a limited temporal God, i.e., to realize the Boethian possession of all times and maintain the distinction of temporality, Pannenberg introduces the doctrine of the Trinity: "This is possible only if the reality of God is not understood as undifferentiated identity but as intrinsically differentiated unity. But this demands the doctrine of the Trinity. Barth finely stressed this and spoke of an 'order and succession' in the Trinitarian life of God which includes a 'before' and 'after.'"[145] However, the traditional doctrine of Trinity has rarely such a function. For example, the Augustinian Trinity, by emphasizing an eternally static relation of the three divine persons, can hardly retain the temporal distinction within the Trinitarian life.[146] Thus, in his next step, Pannenberg has to appeal to Rahner's Rule – the identity of immanent and economic Trinity:

> It corresponds to the realization that the immanent Trinity is identical with the economic Trinity. In virtue of Trinitarian differentiation God's eternity includes the time of creatures in its full range, from the beginning of creation to its eschatological consummation. Barth discusses this in his treatment of the temporality of eternity as pre-, super-, and post-temporality.[147]

Pannenberg claims that he, along with Boethius and Barth, insists on a temporal interpretation of God's eternity by stressing a) the internal differentiation of Trinity and b) the oneness of immanent and economic

---

144. Pannenberg, *Systematic Theology*, volume 1, p. 404.
145. Pannenberg, *Systematic Theology*, volume 1, p. 405.
146. Pannenberg criticizes that Augustine "did not develop the relation between the Trinity and the economy of salvation." See *Systematic Theology*, volume 1, p. 409.
147. Pannenberg, *Systematic Theology*, volume 1, pp. 405-6.

Trinity.¹⁴⁸ Then, Pannenberg explains the functions of the immanent and economic Trinity thus:

> If the doctrine of the immanent Trinity is the basis of the idea of plurality in the life totality of the one God which is eternally present to him, the doctrine of the Trinitarian persons in the economy of salvation is the basis of the existence of a plurality of creatures and their incorporation into the life of God for participation in his eternal glory.¹⁴⁹

So far so good. However, all above is only a prelude for the "absolute future":

> In distinction from creatures, who as finite beings are subject to the march of time, the eternal God does not have ahead of him any future that is different from his present. For this reason that which has been is still present to him. God is eternal because he has no future outside himself. His future is that of himself and of all that is distinct from him. But to have no future outside oneself, to be one's own future, is perfect freedom. The eternal God as the absolute future, in the fellowship of Father, Son, and Spirit, is the free origin of himself and his creatures.¹⁵⁰

What is the "absolute future"? Pannenberg only tells us the resource and origin of this kind of future, however we still have no idea about the concept itself. Perhaps it is clearer in Schwöbel's interpretation:

> Pannenberg argues that the totality of finite being should be thought of as participation in eternity so that the future is conceived as the origin of the totality of finite beings and

---

148. Cf. Pannenberg, *Systematic Theology*, volume 1, pp. 401-10.
149. Pannenberg, *Systematic Theology*, volume 1, p. 407.
150. Pannenberg, *Systematic Theology*, volume 1, p. 410. Cf. Shults, *Reforming the Doctrine of God*, pp. 188-91; Christian Mostert, *God and the Future: Wolfhart Pannenberg's Eschatological Doctrine of God* (London: T & T Clark, 2002), pp. 175-82.

> their being understood as the anticipation of their future. ... Ontologically and epistemologically, Pannenberg's philosophy can be characterized as a *realism of anticipation* which corresponds to and is part of the *eschatological realism* of his theology.[151]

The future, according to another theologian of hope, Moltmann, "works upon the present by awakening hopes and establishing resistance."[152] However, when he easily negates both transcendental and immanent God and interprets God's relation to us totally in the dimension of future by saying that "God is not 'beyond us' or 'in us,' but ahead of us in the horizons of the future opened to us in his promises,"[153] he has gone too far. The concept of the "absolute future" is significant to us because Pannenberg discerns time and eternity according to this absolute future:

> If eternity and time coincide only in the eschatological consummation of history, then from the standpoint of the history of God that moves toward this consummation there is room for becoming in God himself, namely, in the relation of the immanent and the economic Trinity, and in this frame it is possible to say of God that he himself became something that he previously was not when he became man in his son. ...If God wills the independence of his creatures, the success of his creative act depends decisively upon the faithfulness of his creative love, upon the expression of his eternity in the process of time.[154]

---

151. C. Schwöbel, "Wolfhart Pannenberg," in D. F. Ford eds. *The Modern Theologians* (Oxford: Blackwell Publishers Ltd, 1997), p. 187.

152. Jürgen Moltmann, *Theology of Hope: On the Ground and the Implications of a Christian Eschatology*, trans. James W. Leith (Minneapolis: Fortress Press, 1993), p. 227.

153. Jürgen Moltmann, "Theology as Eschatology," in Frederick Herzog eds. *The Future of Hope: Theology as Eschatology* (New York: Herder and Herder, 1970), p 10.

154. Pannenberg, *Systematic Theology*, volume 1, p. 438. Pannenberg's stand is described by Schwöbel as such: "The Kingdom of God is, first of all, the consummation of the community of humankind, and this, radically conceived, includes the resurrection of the dead. Secondly, it is the end of history, which in the context of Christian faith cannot mean its abolition and transition into nothingness, but can only mean the inclusion

Now we may see the result yielded by the "absolute future": the Father does not beget the Son *eternally*. Rather, the Father "became something that he previously was not" in time. This means that God's eternity must be derived from the "absolute future," a temporal term. Thus eternity collapses into one dimension of time – future. What a disastrous result for Barth! Without doubt Barth, like Pannenberg and Moltmann, also emphasizes the importance of the future and eschatology. In *ER*, Barth makes an extremely strong statement in this issue: "If Christianity be not altogether thoroughgoing eschatology, there remains in it no relationship whatever with Christ."[155] Even in *CD* I/2, Barth still favors this dimension of time:

> Now, is not God's future the most intensive presence, incomparably more intensive than anything we regard as present? We have seen with what intensity God's covenant and hiddenness in the Old Testament point to God's coming. In this very intensity they are already present, and Abraham, Moses and the prophets are recipients of revelation in the full sense of the term. But we still have to put it in this way, that they receive the revelation of Yahweh as those who wait for it and hasten toward it. The bearers of the Old Testament revelation, however, do not go to meet the fulfillment that comes, and is already at the door, as those who are actually unconscious of the incompleteness of their situation and its need for fulfillment.[156]

---

of history in God's eternity. Therefore the Kingdom of God is, thirdly, the entering of eternity into time. This last aspect has central significance for Pannenberg: Everything in eschatology revolves around the relationship of time and eternity. Pannenberg's own account of this relationship is based on his ontology. The present reality of everything is constituted from its eschatological future. Therefore the essence of something can only be understood as the simultaneous totality of its appearances, which must be conceived as being "located" in eternity. The process of time is therefore both form of the appearance and the process of becoming of any essence. If eternity is understood as the future perfection of everything, then this future is present in the process of occurring in time as the aim of these processes. Everything that occurs and perishes in time, Pannenberg proclaims, is preserved in God's eternity which includes all temporal events." See Schwöbel, "Wolfhart Pannenberg," p. 201.

155. *ER*, p. 314.
156. *CD* I/2, p. 95.

However Barth has hardly ever been a futurist or a "theologian of Hope."[157] As it is shown in the discussion of "The Third One-sidedness" in this chapter, at least from *CD* II/1 on, Barth is fully aware of any form of one-sidedness about the three dimensions of time and hardly tries to balance them. In his mature doctrine of time and eternity, Barth replaces his extreme stress on eschatology with God's pre-, supra- and post-temporality. Sauter insightfully discerns this change in Barth:

> God is always the coming One does not allow us to locate God in the future, ignoring both past and present, or to see past and present as the prehistory of the future. That Christianity is "thoroughgoing eschatology" cannot be allowed to concentrate attention on what might come to pass or be brought to pass. Barth saw himself be thwarted by this understanding of theology as devoted to the future.[158]

4.3 Conclusion

First, death is not just a miserable end of the creature. In creation the Father sets the Son as our Reconciler and the Holy Spirit as Redeemer. The Father sends them into the salvation history concretely. In this way the Creator enters time from his eternity.

Second, the eschatological hope fulfils our time in two dimensions. Cosmically, the Father creates everything anew and begins the eternal life with us in the Son through the Holy Spirit. Existentially, the noetic eschatological hope breaks into our life and changes us ontologically.

The entire salvation history is a temporal concrete circle from eternity to eternity. We shall appreciate it fully after we finish studying Barth's doctrine of reconciliation and redemption with the entire grand theological structure in front of us. Thus far, we may sum up this chapter in Schwöbel's words:

---

157. Cf. Gerhard Sauter, "Why is Karl Barth's *Church Dogmatics* not a 'Theology of Hope'? Some Observations on Barth's Understanding of Eschatology," trans. Arnold Neufelde-Fast, *SJT* 52: 4 (2000): p. 407.

158. Gerhard Sauter, *What Dare We Hope?: Reconsidering Eschatology* (Harrisburg: Trinity Press, 1999), p. 74.

The eternal is not simply temporalized in the hypostatic union, neither is the temporal eternalized, nor do they coexist in unrelated division and separation. The relationship between the Father, Son and the Spirit is eternal, even though the incarnate Son relates to the Father in the Spirit in the created temporality of a human life. Conversely, Christ relates as the Son to the Father in the Spirit in the Incarnation in the temporal reality of a human life, and this is not denied in asserting that this relationship is eternally the relationship of the Son to the Father in the Spirit. The eternal life of God the creator is disclosed in the reality of the very stuff of creation which is thereby not destroyed, but exalted by grace into the communion of the divine persons.[159]

---

159. Christoph Schwöbel, "Christology and Trinitarian Thought," in Christoph Schwöbel eds. *Trinitarian Theology Today* (Edinburgh: T & T Clark, 1995), pp. 143-4.

CHAPTER 3

The Eternal Concrete Son

Section 1:
Eternity before Time – The Preexistence of the Son

1.1 The Preexistence of the Son

Along with Augustine, Barth also divides time into three parts: past, present and future when he studies the relation between time and eternity. However, he sees the relation from a different perspective. Contrary to Augustine's immanent psychological viewpoint, Barth takes a transcendental object approach. For Barth, the three dimensions of God's time i.e., pre-, supra- and post-temporality, are all related to the eternal Son. Barth, along with Augustine, also develops his doctrine of time and eternity together with the doctrine of creation. When God created the heavens and the earth, he created them in the form of time, thus time is no other thing than the form of the creature which was given by the triune creator through his eternal word, i.e., the preexistent Son.[1] Even before the creation, the preexistent Son was with God the Father.

The preexistence of the Son has plenty of canonical witnesses. Firstly, the eternal being of the Son is portrayed in the Gospels and expressed by Jesus himself: "In the beginning was the Word, and the Word was with God"

---

[1] For two comprehensive treatments of the preexistence of the Son, see R. G. Hamerton-Kelly, *Pre-Existence, Wisdom, and the Son of Man* (Cambridge: Cambridge University Press, 1973); Douglas McCready, *He Came down from Heaven* (Downers Grove: InterVarsity Press, 2005). Cf. also Pannenberg, *Systematic Theology*, volume 2, pp. 363-89.

(John 1:1); "Before Abraham was born, I am!" (John 8:58).[2] Secondly, by Jesus Christ and through Jesus Christ everything was created, including time: "Through him all things were made; without him nothing was made that has been made" (John 1:3); "Through whom he also made the ages" (Heb 1:2).[3] Based on these witnesses, we may roughly identify two kinds of preexistence: the first and classic meaning can be called real or personal preexistence which admits that incarnate Christ was a real and concrete divine person even before the incarnation; the second understanding is called ideal preexistence.[4] Christ's ideal preexistence would be a preexistence of divine intention but would have no reality until intention became actualized in time.[5]

Barth takes the first stand. For Barth, the Son's preexistence is identical with his deity. The deity of Jesus Christ, i.e., the union of the Son with the Father must "be understood as definitive, authentic and essential."[6] The Son is God's concrete word for us. Before everything was created, he was always with the Father and Holy Spirit and the eternal Son's deity remains the same in his incarnation. By incarnation, God's word is revealed to us; by the death and resurrection of the Son, God reconciles himself to us. However, whether before or after the incarnation, Christ *is* the concrete second person of the triune God, thus Jesus cannot possibly be understood as the personification and symbol of an abstract divine being. What he does

---

2. "This 'in the beginning with God' is," Gathercole explains, "crucial because it defines the nature of the beginning – it is not a status of being the first creation; by contrast, the 'beginning with God' gives a qualitative description to the beginning." See Gathercole, "Pre-existence, and the Freedom of the Son in Creation and Redemption," p. 39.

3. This is C. Koester's translation. He points out that the "ages" here may mean both "this age" and "the age to come." Cf. C. Koester, *Hebrews: A New Translation with Introduction and Commentary* (New York: Doubleday, 2001), p. 178.

4. Cf. Hamerton-Kelly, *Pre-Existence, Wisdom, and the Son of Man*, pp. 1-2.

5. McCready also identifies a third kind of preexistence, but it can actually be regarded as the same with the second one. This third interpretation is held by John Hick and Karl-Josef Kuschel, which, in Kuschel's term, can be called "eschatological preexistence." What Kuschel appears to mean is that "the Easter experience" requires some sort of preexistence as its justification. This one is similar to the second, the difference is that the third view relates Christ's existence to God's will and action, not only his thought. Cf. McCready, *He Came down from Heaven*, p. 15-9.

6. *CD* I/1, p. 400.

for us and reveals to us concretely depend on who he is, i.e., his deity and not vice versa. Barth explains:

> The church dogma of Christ's deity as compared with the New Testament statement about Christ's deity says no other than that we have to accept the simple presupposition on which the New Testament statement rests, namely, that Jesus Christ is the Son because he is (not because he makes this impression on us, not because he does what we think is to be expected of a God, but because he is). With this presupposition all thinking about Jesus, which means at once all thinking about God, must begin and end. No reflection can try to prove this presupposition, no reflection can call this presupposition in question. All reflection can only start with it and return to it. … The deity of Christ is true, eternal deity. We see it in his work in revelation and reconciliation. But revelation and reconciliation do not create his deity. His deity creates revelation and reconciliation.[7]

In *CD* I/1, under the title of "The Eternal Son," Barth gives a detailed interpretation of the deity of Jesus Christ according to *Symb. Nicaeno-Constantinopolitanum* in which he locates "the most important record of the church dogma of the deity of Christ."[8] Among the six articles about Jesus Christ's deity in this *Credo*, the third one "*et ex Patre natum ante omnia saecula*," is concerned about his preexistence: "We believe in Jesus Christ as the begotten of the Father before all time. Our starting-point here, too, must be the fact that this is said of Jesus Christ as the Revealer of God and therefore of the God who acts on us and for us in time."[9]

Here Jesus Christ's deity shows his lordship over time. In eternity the Son, as the co-agent of the Father, freely created everything, then for his creatures' sake, the creator enters this world – eternity enters time. Barth's

---

7. *CD* I/1, p. 415.
8. *CD* I/1, p. 423.
9. *CD* I/1, pp. 425-6.

interpretation of the Son's preexistence shows clearly that he sees God's eternity is temporal rather than timeless:

> The phrase "before all time" does not, then, exclude time, whether the *illic et tunc* of revelation as it is attested in Scripture or the *hic et nunc* in which it is to become revelation for us. It does not exclude but includes time, concretely this time, the time of revelation. Hence it does not exclude history; it includes it.[10]

Barth always takes a temporal approach to interpret God's eternity, which is manifested most obviously in Jesus Christ.[11] The eternal Son has never been an abstract idea which can only be reached by pure reason. On the contrary, the Son preexists concretely and really for us. Since the incarnation was in the divine plan even before creation, the time before the incarnation should be regarded as a part of the salvation history rather than an empty chronology. As McCready puts it: "The preexistence of the Son of God is not simply a matter of chronology that he was before his incarnation, but is also qualitative, the one who was incarnated as Jesus of Nazareth is eternally existent as deity."[12]

However, although the Son's preexistence should be understood temporally, that does not mean that God's eternity in any way relies on our time. On the contrary, human time is derived from God's eternity:

> That the Son of God becomes man and that he is known by other men in his humanity as the Son of God are events, even if absolutely distinctive events, in time, within the created world. But their distinction does not itself derive or come from time. Otherwise they would be only relatively distinctive

---

10. *CD* I/1, p. 426.
11. As Hunsinger points out: "Veiled behind Barth's appeal to the particularity of Jesus is the extent to which all dimensions of 'temporality' are subjected to radical reinterpretation according to christological and Trinitarian modes of thought." See Hunsinger, *How to Read Karl Barth*, p. 14.
12. McCready, *He Came down from Heaven*, pp. 16-7.

events, of which there are others. Precisely because they have divine power, because the power of this world is here the power of the world to come, because the power of God's immanence is here the power of his transcendence, their subject must be understood as being before all time, as the eternal Subject, eternal as God himself, himself eternal as God. Jesus Christ does not first become God's Son when he is it for us. He becomes it from eternity; he becomes it as the eternal Son of the eternal Father.[13]

In his *Christology*, Gerald O'Collins explains Christ's preexistence in a very similar way to Barth's argument above:

> The christological doctrine of Christ's preexistence maintains that Christ's personal existence is that of an eternal Subject within the oneness of God, and hence cannot be derived from the history of human beings and their world. His personal being did not originate when his visible history began.[14]

The Son's preexistence has never been an abstract non-temporal eternity. From the beginning the Son was with the Father and with us as well. When we read the part on the Son's "pre-" dimension, we must keep his "supra-" and "post-" dimensions in mind. The Son's preexistence is as concrete as his "real" existence in human history. As Robert W. Jenson puts it: "The eternal 'pre-' of Christ's existence, which is identical with the 'pre-' of predestination, occurs also within time, as the resurrection and as the contingency and divine agency of Israel's and the church's proclamation and prayer, visible and audible."[15] The concrete union of eternity and time in Jesus Christ, which characterizes Jenson's study of Barth, is also appreciated by George Hunsinger:

---

13. *CD* I/1, pp. 426-7.
14. Gerald O'Collins, *Christology* (New York: Oxford University Press, 1995), p. 237.
15. Robert W. Jenson, *Systematic Theology*, Volume 2 (New York: Oxford University Press, 1999), p. 177.

What Jenson sees in contrast is that Jesus Christ in Barth's theology *is* the unity of time and eternity. Eternity is not to be understood in abstraction from Jesus of Nazareth. However difficult the resulting conceptuality might turn out to be (or however illuminating and deep), eternity is defined as inseparable from the particular temporality of Jesus, as ontologically filled and shaped by it. There is neither a general divine nor a general human temporality which takes ontological precedence over the particular temporality of Jesus. No general divine or human temporality has ever occurred in abstraction from his.[16]

Alternatively, Jüngel interprets Barth's teaching of the preexistence of the Son in light of the distinction of the ancient concepts *enhypostasis*[17] and *anhypostasis*.[18] He objects to a "gnoseological" or "ideal" interpretation of the man Jesus' preexistence. If we insist that, as Barth does, the *man* Jesus is in the beginning with God "*in concreto* and not *in abstracto*,"[19] we must understand his preexistence in the sense of *enhypostasis*. Jesus' humanity cannot be understood as a kind of abstract and self-contained general humanity in the sense of *anhypostasis*.[20] On the contrary, his humanity is based on his deity, his unity with God's eternal decision before the incarnation. The total identity of God's word and the *man* Jesus ensures that this preexistence is concrete and temporal.

---

16. Hunsinger, *How to Read Karl Barth*, pp. 16-7.

17. The term "signifies that the human nature of Jesus subsists in the divine Word." See Webster's translator's footnote in Eberhard Jüngel, *God's Being is in Becoming*, trans. John Webster (Edinburgh: T & T Clark, 2004), p. 96. Cf. also John Webster, *Eberhard Jüngel: An Introduction to His Theology* (Cambridge: Cambridge University Press, 1986), pp. 34-6.

18. The term "signifies that Jesus' human nature is not self-subsistent." Ibid.

19. *CD* II/2, p. 98.

20. "Jüngel's exposition," Watts argues, "of the identification of God with the man Jesus in terms of an- and enhypostasia demonstrates Jüngel's approach to the relationship between the Jesus of history and the Christ of the kerygma. It also highlights the identification of God with Jesus as an event. This avoids reducing the relationship between God and Jesus to one highest example of a more general relationship between God and man." See Graham J. Watts, *Revelation and the Spirit: A Comparative Study of the Relationship between the Doctrine of Revelation and Pneumatology in the Theology of Eberhard Jüngel and of Wolfhart Pannenberg* (Milton Keynes: Paternoster, 2005), p. 40.

Jüngel employs these two concepts in order to avoid a timeless eternity. To achieve this, we must distinguish the temporality and eternity in light of eternity. If we make this distinction in light of the temporality, what we may get is only a "projection of a temporal existence into eternity."[21] However, if we see this distinction from God's eternal point of view, Jesus does not preexist for his own sake, but in correspondence [*Entsprechung*] to the Father's election as the Son, thus "in the eternal decision of God in the sense of the *enhypostasis* that this existence really is *temporal* existence."[22] Eternally God elects this man Jesus to be with us and God never makes an opposite decision, i.e., to live by himself in his own eternity. This latter idea even makes God a devil, as Jüngel puts it: "According to Barth, every idea of God makes God a devil when it regards God's deity as the absoluteness of his being and does not see it as, at the same time, an eternally willed relationship to humanity."[23]

Two dangers must be avoided in Jüngel's teaching of *enhypostasis* and *anhypostasis*. The first one is that of making humanity a necessity for God. The divine decision of being with us eternally must be regarded as a free one; otherwise incarnation and humanity inevitably become necessary for God.[24] The second one is a docetic interpretation of *enhypostasis*. More or less, Jüngel's use of *enhypostasis* has eternalized Jesus' humanity. To avoid treating his temporal humanity as a "gnoseological" or "ideal" shadow of his deity, we must, following Webster, repeat once again that the *man* Jesus is the *God* for us alike.[25]

---

21. Jüngel, *God's Being is in Becoming*, p. 96.
22. Jüngel, *God's Being is in Becoming*, p. 96.
23. Jüngel, "'…keine Menschenlosigkeit Gottes…' Zur Theologie Karl Barths zwischen Theismus und Atheismus, " *Evangelische Theologie* 31 (1971), p. 386. Trans. by John Thompson.
24. Thompson charges Jüngel that he "comes dangerously close to making incarnation and cross a necessity for God." See Thompson, "Jüngel on Barth," in John Webster eds. *The Possibilities of Theology: Studies in the Theology of Eberhard Jüngel* (Edinburgh: T & T Clark, 1994), p. 175. Cf. also Watts, *Revelation and the Spirit*, pp. 66-7.
25. Webster, *Eberhard Jüngel*, p. 36. However, Williams argues: "Jüngel in effect proposes a solution whereby God eternally 'forsees' the man Jesus, and, although he denies that the preexistent being of Jesus is 'gnoseological' or 'ideal', it is hard to see what else such a 'forseen' existence could be. " See R. D. Williams, "Barth on the Triune God," in S. W. Sykes eds. *Karl Barth: Studies of His Theological Method* (Oxford: Clarendon Press, 1979), p. 179.

Hans Küng also takes a traditional way to interpret the preexistent Logos. His approach draws the distinction of *sub specie temporis* and *sub specie aeternitatis*: "The theologian cannot therefore consider the incarnation only *sub specie temporis*, he also must attempt to see it *sub specie aeternitatis*."[26] Thus from our temporal point of view, we can separate the Logos and the incarnate Son, so that we would ask questions like 1) "how the Logos was *before* the Incarnation?"[27] However, from God's eternal standpoint, there is no distinction between "pre" and "post," then under this aspect the most we can ask is 2) "What would the Logos be without the incarnation?"[28] It is obvious that Küng's understanding of God's eternity is similar to Boethius' "classical definition," i.e., a timeless eternity. The difference between 1) and 2) can easily be reduced to the one between an A-series statement and a B-series statement. What makes Küng's approach special is that he relates the Logos to the *eternal Trinitarian self-knowledge*: "God has of himself only a single and individual knowledge through which he knows himself as the one who freely became man in the Son. Hence the eternal Logos knows himself as Logos only by knowing himself simultaneously as incarnate; and only as Logos incarnate is the eternal Logos known also by the Father and the Holy Spirit."[29]

In Thompson's opinion, Küng's interpretation of Barth is "more illuminating than Jüngel's use of '*enhypostasia*.'"[30] Thompson also charges that Jüngel's approach is in danger of "a God *per se* in whom nature and will do not coincide."[31] This charge is difficult to hold since Jüngel's approach stands or falls on the identity of God's will and nature in Jesus Christ. Were it not for this identity, Jesus' preexistence would have inevitably become timeless and abstract. Thus while Küng's interpretation is perhaps much easier to understand, nevertheless it is definitely not more "illuminating."

---

26. Hans Küng, *Justification: The Doctrine of Karl Barth and a Catholic Reflection*, trans. Thomas Collins, Edmund E. Tolk and David Granskou (London: Burns & Oates, 1964), p. 275.
27. Küng, *Justification*, p. 278.
28. Küng, *Justification*, p. 278.
29. Küng, *Justification*, p. 279.
30. John Thompson, "Jüngel on Barth," p. 166-7.
31. Thompson, "Jüngel on Barth," p. 166-7.

1.2 Preexistence and Predestination

By reinterpreting the traditional Reformed doctrine of predestination in light of Christology and the doctrine of election, Barth does fill the old bag with new wine. Since the abstract determining-determined, positive-negative, creator-creature dualism in the old doctrine has acquired a concrete mediator, who is no less than God himself and no less than human also, it looks never so real and vivid. Jesus Christ, as the electing God and elected man alike, synthesizes the subject and object of the eternal election of grace. Barth insists that we must understand predestination in light of this synthesis which contains both ontological and epistemological meaning: ontologically, Jesus Christ was the One with God in the beginning;[32] epistemologically, we can know nothing about God's eternal will apart from this man.[33]

A doctrine of election undergirds the entire relationship between God and humans. In God's eternal election all those men in the Bible, even the reprobated and heathen are elected.[34] However, God's eternal will and his contemporary work in man must be acknowledged in the one concrete person – Jesus Christ.[35] In his doctrine of election, Barth points out that,

> before all created reality, before all being and becoming in time, before time itself, in the pre-temporal eternity of God, the eternal divine decision as such has as its object and content the existence of this one created being, the man Jesus of Nazareth, and the work of this man in his life and death, his humiliation and exaltation, his obedience and merit… in and with the existence of this man the eternal divine decision has as its object and content the execution of the divine covenant

---

32. "In the beginning with God was this One, Jesus Christ. And that is predestination." See *CD* II/2, p. 145.
33. In Barth's word, "[a]ll that this concept contains and comprehends is to be found originally in Him and must be understood in relation to Him." See *CD* II/2, p. 145.
34. Cf. *CD* II/2, p. 149.
35. This is what Hunsinger called "particularism," which "meant that the incarnation was conceivable only in its inconceivability; that eternity had to be radically reconceived in incarnational and Trinitarian terms, but without losing the ontological difference between Creator and creature." See Hunsinger, *How to Read Karl Barth*, p. 19.

with man, the salvation of all men. In this function this man is the object of the eternal divine decision and foreordination.[36]

At this point, Barth criticizes that the "older theologians," represented by Calvin and Thomas Aquinas,[37] did not treat predestination and Christology properly. Although they recognized man as the object of the eternal predestination, the man in their mind is man in general or the sum of individuals rather than the specific man – Jesus Christ; although they knew the continuity of predestination and Christology, they understood the two reversely, i.e., understanding Christology in light of predestination and not vice versa. Barth argues that:

> Quite naturally, too, they thought of man as the specific object of the eternal predestination. But it was man in general, or the race as a whole, or the sum total of individuals. It was not man as the one who is identical with Jesus Christ. Certainly they found a continuity between the eternal presupposing of the divine work and its centre and *telos* in Jesus Christ. But as they understood Scripture the relationship between the two was reversed. The eternal predestination was set up as a first and independent entity standing over against the center and *telos* of the divine work and of time: a different encounter between God and man from that which became temporal event in Jesus Christ. As they saw it, the second decision and all that it involved followed on the first.[38]

This double predestination, for Barth, means that God's eternal will contains a twofold reference: God elected himself and humans. On one hand, God elected himself in Jesus Christ, the one who is identical with God's eternal will and word. On the other hand, God elected Jesus the man, the very man as descendant of David, through whom his word is spoken in

---

36. *CD* II/2, p. 116.
37. Cf. *CD* II/2, p. 149.
38. *CD* II/2, pp. 149-50.

this world.[39] Out of God's self-giving love, he deserted himself in order that man can gain him. Thus God did not predestine both salvation and reprobation for man. On the contrary, he ascribed to man the former and to himself the latter. However, Jenson reminds us: "the event of the eternal predestination and of Jesus Christ's preexistence therein, is not identical with the history of salvation. Nor is the eternal preexistence of the Godman exhausted in his immediacy to God's all-encompassing eternity."[40] The power of God is revealed in Jesus Christ as self-emptying and self-giving love rather than domination and conquest. God gives not primarily some created material, but his only Son, i.e., his very self. For the "older theologians," since there was a gap between predestination and Christology, they did not believe in a self-developing God, but in a God who is eternally unchangingly himself and *then*, Jesus Christ was foreordained by the eternal Father for the soteriological purpose. However Barth insists that if God gives himself to us, it is because there is a will already there within God himself in all eternity. Indeed, this will constitutes our knowledge of God. Only because God is in himself a God who gives himself can we know that he is so for us. When God reaches out to us and gives his Son to us, he does not become a different kind of God or change a new divine purpose. He is simply being himself to us eternally. The eternal Son in human history is the very same one who is with the eternal Father by the very same eternal will: "the eternal will of God which is before time is the same as the eternal will of God which is above time, and which reveals itself as such and operates as such in time. In fact, we perceive the one in the other. For God's eternity is one."[41]

Furthermore, Barth reproaches the old theology for being based on "a doctrine of God which was pagan rather than Christian."[42] When predestination was separated from Christology, it became an "isolated and given enactment which God had decreed from all eternity"[43] and thus God inevitably imprisoned himself in his own decree and committed himself in time.

---

39. Cf. Colwell, *Actuality and Provisionality*, pp. 231-63.
40. Jenson, *Cur Deus Homo?*, p. 86.
41. *CD* II/2, p. 156.
42. *CD* II/2, p. 181.
43. *CD* II/2, p. 181.

1.3 Conclusion

In Barth's opinion, the preexistence of the Son has the following characteristics: firstly, the preexistence of the Son is temporal rather than timeless. The fact that Jesus Christ exists "before all time" does not exclude but includes time and this time is concretely revealed in our history. Secondly, the eternal Son enters time not out of any abstract necessity, but out of God's concrete free self-giving love. The eternal Son's temporality cannot be taken for granted. On the contrary, "it is grace, mystery, a basis that we must recognize in the fear of God."[44] Thirdly, the eternal Son preexists concretely for us. Based on the deity of God, the Son exists for our salvation. By doing this, he even willingly goes to the "far country," i.e., our human time.[45] Fourthly, human time is derived from the Son's eternity and not vice versa. In other words, the Son's deity defines our humanity and not vice versa. When he enters time from eternity, the fallen human nature is reconciled and redeemed, but his deity remains distinctive from our humanity, his eternity remains distinctive from our temporality.

Section 2:
Eternity in Time – The Incarnation of the Son

2.1 The Incarnation of the Son as the Turning Time

The first dimension of the eternal Son's time is his pre-temporality; the second is his "supra-temporality." This part is one of the best presentations Barth gives of the topic.[46] At first, Barth discerns time and eternity as the form of the creature and the form of the creator:

---

44. *CD* I/1, p. 426.

45. "Certainly the statement about the preexistence of Jesus Christ," Barth argues, "is only an explication of the statement about his existence as the Revealer and the Reconciler, as the God who acts in us and for us in time. But just as truly the statement about his existence is only an explication of the statement about his pre existence. This One, the Son of God who exists for us, is the Pre existent. But only this One, the preexistent Son of God, is the One who exists for us." See *CD* I/1, p. 426.

46. For Barth's teaching on incarnation and time, see Thomas F. Torrance, *Space, Time and Incarnation* (London: Oxford University Press, 1969); John Thompson, *Christ in Perspective: Christological Perspectives in the Theology of Karl Barth* (Edinburgh: The Saint Andrew Press, 1978), pp. 20-33.

Time, in contradistinction to eternity, is the form of existence of the creature. For its part, of course, eternity is not merely the negation of time. It is not in any way timeless. On the contrary, as the source of time it is supreme and absolute time, i.e., the immediate unity of present, past and future; of now, once and then; of the center, beginning and end; of movement, origin and goal. In this way it is the essence of God himself; in this way God is himself eternity. Thus God himself is temporal, precisely in so far as he is eternal, and his eternity is the prototype of time, and as the Eternal he is simultaneously before time, above time, and after time. But time as such, i.e., our time, relative time, itself created, is the form of existence of the creature; it is, in contradistinction to eternity, the one-way sequence and therefore the succession and division of past, present and the future.[47]

However, "supra" here does not mean separation. On the contrary, God sustains our temporality like a mother embraces her baby.[48] From our point of view, time is separated from its own beginning and end, but time cannot be separated from eternity.[49] The point of contact here, once again, is Jesus Christ. When the Son of God was born unto us, the time is "secured," "fulfilled," and "revealed". Jesus thus is the center of time.[50] By circling around him, time is no longer empty time, that is, time without eternity, but also remains as time. The time itself can be distinguished, or created anew by Jesus into two spheres – the real past and the real future. In his death he

---

47. *CD* III/1, p. 71.
48. In very touching language, Barth describes the image of time and eternity as thus: "Time itself is in eternity. Its whole extension from beginning to end, each single part of it, every epoch, every lifetime, every new and closing year, every passing hour: they are all in eternity like a child in the arms of its mother." See *CD* II/1, p. 623.
49. For Barth, eternity is always real duration, there is no difference among beginning, middle and end. When time is related to eternity, it is not separated from its beginning and end.
50. Upon Jesus' time as the "center," "heart" and "fulfillment" of time, Barth explains: "The fact that in his life all time comes to fruition means that all time before it moved towards it and all time after it moved away from it." See *CD*, III/2, p. 461. Cf. also *CD* II/1, p. 629.

buried the old man in the past, and in his resurrection he brings the new man into the future. He is the "turning" of time, and when we are related to him, we are also in this turning both ontologically and epistemologically.[51] Barth borrows Luther's *simul iustus et peccator* to explain this turning.[52] For Luther, perhaps later Luther, justification is a lifelong process rather than a "once for all" event.[53] In the faith of Jesus, God does not punish our sins, but our sins do exist in us. That means "righteous and sinner alike". For Barth, this *simul* is unbalanced because we do not stand between the two spheres – the past, the old man and the future, the new man by ourselves. Rather Jesus Christ stands between them before us, or, instead of us. Thus, past and future are not empty for us any more since they have been filled by Jesus the Son of God.

The consequence of God's supra-temporality is twofold. Firstly, we are free from tyranny of the past and its condemnation. Rather, we are free to the extent we locate it in Jesus. All that should be remembered are "all his benefits" (Ps 103:2). Since our old sinful self has been redeemed by the incarnate son, "from what is really past, from what can disappear and be taken from us, we have to be set free and we are set free. To be able to look back to its disappearance, and no longer to have to keep it as a thing present, is a new reason for thankfulness and not for sorrow."[54] Secondly, we should not worry about our future. If future is still empty time, worry and fear are inevitable. However, like our past, our blessed future has already been prepared before us by the eternal Son thus it becomes "the coming new age with all its benefits for which we are set free in Jesus Christ. As men set free in this positive way we can look and move to the future – this

---

51. As Torrance says, "[i]t is the incarnation, the concrete reality of God in space and time, that enables Barth to think out the ontic as well as the cognitive basis for theological activity." See Torrance, *Karl Barth: An Introduction to His Early Theology*, p. 193.

52. Cf. *CD* II/1, p. 627.

53. For Luther's teaching on *simul iustus et peccator*, see Bernhard Lohse, *Martin Luther's Theology: Its Historical and Systematic Development*, trans. and eds. Roy A. Harrisville (Minneapolis: Fortress Press, 1999), pp. 76, 302; Paul Althaus, *The Theology of Martin Luther*, trans. Robert C. Schultz (Philadelphia: Fortress Press, 1966), pp. 242ff.

54. *CD* II/1, p. 627.

is the meaning of the evangelical admonition not to worry."⁵⁵ On this redeemed past and fulfilled future, Hunsinger has an excellent comment:

> Grounded in him, who died in our place and who was raised to establish us in his place before God, our present existence is determined simultaneously by his death and resurrection. As determined by his death, our existence as sinners, as those who are at war with grace and who are consequently abandoned by God, is completely past. It is past that is truly past, because (though it would otherwise have been our future) it came to be the past by his death. As determined by his resurrection, on the other hand, our existence as those who are saved, as those who are bestowed with grace and accepted into fellowship with God, is an existence that is completely future. It is the future that is truly future, because (though it would not otherwise be ours) it came to be ours by his resurrection. Here and now, therefore, we are at once sinners whose existence is completely past and the saved whose existence is completely future.⁵⁶

Since our time has a turning, a center in Jesus Christ, the one who lives in such a turning is the one who lives in real time.⁵⁷ Although it is not eternity, it is a time fulfilled and secured by eternity and not far from eternity. On the other hand, this fulfilled time does not lose its distinction from eternity. The time retains its temporality even after being redeemed by the eternal Son. As Hunsinger argues, "temporal distinctions are not conceived as being absent from eternity, but rather as being (mysteriously) present with a simultaneity that does not efface their sequence."⁵⁸

---

55. *CD* II/1, p. 628.
56. Hunsinger, *How to Read Karl Barth*, p. 126.
57. As Hunsinger puts it, "we are placed, rather, in a moment of existential turning – a turning from the past that is really past, to the future that is really future, because the former has really been abolished and the latter really established apart from us in Jesus Christ." See Hunsinger, *How to Read Karl Barth*, p. 126.
58. Hunsinger, *How to Read Karl Barth*, p. 241.

2.2 The Incarnation and the Triune God

The Son's incarnation is based on his preexistence. From all eternity the triune God elects the Son's incarnation in time, which means the Lord of time comes into time. The Son thus links the eternity and time by becoming temporal in our time from his eternity, as Zizioulas rightly points out: "Both the Father and the Spirit are involved in history, but only the Son *becomes* history."[59] The incarnation makes God put on the humanity and thus eternity put on the form of time.[60] Thus Barth writes:

> The fact that the Word became flesh undoubtedly means that, without ceasing to be eternity, in its very power as eternity, eternity became time. Yes, it became time. What happens in Jesus Christ is not simply that God gives us time, our created time, as the form of our own existence and world, as is the case in creation and in the whole ruling of the world by God as its Lord. In Jesus Christ it comes about that God takes time to himself, that he himself, the eternal One, becomes temporal, that he is present for us in the form of our own existence and our own world, not simply embracing our time and ruling it, but submitting himself to it, and permitting created time to become and be the form of his eternity.[61]

When this happens, although the electing God has become the elected man, God's identity remains unchanged: this incarnate Son is exactly the very eternal Son; eternity in our time is still God's authentic eternity. However, upon the priority of God's being (i.e., the triune God himself) and God's acts (e.g., God's election and incarnation), there is an argument

---

59. Zizioulas, *Being as Communion*, p. 130.

60. As Gunton puts it: "If we take seriously the implication of this doctrine [the Trinitarian context of Christology] for our understanding of God, we shall not so easily abstract our Christology from eternity or our God from involvement in space and time. If God is triune, and oriented from all eternity to what happened in Jesus of Nazareth, we shall not be tempted to conceive him or the world in terms that exclude the interrelationship of eternity and time." See Colin Gunton, *Yesterday & Today: Study of Continuities of Christology* (London: SPCK, 1997), p. 136.

61. *CD* II/1, p. 616.

between two contemporary Barthians: Edwin Chr. van Driel and Bruce McCormack. McCormack insists that we must understand all other doctrines in light of election and not vice versa. Even the position of the doctrine of election in Barth's system, i.e., in his doctrine of God rather than in his doctrine of creation, indicates its crucial significance.[62] Van Driel does not question the preexistence and eternity of Jesus Christ, and also agrees that there is nothing "before" or "after" eternal Son, even the triune God himself. However, van Driel cannot understand how an act can be logically and ontologically "prior" to a being, even if that act is a divine and eternal act.[63] He also denies that the eternal act of election and incarnation can "constitute" the divine being, that is, the Trinitarian God.[64] On the contrary, van Driel argues, Barth's teaching does support the reverse case, i.e., "the incarnation does not constitute divine being, but the divine being constitutes the incarnation."[65]

McCormack cannot tolerate such a division between God's being and God's acts,[66] and thus make one part prior to the other. If God, as Molnar says, would still be triune without us,[67] the separation of immanent Trinity and economy Trinity is inevitable. In van Driel's argument, McCormack points out, there is such a two-event structure – the event in which God is naturally and necessarily triune and, second, the event in which God chooses to be God "for us" in Jesus Christ.[68] If we discern such a twofold structure in the triune God, that is, discerning his being and action, and emphasizing the former, no matter temporally or ontologically, we may

---

62. See Bruce McCormack, "Seek God where he may be found : a response to Edwin Chr. van Driel," *SJT* 60: 1 (2006): pp. 77-8.

63. "When McCormack speaks about what the Logos was 'prior' to election, he does not talk about a temporal 'prior', but a logical and ontological 'prior'. If God is eternal, as previously discussed, there is no temporal differentiation in God. But there still might be a logical and ontological differentiation in the divine being." See Edwin Chr. van Driel, "Karl Barth on the Eternal Existence of Jesus Christ," *SJT* 60: 1 (2007): p. 51.

64. Van Driel, "Karl Barth on the Eternal Existence of Jesus Christ," p. 52.

65. Van Driel, "Karl Barth on the Eternal Existence of Jesus Christ," p. 52.

66. In his opinion, both God's being and God's acts are included in the same triune God. Cf. McCormack, "Seek God where he may be found," p. 76.

67. McCormack, "Seek God where he may be found," p. 76.

68. McCormack, "Seek God where he may be found," p. 76.

separate eternity and time, therefore making God's eternity timeless, as McCormack argues:

> Once this two-event structure is in place, the only way to avoid temporalizing the relation between them is by making the first to be timeless. Applied to Barth, such a timeless understanding of the triunity of God would make Barth's actualistic ontology, his emphasis on divine suffering, etc. impossible.[69]

Ironically, this disastrous result is exactly what van Driel believes Brunner's and Berkouwer's interpretations of Barth lead to. When Brunner and Berkouwer put revelation "posterior" to divine election and self-giving,[70] the revelation does not mean the process of actualization itself, but only making what has been already actualized known:

> Divine self-revelation and divine self-giving relate herein as content and form. It is for this reason that Barth can speak, somewhat later in *CD* II/2, of what took place in the temporal life of Jesus Christ as 'the eternal will of God temporally actualized and revealed'. On Brunner's and Berkouwer's interpretation this would not make sense, Revelation, yes, but no actualization.[71]

Van Driel thinks the reason for this is that both Brunner and Berkouwer treat the relation between revelation and election *temporally*. With such a precaution in mind, when he develops his own interpretation on the relation between election and Trinity, he stresses that the priority of the triune God to God's election must be understood *logically* and *ontologically*. However, such a methodological shift is insufficient for McCormack. He may argue that the term employed by him – constitute – can be interpreted

---

69. McCormack, "Seek God where he may be found," p. 76.
70. Cf. van Driel, "Karl Barth on the Eternal Existence of Jesus Christ," p. 47
71. Van Driel, "Karl Barth on the Eternal Existence of Jesus Christ," pp. 47-8.

logically and *ontologically*.⁷² It is unnecessary that there must be triune God first, who then elects and incarnates himself. God's eternal will of election is identical with himself either *temporally* or *logically* and *ontologically*. If the election is understood as an event posterior to the divine being, although not temporally, but *logically* and *ontologically*, the similar disastrous result – timeless eternity – remains inevitable.

Gunton's stand on this issue is weaker than McCormack's and more coherent with van Driel's. For Gunton, Christology does not "constitute" Trinity but "presupposes" the triune God.⁷³ The doctrines of Trinity and Christology are interdependent: *ontologically* Christology presupposes Trinity, *epistemologically* Trinity requires the incarnate Christ:

> The two doctrines, of God and of Christ, offer each other mutual support, or, rather, are dependent upon one another. Without a presupposed Trinity, the doctrine of the incarnation becomes an absurdity. With it, the point of the doctrine of the Trinity comes to be further realized.⁷⁴

However, Christology should not be confined to the merely epistemological, for it has ontological meaning to this world as well. As "eternal

---

72. Cf. Bruce McCormack, "Grace and Being: The Role of God's Gracious Election in Karl Barth's Theological Ontology," in *The Cambridge Companion to Karl Barth*, pp. 92-110; "Barth's grundsätzliche Chalkedonismus?" *Zeitschrift für Dialektische Theologie* 18 (2002): pp. 151-7.

73. "Although confessions of Jesus of Nazareth's temporal-eternal significance do not presuppose the doctrine of the Trinity, they inevitably lead to it. For they presuppose the reality of a God who is able to become spatio-temporal without loss of his divinity, of an eternal who is able to differentiate himself to become other than he is… But the impact of the reality of Jesus compels us to say that God is not to be understood as the bare negation of our time and space – as utterly timeless and spaceless – but as being eternally in himself that relatedness to the other which actualizes itself in our history. And that is one of the things meant when we say that God is triune, one in three ways of being." See Gunton, *Yesterday & Today*, pp. 134-5.

74. Colin Gunton, *Christ and Creation* (Grand Rapids: Wm. B. Eerdmans, 1992), p. 76.

mediator,"⁷⁵ towards above, the incarnate Son does not "constitute" Trinity; towards below, he does "constitute" worldly realities.⁷⁶ As Barth puts it:

> This Word is the ground of our being beyond our being; whether we hear it or not, whether we obey it or not, it is in virtue of its superior existence that our existence is a reality. This Word came to us before we came or not, and as we come or not. Our coming or not coming is possible only because this Word is real. The same Jesus Christ through whom God unites us to himself even while we are his enemies has already united us to himself as those who belong to him because he alone holds us over the abyss.⁷⁷

In this sense, Gunton points out, in Barth's doctrinal system, "both creation and redemption are embraced within the concept of election."⁷⁸ One of Gunton's main goals here is to move the centrality of time back to the present from the "overrated" future.⁷⁹ By doing this, he needs to keep a delicate balance between the pre-temporal dimension and the post-temporal, neither too protological (like Barth) nor too eschatological (like Pannenberg).⁸⁰ The presentism Gunton desires, compared with Augustinian presentism aforementioned in chapter 1, needs to be more Trinitarian than Christological;⁸¹ more objective and real than psychological.

---

75. Gunton, *Christ and Creation*, p. 90.

76. "The incarnation is constitutive of certain worldly realities, it achieves things. … Simply, the incarnation achieves its redemptive end by a form of divine immanence in the world. The form that immanence takes is what must concern us now." See Gunton, *Christ and Creation*, p. 90. For Gunton's "Christology from below" and "Christology from above", Cf. *Yesterday & Today*, pp. 10-55.

77. *CD* I/1, p. 444.

78. Gunton, *Christ and Creation*, p. 95.

79. Under the title of "A Plea for present," Gunton argues that "we require a reaffirmation of the centrality of the present for those whose createdness makes them creatures who know little of the past and even less of the future." See Colin Gunton, *The One, The Three and The Many: God, Creation and the Culture of Modernity* (Cambridge: Cambridge University Press, 1993), p. 93.

80. Cf. Gunton, *The One, The Three and The Many*, pp. 159-60.

81. In Gunton's opinion, this is also the case of Barth. In next *chapter*, we shall face another severe accusation by Gunton on Barth: Barth's doctrine of election is conceived

Another contribution by Gunton is his excellent resolution of the problem of subordination in light of the union of time and eternity:

> If we are to achieve a positive Christology that does not fall prey to the absolutism of time or eternity, we must hold firmly to the bipolarity of the New Testament's approach: that this life is both fully temporal and yet is the place where the eternal is present. One way in which this is expressed is by those passages which speak of the subordination of Jesus to the Father. Thus the Synoptic Gospels depict a pattern of obedience, while the Fourth Gospel juxtaposes expressions of the subordination of Jesus to the Father ('the Father is greater than I', John 14:28) with assertions of their equality (John 10:30). In these depictions, as well as in passages like Philippians 2, the writers are not expressing an ontological subordination, as in Arianism – for the obedience, humiliation and death are the way by which Jesus works out his divine calling – but showing that what happens here takes its origin in the eternal. It is the divine love, that which exists to all eternity, that is here to be touched and heard. This is the point of the metaphor of sending in Paul and of setting by both John and Hebrews of the life of Jesus in the context of eternity. What happens with Jesus of Nazareth is first of all to be understood as the good news of the movement into time of the eternal.[82]

From Gunton's new perspective, the subordination is transformed naturally into the fulfillment of time by eternity, thus it disappears in the process of the fulfillment and redemption of time. The Son's "obedience," "humiliation" and "death" are true and concrete in time, but they are out of God's self-grounded decision from all eternity. From a static "being" point of view, the incarnate Son subordinates to the Father; from a dynamic

---

rather binitarianly than Trinitarianly, "as something happening between Father and Son. The Spirit contributes nothing structurally as in much of Barth's theology." See Gunton, *Christ and Creation*, p. 90.

82. Gunton, *Yesterday & Today*, pp. 127-8.

"becoming" point of view, the incarnation is based on and leads to the triune God's eternal will which, out of God's free gracious decision, is always for us. As the Son preexists for us from eternity, he also incarnates with us from eternity. In Barth's view:

> Already in the eternal will and decree of God he was not to be, nor did he will to be, God only, but Emmanuel, God with man, and, in fulfillment of this "with," according to the free choice of his grace, this man, Jesus of Nazareth. And in the act of God in time which corresponds to this eternal decree, when the Son of God became this man, he ceased to all eternity to be God only, receiving and having and maintaining to all eternity human essence as well. ...For he is not God to us, nor can he be known or glorified or loved or worshipped by us as God, except in and with the human flesh assumed by his Son as the Mediator of the covenant.[83]

In Thompson's opinion, here Barth expresses clearly the union of God and man in Jesus Christ. The union decided and started by God from all eternity, the Son of Man is no less than the Son of God who was given for us. Thompson comments:

> Nothing could be clearer or more explicit than this. God is no non-human God, because he has, from all eternity, in his free election of grace, determined himself for man and for himself. To use Barth's metaphors, God is God clothed with our humanity because he has revealed himself to be God precisely in his union with man in the incarnation and atonement.[84]

---

83. *CD*, IV/1, pp. 100-1.
84. Thompson, *Christ in Perspective*, p. 103.

2.3 Incarnation as the Reconciliation between Time and Eternity

When the eternal Son comes into time, our time could not remain the same. Now our time may ground itself on its true foundation – God's eternity – for the first time. Human time has no chance to redeem itself: it can neither break the limit of each individual's actual lifespan, nor resolve the alienation of its own past, present and future. Only when God's eternity comes into our time, is there a real reconciliation between time and eternity and thus between time and itself. In this passage Torrance makes it obvious what the incarnation really means to our time:

> The eternal Word-and-Reason of God has become human flesh, personally penetrating into and participating in the contingent intelligibilities of our existence, in such a way as to bring God himself to bear directly and intimately upon us within the subject-subject and subject-object relations in which we live our daily life, so that our personal contact with God and our personal knowledge of him may be objectively and durably grounded on the internal being and reality of God.[85]

From our point of view, only on this firm rock – the incarnation of the eternal Son – does our time stand a chance to reconcile with eternity and thus with itself. From God's point of view, by incarnation the Son puts on the form of time but transcends it alike. It is this twofold relation with time that makes the Son become the contemporary of all men and all time. First of all, he has a certain lifespan like you and me and every event in his life had its specific "time." It is not an exaggeration if we say that in the incarnation of the eternal Son, the concretion of God's temporality reaches its ultimate climax. The biblical narrative may show us how the evangelists are interested in the details of Jesus' lifetime. Barth marvels at the exactness of Jesus' life recorded in the Bible:

---

85. T. F. Torrance, *Space, Time and Resurrection* (Edinburgh: T & T Clark, 1976), p. 21.

It is in this history, and therefore in time, that the fullness of time is reached and only so. The Gospels distinguish the life of Jesus from myths proclaiming timeless truth by underlining, though not overstressing the temporal limitations to which Jesus was subject. Palestine, Galilee and Jerusalem are the indispensable background to his life, giving him a concrete relationship to his contemporary social environment and a definite place in history (Luke 2:1f., 3:1f.). The inclusion of Pontius Pilate in the Creed means, *inter alia*, that the church wished to pinpoint the death of Jesus as an event in time. And it is worth noting that the Synoptists record the precise time of the events of the passion almost to the minute – the cockcrow (Mark 14:68 and *par*), the morning (Mark 15:1), the third hour (Mark 15:22), the sixth hour, the ninth (Mark 15:33 and *par*) and the evening (Mark 15:42 and *par*).[86]

Another aspect of the concretion of Jesus' time can be found in the likeness between Jesus' time and our time. The time of the incarnate Son has the real characteristics of our time, i.e., the beginning, duration and end:

> [I]n the first instance the time of Jesus is also a time like all other times that it occurred once and once for all; that it had beginning, duration and end; that it was contemporary for some, future for others, and for others again, e.g., for us, past. Only a docetic attitude to Jesus can deny that his being in time also means what being in time means for us all. Our recognition of his true humanity depends on our acceptance of this proposition. Even the recognition of his true deity, implying as it does the identity between his time and God's, does not rule out this simple meaning of his being in time. On the contrary, it includes it.[87]

---

86. *CD*, III/2, p. 441.
87. *CD*, III/2, pp. 462-3.

Jesus' time is definitely a concrete and real time rather than an abstract and imaginary time. At the same "time," Jesus' time is beyond human time, that is, Jesus still transcends all times from all his eternity. The three divisions of time, in the case of humans, are alien each other. There are impassable boundaries between them. However, Jesus is simultaneous to all three divisions of time. His three divisions are not strict divisions, but communicative parts which belong to a coherent whole. On one hand, his present reminds us of his past, that is, his preexistence, those prophecies and anticipations about him; on the other hand, his present stimulates our expectation of his future, his glorious return. Barth characterizes his view this way:

> "Jesus Christ lives" means that history takes place today in the same way as did that yesterday – indeed, as the same history. Jesus Christ speaks and acts and rules – it all means that this history is present. Whether confessed and acknowledged or not, it is the great decisive event of today. It is the most up-to-date history of the moment. ...It took place then, at its own time, before we were, when our present was still future. And it has also a forward reference. It is still future and will still happen – "even unto the end of the world." In other words, when we say that Jesus Christ is in every age, we say that his history takes place in every age. He is in this *operatio*, in this event.[88]

In all three divisions of time, Jesus' identity remains unchanged. If we separate Jesus' past and future from his present, and thus are interested in the historical Jesus or focus on his return in glory, without knowing the fact that "He is" both in his past and future, we surely belong to an "unspiritual community."[89]

Some problems may rise from the similarity of our time and Jesus' time: how similar are they on earth? Isn't it that our redeemed and fulfilled time is so eternity-like that they may confuse each other? Douglas Farrow thinks so. He charges that in Barth's teaching, when the eternal Son puts on the

---

88. *CD* IV/2, p. 107.
89. Cf. *CD*, III/2, p. 468.

form of time, time also puts on the form of eternity. Further, he argues that the confusion of time and eternity is the "remnant of natural theology in Barth." Let us see Farrow's argument first:

> But he (Barth) is wrong to attempt to articulate that eternity as real or authentic time, that is, as pure duration, a perichoretic 'simultaneity of beginning, middle and end.' To do so is only to repeat the common error of venturing a model of eternity (of the Trinity!) by way of negative judgment on time. If that negative judgment were not obvious enough from the claim that 'eternity is just the duration which is *lacking* to time,' it would become so from the fact that the incarnation is brought in precisely as the salvation of time. By taking time and making it a form of his eternity, God lends to it the duration it lacks. And what is this durable time? It is finite creaturely time – the time appointed to each of us between birth and death – but time that does not pass away. It is time fixed in God as in a secure bracket, its beginning, middle and end gathered up by the Trinity into a proper perichoresis. It is plainly time for God, in other words, but we are justified in asking how far it is time for man; for it is time in which the creature's possibilities are already 'exploited and exhausted.'
>
> This circular reasoning from time to eternity and back again we must regard as an unfortunate remnant of natural theology in Barth. We cannot square it either with scripture or with Barth's own best insight, but only repeat that it is closely bound up with his actualism. Since the incarnation does not merely accomplish atonement but is atonement, Barth's crucial distinction between created time and fallen time tends to melt away; but that is the very distinction which should have prevented him from seeing the problem of time in terms of its not being eternity, and so from misconstruing eternity as the saviour of time.[90]

---

90. Douglas Farrow, *Ascension and Ecclesia: On the Significance of the Doctrine of the*

Here Farrow more or less neglects the "for us" dimension in Barth's doctrine. His one-sided interpretation of the salvation of time as "plainly time for God" rather than time for us inevitably leads to timeless and abstract eternity which Barth repudiates in his doctrine with all his strength. It is true that "we are justified in asking how far it is time for man." Actually, Torrance asks a similar question in his *Space, Time and Resurrection*: "But what about *the individual*, and what about the death of the believers?"[91] In order to answer this question, Torrance tells us, "we must think Christologically."[92] As the mediator and reconciler of God and man, he is not far from either side. "A proper perichoresis" does not only exist in Trinity, but also resides between the triune God and us.[93] The atonement of time is firstly and mainly for us rather than for the triune God himself, since the aim of the reconciliation of time and eternity and time within its own three directions – past, present and future – is not to make time eternity-like, but to make our time "new." After time reconciled with eternity and itself, the believer exists in a twofold time: worldly time which decays and passes away and Christological time which is renewed day by day.[94]

2.4 Conclusion

From his argument above, we may identify some main "motifs"[95] of Barth's theological approach on this topic. The first one is "concretion." There is no other dimension of God's temporality which is more concrete than the

---

Ascension for Ecclesiology and Christian Cosmology (Edinburgh: T & T Clark, 1999), p. 291. Emphasis by Farrow.

91. Torrance, *Space, Time and Resurrection*, p. 102. Emphasis by Torrance.

92. Torrance, *Space, Time and Resurrection*, p. 102.

93. "Because the life," Hunsinger argues, "which Jesus Christ lives is always an eternal life, his past and present and future must not, Barth argues, be separated from one another abstractly. Instead, they must be seen concretely in the unity that is proper to them. This unity is again understood as a complex action, and its complexity is indeed that of the Trinitarian pattern in its paradigmatic form. That is, the (active) complex unity of eternity itself (and therefore of Jesus Christ's eternal life) is conceived as 'perichoretic.'" See *How to Read Karl Barth*, pp. 240-1.

94. Cf. Torrance, *Space, Time and Resurrection*, pp. 100-2.

95. This term is borrowed from George Hunsinger. In his *How to read Karl Barth*, he employs four main "motifs" to study Barth's theological system: actualism, particularism, objectivism and personalism (Cf. *How to Read Karl Barth*, pp. 30-42.). Actually, all these four motifs are related to "concretion."

one of the incarnate Son. Only by incarnation, the Son's preexistence for us actualizes in our time and space; only by incarnation, the Son's salvation assumes historic reality. This is also a main characteristic of the whole Barthian theology, as Gunton points out: "Barth fought a lifelong battle against what he called abstraction: the treatment of any topic out of relation to the fact that the divine action which provides the basis and possibility of theology is action in relation to the world."[96]

The second motif is "simultaneity." In incarnation, the Son comes into time and transcends time at the same time. By reconciling time and eternity, as well as time and itself, Jesus becomes contemporary of all times and thus he reveals his lordship over all times. Jesus lives and "is the eternal salvation of all men in their different times."[97]

The third one is "wholeness." The Son's pre-, supra- and post- existential states, as three aspects of one mutual related state, resist being studied independently. When we treat one, we must bear the other two in mind, as we always do in studying doctrine of Trinity. Once again, this motif can be applied to all Barth's works. And let us quote Gunton again: "Karl Barth is a systematic theologian in the respect that nothing written in one place is said without implicit or explicit reference to other theological themes."[98]

Section 3:
Eternity after Time – The Resurrection of the Son

3.1 Jesus' Resurrection as Historical Event

In the last two sections we have already seen God's purpose for us through the preexistence and incarnation of the Son. However, from nowhere else has the fulfillment of this purpose been manifested more clearly than in

---

96. Gunton, "Salvation," in *The Cambridge Companion to Karl Barth*, p. 143.
97. *CD* III/2, p. 441. Here we should also compare Barth's statement with Farrow's "[s]ince the incarnation does not merely accomplish atonement but is atonement, Barth's crucial distinction between created time and fallen time tends to melt away." See Farrow, *Ascension and Ecclesia,* p. 291. For Barth, of course "the incarnation does not merely accomplish atonement but is atonement," and in vain we would find the reason why "Barth's crucial distinction between created time and fallen time tends to melt away."
98. Gunton, "Salvation," p. 143.

the resurrection and ascension of the Son.[99] As the manifestation of God's purpose in human history, the resurrection, like the preexistence and incarnation, is temporal rather than timeless. It is an event in time and space.[100] However, the earlier Barth, when he is still unrelieved by his dialectic approach to the historicity of the event of resurrection, holds the opinion that Jesus' resurrection is something outside of our history, for there is only one tangent touching point between resurrection and history. Thus he argues:

> The Resurrection is the revelation: the disclosing of Jesus as the Christ, the appearing of God, and the apprehending of God in Jesus. The Resurrection is the emergence of the necessity of giving glory to God: the reckoning with what is unknown and unobservable in Jesus, the recognition of him as Paradox, Victor, and Primal History. In the Resurrection the new world of the Holy Spirit touches the old world of the flesh, but touches it as a tangent touches a circle, that is, without touching it. And, precisely because it does not touch it, it touches it as its frontier-as the new world.[101]

In *CD*, Barth does full justice to the resurrection event by admitting that it is a divine act, which happens in our space and time. The Father's eternal love raises the obedient Son from the dead in Easter history; such an event witnesses the continuity of God *ad intra* and God *ad extra*. In this event, the Son is passive rather than positive. Barth maintains that although the resurrection is an actual event in Jesus' earthly life, it is an event that *happens*

---

99. For Barth's teaching on the resurrection and time, see Torrance, *Space, Time and Resurrection*; Dawson, *The Resurrection in Karl Barth*; Adam Eitel, "The Resurrection of Jesus Christ: Karl Barth and the Historicization of God's Being ," *IJST* 10: 1 (Jan 2008): pp. 36-53.

100. Cf. *CD* IV/1. pp. 336-7.

101. *ER*, p. 30. Pannenberg rightly points out that "according to Karl Barth, Jesus' resurrection is not a completely new event with its own decisive importance, but still only the 'revelation' of Jesus' history consummated on the cross. Barth expressed this idea most clearly in 1922 in the second edition of his *The Epistle to the Romans*... However, Barth's position in the *Church Dogmatics* is distinguished from his own earlier position and from that of Bultmann in that he permits the event of revelation, the nonhistorical relation of Jesus' whole life to its origin of God, to be a particular event in the temporal course of Jesus' history." See Pannenberg, *Jesus–God and Man*, p. 111.

to him. The resurrection was the act of the eternal Father since: "the Subject of the resurrection is not simply θεός, according to the regular usage, but θεός πατήρ."[102] Like all other dead people, Jesus is dead and buried in the tomb. He did not rise from the dead by himself; it is the Father's gracious act that brings the obedient Son back from the empty grave. In this event the eternal Father-Son relationship is manifested in Jesus' earthly existence, as Eitel puts it:

> As the One who eternally 'issues' the Son, the Father gives life and glory to the Son in time because he is the One who has always done so in eternity. The Father does all of this precisely because this *is* the Father's eternal act of being. For Barth, the entire sweep of Jesus Christ's earthly existence was grounded in this eternal intra-triune Father–Son relationship. Therefore, all of Jesus' life was the revelation of God's eternal act of being.[103]

In the event of resurrection, the eternal God interferes with our temporality with a purpose that our time may be reconciled to his eternity. The resurrection of the Son defeats the death which once was the ultimate form of the negation of the life. Now the risen Jesus negates this negation in a historical event, an event happens to him *among* us, therefore the Father's unfailing love in the Son is also poured upon us. By this eternal act in our history, our temporality is changed once for all: the death becomes past and eternal life becomes our future. In this sense Dawson writes:

> Jesus Christ in his completed being and action is not content to remain enclosed within himself, concealed in the darkness of his crucifixion. The nature of his being is such that it reaches out beyond itself, illuminating and embracing the sphere of other men and women, revealing to them his own identity, and hence the true identity of other men and women in him,

---

102. *CD* IV/1. p. 303. Cf. also Eitel, "The Resurrection of Jesus Christ," p. 38.
103. Eitel, "The Resurrection of Jesus Christ," p. 43.

with the result that these others respond in a corresponding embrace of him and themselves as they are in him and in so doing participate in his newness of life. The event of the resurrection is the specific act of this revelation in which Jesus Christ is at once the sovereign subject of this revelation and its peculiar content.

The implications of this comprehensive statement are varied and profound. The first that we shall consider here is the manifestation of the teleological determination of the being of Jesus Christ. That is, in the revelation of his own reconciled being and action he has historical density. His is not a static, timeless reality, but one with and in time.[104]

As a historical event, on the one hand, the resurrection shares the same characteristics with the preexistence and incarnation: temporal rather than timeless; concrete rather than abstract; out of freedom rather than necessity. On the other hand, the resurrection is unique: the incarnate Son is only contemporaneous with the people of his lifetime; the resurrected Son is the contemporary of all human beings.[105] The meaning of the resurrection of the incarnate Son within our time and space, which came into being through him, cannot be confined in Jesus' lifetime. His triumphant resurrection breaks the limit of human lifespan, and thus brings the end time to every man. Everybody may encounter the Lord of time in his own time and his time is thus fulfilled by the risen Son. This is the eschatological aspect of the resurrection: Jesus continues to relate to us with us in our time

---

104. Dawson, *The Resurrection in Karl Barth*, p. 176. In Barth's words, "[a]ccording to the resurrection the death of Jesus Christ as the negative act of God took place with a positive intention. It had as its aim the turning of man to himself, his positing afresh, his putting on of a new life, his freeing for the future. And, according to the prior death of Jesus Christ, the resurrection has this negative presupposition in a radical turning of man from his old existence, in a total removing of man in his earlier form, in his absolute putting off, in his complete freeing from the past." See *CD* IV/1. p. 310.

105. The resurrection ensures that Christ does not merely live in his earthly time but is fully present to people of all times, as Dawson says that, "in the resurrection the life history of Jesus Christ from Bethlehem to Golgotha is taken up and made contemporaneous with all times is Barth's dominant theme at this point." See Dawson, *The Resurrection in Karl Barth*, p. 64.

as the risen Son who will return to complete the eternal Father's salvation history at his second *parousia*. As Torrance puts it:

> Such a resurrection of the incarnate Word of God within the creation of time and space which came into being through him is inevitably an event of cosmic and unbelievable magnitude. So far as the temporal dimension of creation is concerned, it means that the transformation of all things at the end of time is already impinging upon history, and indeed that the consummation of history has already been inaugurated. …The resurrection of Jesus heralds an entirely new age in which a universal resurrection or transformation of heaven and earth will take place, or rather has already begun to take place, for with the resurrection of Jesus that new world has already broken into the midst of the old.[106]

The temporality of human beings locates in his relation with God and his "fellow-men" and we can only know this in the Word of God, i.e., Jesus Christ.[107] When Jesus the eternal Son comes into time, he takes the form of time. Jesus, as the "eternal content," cannot separate from this temporal form, otherwise it will lead to abstraction and lose Jesus' lordship over time, as Barth reminds us: "We should lose Jesus as the Lord of all time if we ignored him as a man in his own time."[108] On the other hand, Jesus is not only a man in his own time for his deity penetrates all times. While Jesus' earthly time ends on the cross, in the resurrection his eternal time enlightens all times before and after his lifetime. Thus Hunsinger comments: "Its historical occurrence takes place in the genuine sequence of past, present, and future as real temporal forms. Therefore, just as the reality and sequence of these forms is presupposed by their simultaneous integration in eternity, so their simultaneous integration lends these forms

---

106. Torrance, *Space, Time and Resurrection*, p. 31.
107. Cf. *CD*, III/2, pp. 438-9.
108. *CD*, III/2, pp. 440-1.

a transcendental uniqueness and power peculiar to the one life act of this person."[109]

Jesus, Son of Man and Son of God alike, comes to our time from his eternity, therefore makes himself the contemporary of all times. In eternity he is begotten for us; his deity is pre-, supra- and post-humanity. It is his double-nature that makes him a man who is contemporaneous with all men:

> The twofold answer which he gives, to God on the one hand and to men on the other, makes him the contemporary of all men, whether they have lived, live or will live. The way in which he is their contemporary varies according to whether they live with him, lived before him or will live after him. Yet he is the contemporary of them all because he lives for God and for them all. ...His time acquires in relation to their times the character of God's time, of eternity, in which present, past and future are simultaneous. Thus Jesus not only lives in his own time, but as he lives in his own time, and as there are many other times both before and after him, he is the Lord of time.[110]

Do not such descriptions as "contemporary of all men," "present, past and future are simultaneous" make eternity timeless? Indeed from this passage we may understand why Jesus is the Lord of eternity rather than the Lord of time. What is the difference between an eternal God who once lived in time and the One never? Whether he lived in time or not, we can always say that the eternal God is simultaneous to present, past and future. That is traditional understanding of eternity. Had he not lived in time for some thirty years, he would still have reigned over our time from all eternity, though, in an abstract way, which Barth fought against for his entire life. If we want to say something more, e.g., he is the Lord of time, we must know the different way in which he interacts with time. When eternal God lives

---

109. Hunsinger, *How to Read Karl Barth*, p. 242.
110. *CD*, III/2, p. 440.

in time, his temporary form must be different from our temporary form. The difference can be found in Jesus' resurrection and ascension:

> But the history of the man Jesus, this salvation history, cannot be recounted unless we remember that the New Testament has something more to say of him, though still in the form of history, at the very point where the history of any other man would inevitably stop. For Jesus has a further history beginning on the third day after his death and therefore after the time of his first history had clearly come to an end. In temporal sequence, it is a second history – or rather, the fragments of a second history – of Jesus. It is the Easter history, the history of the forty days between his resurrection and ascension. The second stage of our investigation, more difficult, but rewarding, leads us inevitably to this point. For unless we wilfully ignore the clear indication of the New Testament sources, we are bound to recognise that this is a key position for our whole understanding of the man Jesus in his time. It shows us as nothing else can, according to the New Testament, that even as a man in his time Jesus is the Lord of all time.[111]

In Easter time Jesus appeared to people as true man,[112] but especially in the mode of God. It is in those forty days his disciples and other people witnessed and recognized that God was present in this very man. Resurrection breaks the limit of time, and thus reveals that Jesus, as the eternal God, is the Lord of time. Moreover, in Easter time Jesus shared his eternity with

---

111. *CD*, III/2, p. 441. Jesus' resurrection is so unique that it creates a new history and opens future for us, in this sense Dawson comments: "Barth underscores the biblical witness to the fact that this Jesus who, like every other human being has his time as the definite and completed whole of his beginning, duration and end, also has a further history beginning on the third day after his death. This is a history that Barth calls 'the fragments of a second history,' that is, the Easter-history comprised of the forty days between Jesus resurrection and his ascension." See Dawson, *The Resurrection in Karl Barth*, p. 70.

112. Barth employs two examples to show how real Jesus' resurrected body is: when Jesus appears to the disciples on the road to Emmaus and to "doubting" Thomas, he asks them to behold, even touch his physical body. Cf. *CD*, III/2, p. 448.

those who live in time and thus changed their time once for all, that is, reconciling human time with God's eternity. Barth thus argues:

> He was then the concrete demonstration of the God who not only has authority over man's life and death, but also wills to deliver him from death. Moreover – and this is what interests us especially in this connection – he was the concrete demonstration of the God who has not only a different time from that of man, but whose will and resolve it is to give man a share in this time of his, in his eternity.[113]

Jesus' time, as the fulfillment of all times, not only establishes our time ontologically, but also epistemologically.[114] Although we cannot live beyond our own time, like the resurrected Son did, we do encounter the redeemed time concretely here and now. On one hand, our time remains under a "not yet" circumstance, awaiting the eschatological redemption; on the other hand, the ultimate triumph of the Son's salvation has already begun inside us. Hunsinger's excellent explanation of this theme in Barth deserves a full quotation:

> The truth of our being in Christ, as Barth understands it, is not only real and hidden; it is also yet to come. It defines and determines the future promised to us, and actualized for us, in him. Jesus Christ is not the inclusive human being without also being the eschatological human being. We are not only included in his being, in his humanity, in his history, in his transition from shameful death to glorious resurrection, in his transformation of the old creation into the new. We are also confronted by his being, here and now, as the real but hidden

---

113. *CD*, III/2, pp. 450-1.
114. "As St. Paul understood it, for example, the resurrection of Jesus Christ did not take place for himself alone, but for us whom he had assumed into a unity of nature with himself, so that in a profound sense we have already been raised up before God in him: to what has objectively taken place in him there is a corresponding subjective counterpart in us which as such belongs to the whole integrated reality of the resurrection event." See Torrance, *Space, Time and Resurrection*, pp. 38-9.

future of our own being, as the pledge that our resurrection in him and with him to the glorious liberty of the children of God is already ours today. We are confronted by his being as the promise that our transformation as he has accomplished it from old creation to new will not always remain hidden but will one day be manifest fully in the light of his resurrection and in the glory of his eternal life. We are confronted by his being here and now as the new being of our common future.[115]

3.2 Jesus' Resurrection as Eternal Event

From a temporal point of view, Jesus' resurrection breaks all boundaries between past, present and future, making him the contemporary of all humans in all time. Although the resurrection is an event that happens in our concrete time and space, it is at the same time something extraordinary in history: it is not the *natural* result of Jesus earthly life and his empirical death. Therefore, besides a historical side of this event, there must be an eternal side as well. From an eternal point of view, the resurrection event, together with the preexistence and incarnation of the Son, belongs to the same coherent salvation history:

> The resurrection is the event of the revelation of the Incarnate, the Humiliated, the Crucified. Wherever he gives himself to be known as the person he is, he speaks as the risen Christ. The resurrection can give nothing new to him who is the eternal Word of the Father; but it makes visible what is proper to him, his glory.[116]

---

115. Hunsinger, *How to Read Karl Barth*, pp. 124-5. Torrance's opinion is very similar to Hunsinger's here: "Our resurrection has already taken place and is fully tied up with the resurrection of Christ, and therefore proceeds from it more by way of manifestation of what has already taken place, than as new effect resulting from it. That is why the New Testament speaks so astonishingly of our having already tasted the powers of the age to come (Heb 6:5), for in Christ we are already living 'in the end time.'" See Torrance, *Space, Time and Resurrection*, p. 37.

116. *CD* I/2, p. 111.

No matter how amazing, supernatural and even unbelievable the resurrection event is, it by no means "constitutes" or "establishes" Jesus' eternity.[117] There is no gap within the salvation history, between God *ad intra* and God *ad extra*, between God's past, present and future. The Son's resurrection violates the natural law in human history, however it witnesses the Son's obedience of the Father's eternal will. Torrance thus argues: "The teaching of the New Testament makes it clear that we cannot isolate the resurrection from the whole redeeming purpose of God or from the decisive deed of God in the incarnation of his Son which ran its full course from the birth of Jesus to his crucifixion and triumph over the powers of evil."[118]

While Barth maintains the continuity of Jesus' preexistence, incarnation and resurrection, he also admits that there is something special in the resurrection event even from an eternal perspective. The account of the Resurrection is considered as a witness that God's eternity interfaces with the time of the creature given in the person of Jesus. The Easter history gives expression to the encounter of God's eternal time with human time. Although it adds nothing new to the triune God's eternal will in creation, it does "make visible" what eternity achieves for human temporality in Jesus Christ. In his resurrection the Son realizes what is ordained by the Father in eternity and bestows it to us. No doubt this encounter of time and eternity changes our temporality ontologically, however, according to Barth, does this event have any impact on God's own being and eternity? On this issue there are different interpretations between Eitel and Dawson. In Dawson's opinion, the death of Son inevitably threatens the perfect unity of Godhead because "it constitutes as such the supreme challenge to God's eternal life, pressing for the reversal of the self-differentiation of God as Father, Son and Holy Spirit."[119] In order to conquer this assault, the Son has to be raised from the death. In this sense Dawson confirms that the resurrection is nothing other than the "reassertion" or "reaffirmation" of

---

117. For example, Pannenberg says that, "Jesus' unity with God was not yet established by the claim implied in his pre-Easter appearance, but only by his resurrection from the dead." See Pannenberg, *Jesus–God and Man*, p. 53.
118. Torrance, *Space, Time and Resurrection*, p. 46.
119. Dawson, *The Resurrection in Karl Barth*, p. 218.

triune God's being.[120] Eitel acknowledges that there is nothing in God's own being that needs to be reasserted or reaffirmed. Since the physical resurrection is already in God's eternal plan before the creation, what the Father and the Son actualize in this event is the "historicization" of the *telos* of the intra-divine life. Eitel's argument runs thus:

> On Dawson's reading, Barth conceives the resurrection as the 'reassertion' or 'reaffirmation' of God's triune being in the face of death. While Dawson's valuation of Barth's suggestive remarks is in some sense correct, it misses the more nuanced trajectory of Barth's resurrection–Trinitarian correspondence. As I have shown, the resurrection is presented, not as the *reaffirmation* of the intra-divine life – but rather as its *telos*. The resurrection does not 'reassert' God's eternal being; it is an event always already grounded in the singular and eternal *affirmation* of God's eternal being as a being for space and time.[121]

Actually, the difference between Dawson and Eitel lies in the fact that Dawson approaches this issue from a temporal, bottom-up perspective, whereas Eitel approaches from an eternal, top-down perspective. When we look at God's eternity from our temporal perspective, the unity of triune God is threatened by the death of the Son for the Son is isolated from the Father and the Holy Spirit; when we try to look at this problem from God's eternal point of view, both the crucifixion and the triumph of the death are pre-ordained in eternity as parts of the same salvation history. Eitel's interpretation will not lead to Docetism since he never challenges the reality and historicity of the resurrection. However, there is a disastrous result which Dawson's approach cannot avoid, that is, if the unity of triune God is really under the assault of the death and the only way out is the resurrection of the Son, the resurrection becomes a necessity rather than the free

---

120. Cf. Dawson, *The Resurrection in Karl Barth*, p. 219-21.
121. Eitel, "The Resurrection of Jesus Christ," p. 45.

act of eternal God. By no means Barth would accept such an explanation on his thought.

3.3 Conclusion

Firstly, like his preexistence, the eternal Son's resurrection is as concrete as his incarnation. In the Easter event, his voice is heard, his body is seen, even his wounds are touched. Secondly, the resurrected Son has conquered the power of death, thus breaks the limit of the form of time and becomes the contemporary of all human beings in all times. Thirdly, the resurrected Son brings the triune God's eschatological salvation to our own time, so that we can live in real expectation rather than in despair. Fourthly, the tension between our "not yet" ontological situation and the triune God's future salvation cannot be effaced by us, however it must remain as a dynamic encounter which comes to us from the Son's side.[122]

---

122. As Hunsinger reminds us, "[t]he truth that is in him is not yet in us; the actuality which is ours in him is not yet actualized in us. Nor can it be produced or actualized by us. ...It encounters human beings as the present truth of their future salvation." See Hunsinger, *How to Read Karl Barth*, p. 125.

CHAPTER 4

The Eternal Concrete Holy Spirit

Section 1:
The Eclipse of the Spirit

1.1 The Eclipse of the Spirit?

The first task to undertake when studying Barth's pneumatology should only be apologetics.[1] Barth demands of his interpreters the exacting task of asking particular questions: "Forgetting the Spirit?"[2], "You wonder where the Spirit went?"[3], "Is there nothing the Spirit can do that the Son can't do better?"[4] If the doctrine of the Holy Spirit is the "orphan doctrine" of Christian theology,[5] pneumatology is doubtless also the orphan doctrine of the *Church Dogmatics*. While Barth has authored more than one book with "Spirit" in the title,[6] some 2100 pages with "Spirit" in

---

1. Cf. Eberhard Busch, *The Great Passion: An Introduction to Karl Barth's Theology* (Grand Rapids: William B. Eerdmans Publishing Co., 2004), pp. 219-20; Eugene F. Rogers Jr., *After the Spirit: A Constructive Pneumatology from Resources outside the Modern West* (Grand Rapids: William B. Eerdmans Publishing Co., 2005), pp. 19-23, 33-6; Rogers, "The Eclipse of the Spirit in Karl Barth," in John McDowell and Michael Higton eds. *Conversing with Barth* (Aldershot: Ashgate, 2002), pp. 173-90.

2. Busch, *The Great Passion*, p. 219.

3. Robert W. Jenson, "You Wonder Where the Spirit Went," *Pro Ecclesia* 2: 3 (1993): p. 296.

4. Rogers, *After the Spirit*, p. 19.

5. This was observed by Adolf von Harnack, see Hunsinger, "The Mediator of Communion," p. 148.

6. Barth, *Come Holy Spirit*, trans. Richard Ernst and Honrighausen (New York: Round Table Press, 1939) and *The Holy Spirit and the Christian Life*, trans. R. Birch Hoyle (Louisville: Westminster/John Knox Press, 1993).

bold-face theses,[7] and there are at least two secondary books devoted to the Spirit,[8] two interwoven critiques of Barth still need to be considered: first, that Barth's pneumatology subsides into Christology; second, that Barth confines the function of the Holy Spirit strictly to the noetic. The first critique is fully presented in Rogers' *After the Spirit*:

> The upshot of two centuries of Trinitarian revivals seems to be this: Anything the Spirit can do, the Son can do better. If the Spirit sanctifies, that is more specifically expressed as following the Son. If the Spirit empowers the subjective human response, that is more concretely expressed as the power of the Son. If the Spirit consummates life together with God, that is more biblically expressed as the wedding of the Lamb. If the Spirit gathers the community, that community is of course better named as the body of Christ. If the Spirit distributes various gifts, then they are better coordinated as gifts that make members of the body of Christ. …It comforts Christians while Christ is absent, but Christ is not really absent.[9]

Indeed, Christ is never really absent, neither is the Spirit. For Barth, the work of Christ is the objective reality of revelation, whereas the work of Holy Spirit is the subjective reality of revelation.[10] In revelation, Jesus Christ's soterial work is effected to us through the work of the Holy Spirit, thus the subjective "in Spirit" is the coordinate of the objective "in Christ." God's grace is manifested both in the objective revelation in Christ and man's subjective appropriation of this revelation through the Holy Spirit.

---

7. Cf. Rogers, *After the Spirit*, p. 19.

8. Philip J. Rosato, *The Spirit as Lord: The Pneumatology of Karl Barth* (Edinburgh: T & T Clark, 1981), and John Thompson, *The Holy Spirit in the Theology of Karl Barth* (Allison Park: Pickwick Publication, 1991).

9. Rogers, *After the Spirit*, p. 33.

10. "When we keep in view the subjective aspect of the central concept of revelation," Barth says, "we have spoken then of the special work of God the Spirit, of the wonder of the love in the outpouring of the Holy Spirit." See Barth, *The Holy Spirit and the Christian Life*, p. 6. Cf. Otto Weber, *Karl Barth's Church Dogmatics*, trans. Arthur C. Cochrane (London: Lutterworth Press, 1953), pp. 50-1.

In this reality we are free to be eternally God's children and to know, love, and praise him in his revelation. The Spirit as subjective reality of God's revelation makes real and concrete God's eternal grace in our time. As Barth puts it:

> This is how God works in the specific event which forms the center and meaning and goal of all creaturely occurrence: objectively, proceeding from God by His Word; and subjectively, moving towards man by his Holy Spirit. ...Every time that God shows forth his power to the men of his choosing, and through them to others, every time, then, that he acts, he does so in the following way: his Word goes forth to these men, to be received by them in the power of his Spirit; his Spirit is given to these men, to receive his Word of power.[11]

Had Barth followed this approach to interpret the relation between the Word and the Spirit from beginning to the end, we would have a Barthian Christological Pneumatology or Pneumatic Christology.[12] Busch argues that Barth seeks two centers in Christian theology: Word and Spirit, and "if it were to make either the former or the latter the center, it would become either metaphysics or mysticism."[13] Although it is difficult to charge Barth's theology with "metaphysics" or "mysticism", yet to read all his *CD* is to be persuaded of the basic justice of John Thompson's judgment:

> It does not mean that there is no theology except Christology, that all other theology is absorbed and assumed into it. Barth's *Church Dogmatics* is a massive proof to the contrary. It means rather that all aspects of theology and dogmatics must be

---

11. *CD* III/3, p. 142. Thompson gives a brief summary of the Spirit's function: "Since God and humanity are one though distinguished in Jesus Christ, only by the Spirit can this truth be known." See Thompson, *The Holy Spirit in the Theology of Karl Barth*, p. 8.
12. Rosato does discuss the "possibility of a Spirit Christology" in *CD* III/3, Cf. Rosato, *The Spirit as Lord*, p. 184.
13. Busch, *The Great Passion*, pp. 219-20.

dynamically related to this living and concrete center and be determined throughout by it.¹⁴

Evidently, there is an imbalance between Christology and Pneumatology in Barth. The problem is: does the imbalance of the Word and the Spirit lead to the latter being subordinate to the former? The answer must be "No." On one hand, Barth argues that the Spirit is never separated from the Son or the Word: he cannot be seen as another center alongside the Son, for the Spirit is the Spirit of Jesus Christ and "there is no special or second revelation of the Spirit alongside of that of the Son."¹⁵ On the other hand, the Spirit cannot be confused with the Son: in one revelation, "the Son or Word represents the element of God's appropriation to man and the Spirit represents the element of God's appropriation by man."¹⁶ Furthermore, ontically God the Spirit is different from God the Father and God the Son.¹⁷ All in all, a close study of Barth's teaching on the relation between the Son and the Spirit shows that he denies any kind of subordinationism. As Hunsinger rightly points out:

> Barth intended to develop a doctrine of the Holy Spirit's saving work that would be rigorously Christocentric, yet without becoming deficient in its grasp of essential Trinitarian relations. No subordinationism, whether implicit or explicit, could be tolerated. Christ's reconciling work was not to be devalued but rather upheld as 'intrinsically perfect,' yet no 'subordinationist' displacement could be allowed of the Spirit's own special work of redemption.¹⁸

---

14. Thompson, *Christ in Perspective in the Theology of Karl Barth*, p. 1. As for Rosato's attempt "to give Barth a primarily pneumatic slant," Thompson refutes that, "Pneumatology is a very important aspect of theology but not the whole of it. It is integrated into and integral to the whole content of the *Church Dogmatics* but is never its primary thrust" (p. 8).
15. *CD* I/1, p. 474.
16. *CD* I/1, p. 474.
17. Cf. *CD* I/1, pp. 474-80.
18. Hunsinger, "The Mediator of Communion," p. 150.

If Barth can avoid the first critique, can he avoid the second one as well? Does Barth's pneumatology only have noetic consequences? At first glance, Barth indeed develops his pneumatology mainly within the frame of the doctrine of revelation:

> It is God's reality in that God himself becomes present to man not just externally, not just from above, but also from within, from below, subjectively. It is thus reality in that he does not merely come to man but encounters himself from man. God's freedom to be present in this way to man, and therefore to bring about this encounter, is the Spirit of God, the Holy Spirit in God's revelation.[19]

Our relationship with God, which is accomplished by the Holy Spirit in divine revelation, is a personal relationship. In this encounter the divine revelation imparts itself to us. However without the Holy Spirit we are unable to acknowledge the truth established by Jesus. That is to say, the two subjects in this encounter – the triune God and human being – cannot be seen as the equal partners, even noetically. Human beings have no capacity in themselves to acknowledge Jesus Christ's soterial work for them. Barth argues:

> When men belong to Jesus Christ in such a way that they have freedom to recognize His word as addressed also to them, his work as done also for them, the message about him as also their task; and then for their part, freedom to hope for the best for all other men, this happens indeed, as their human experience and action, and yet not in virtue of their human capacity, determination and exertion, but solely on the basis of the free

---

19. *CD* I/1, p. 451. For example, Thomas Freyer charges that for Barth the function of the Holy Spirit is confined to noetic realization of the ontic work accomplished by Jesus Christ. Cf. Thomas Freyer, *Zeit – Kontinuität und Unterbrechung: Studien zu Karl Barth, Wolfhart Pannenberg und Karl Rahner* (Würzburg: Echter, 1993), pp. 176-81. Cf. also Rosato, *The Spirit as Lord*, p. 82.

gift of God, in which all this is given to them. In this giving and gift God is the Holy Spirit.[20]

Following Augustine,[21] Barth understands the Holy Spirit as God's eternal gift in divine revelation. Barth employs both agential[22] and non-agential[23] language to describe the Holy Spirit. Hunsinger makes it clear that the role of the Holy Spirit in the eternal trinity has a twofold character: "Following Barth's pattern of usage, we might say that the Spirit 'mediates' the communion between the Father and the Son. We would then say that the Spirit is the 'mediator' of this communion, but we might also want to say that the Spirit is equally its 'mediation,' or even that the Spirit just *is* this communion itself."[24] This twofold ontic agency of the Holy Spirit determines that the work of the Holy Spirit cannot be, for Barth, restricted to the noetic aspect of man's acknowledgment of the revelation. Indeed, both Barth himself and some outstanding interpreters of his pneumatology, such as Busch, Hunsinger and Rosato, emphasize the ontic aspect of an established truth concerning mankind. Barth says: "What we have is a divine noetic which

---

20. Barth, *Dogmatics in Outline*, trans. G. T. Thomson (London: S. C. M. Press, 1949), p. 137. On human's incapacity for God's revelation, Busch has an excellent argument: "As Barth sees it, the Holy Spirit overturns the pillar of the modern doctrine of the spirit, namely, the assertion that there is a capacity for God as a given in the human person. The human incapacity to make oneself into a participant in revelation is not a universally acknowledged truth. Humans will dispute it hotly. Only in the experience of the Holy Spirit does God 'rid him of any idea that he possesses a possibility of his own for such a meeting' (*CD* I.2, p.234). Indeed, the whole idea that the Holy Spirit sanctions the view that we are equal partners with God is unmasked as a lie." See Busch, *The Great Passion*, pp. 225-6.

21. Augustine writes on the role of the Holy Spirit thus: "We should not be disturbed at the Holy Spirit, although he is coeternal with the Father and the Son, being said to be something from a point of time, like this name we have just used of "donation." The Spirit, to make myself clear, is everlastingly gift, but donation only from a point of time." See Augustine, *The Trinity*, trans. Edmund Hill (New York: New City Press, 1991), p. 200.

22. For the agential role of the Holy Spirit Barth describes that "[w]ith the Father and the Son he is the one sovereign divine Subject, the Subject who is not placed under the control or inspection of any other, who derives his being and existence from himself." See *CD* I /1, p. 469.

23. For the non-agential role of the Holy Spirit Barth writes that "he is the common element, or, better, the fellowship, the act of communion." See *CD* I/1, p. 470.

24. Hunsinger, "The Mediator of Communion," p. 153.

has all the force of a divine ontic."[25] This noetic-ontic change means that once the creature participates in the divine revelation, he cannot remain the same. Firstly, the Holy Spirit reveals the real ontic identity of human for the first time in his or her life, namely, creature as he or she is, he or she is elected by God the Creator as his partner. As Rosato puts it: "The Spirit is God as he realizes in time his eternal redemptive and creative turning to man. In doing so, the Spirit reveals himself as the God who transcends the world of man and who nevertheless intimately encounters man and lends him the ability to be what he is called to be from eternity: the free and loving covenant partner of God."[26]

Secondly, by participation of the divine communion through the Holy Spirit, the ontic situation has been eventually changed. In the eternal immanent Trinity, the Holy Spirit initiates the divine communion; in temporal economy Trinity, the Holy Spirit draws us into this communion in a concrete way, therefore changes our existential state fundamentally. As Rosato puts it: "As the Spirit creates eternal community between the Father and the Son, he also creates temporal community between God and man. …In historical revelation the Spirit lends a new potentiality to man by initiating him into the prepared communion between God and man which existed antecedently in the Spirit's own eternal communion with the Father and the Son."[27] The Holy Spirit is also believed to be active especially in the life of the Son. It is in the Holy Spirit Jesus and man present and impart each other, thus the acceptance of God's eternal gift in our time enables man to come back to the triune communion, like the prodigal son comes back home. Certainly this mutual impartation should not be confined in the epistemological area, since our existential situation is created, sustained and redeemed by the activities of the Holy Spirit in an ontological way as well, as Hunsinger writes: "As disclosed by the Spirit, in other words, the knowledge of Jesus is not something merely cognitive, for it claims those who are addressed by the gospel as whole persons. In the power of the Spirit through the proclamation of the gospel, Jesus is present to believers

---

25. *CD* IV/3, p. 297. Cf. Busch, *The Great Passion*, p. 225.
26. Rosato, *The Spirit as Lord*, p. 104.
27. Rosato, *The Spirit as Lord*, p. 27. Cf. also Donald G. Bloesch, *The Holy Spirit: Works and Gifts* (Downers Grove: InterVarsity press, 2000), pp. 226-8.

and believers to him. ...Mutual self-presence becomes the basis for mutual self-impartation."[28] It is the same Spirit who speaks, acts and intercedes for us in our time from eternity,[29] assuring that God's word can renew us continuously. As Barth puts it in an earlier work:

> But as the Scriptural announcement of God's revelation must be ever increasingly *becoming* the voice of the living God to us, seeing that God is continually saying to us what he said by the mouth of prophets and apostles once for all, so too the outer and inner constraints of our existence must be ever *acquiring* the character of divine indications, duties and promises through the divine speech to us.[30]

In conclusion, although there is an asymmetry in Barth's Christology and Pneumatology, the charge of subordinationism cannot be held as viable; although Barth emphasizes the noetic function of the Holy Spirit in revelation, we cannot neglect its ontic consequences. As such this makes "the eclipse of the Spirit" in Barth's theology an overstatement.

1.2 Some Further Charges

The critique aforementioned is the most common charge on Barth's Pneumatology, however there are some further critiques. Besides the subordination of the Holy Spirit, Wolfgang Vondey further charges Barth with two other kinds of subordination, i.e., the subordination of eschatology and the subordination of temporality:

> [T]he confrontation of time with eternity is radically determined by the work of God in Christ; pneumatology is

---

28. Hunsinger, "The Mediator of Communion," p. 161.
29. In Hunsinger's words, "[t]he Spirit who enabled Christ alone to accomplish our salvation as a finished work there and then is the very Spirit who enables us to participate in it and attest to it here and now." See Hunsinger, "The Mediator of Communion," p. 158.
30. Barth, *The Holy Spirit and the Christian Life*, p. 9. In this sense, Hunsinger says that the "Holy Spirit is God insofar as God is eternally communion." See "The Mediator of Communion," p. 154.

subsumed under Christology. In addition, the Spirit directs humankind back in time to Christ but does not point forward to the completion of God's work of salvation in the future; eschatology is subsumed under soteriology. Finally, Barth speaks of the work of the Holy Spirit in time as the historical self-communication of God that is itself subject to time; temporality is subsumed under history. In other words, Barth can speak of the 'Spirit in history', but he does not know the 'Spirit of history'.[31]

Here the second critique, namely, that eschatology is subsumed under soteriology, appears justified at first glance, considering that Barth indeed emphasizes the Spirit's work which is based on the cross and resurrection: "[i]n the context of the New Testament witness the non-identity between Christ and the Holy Spirit seems to be as necessarily grounded as possible. Thus we find the Holy Spirit only after the death and resurrection of Jesus Christ or in the form of knowledge of the crucified and risen Lord, i.e., on the assumption that objective revelation has been concluded and completed."[32] However, Barth criticizes and tries to avoid any sense of such a one-sidedness through over emphasizing the past, or the present, or the future in pneumatology as in Christology. Rather any sense of such a one-sidedness may disappear if we study Barth's eschatology in light of pneumatology fully. We are going to do this in section 4 of this chapter.

The third charge, that "temporality is subsumed under history," more specifically, the relationship between temporality and eternity, can also be resolved if we consider the activities of the Holy Spirit in our time, in the

---

31. Wolfgang Vondey, "The Holy Spirit and Time in Contemporary Catholic and Protestant Theology," *Scottish Journal of Theology* 58: 4 (2005): p. 398. Cf. D. Lyle Dabney, *Die Kenosis des Geistes: Kontinuität zwischen Schöpfung und Erlösung im Werk des Heiligen Geist* (Neukirchen-Vluyn: Neukirchener, 1997), pp. 32-4.

32. *CD* I/1, p. 451. Gunton approves this charge also when he says that "[a]ny weakness in the discussion of the Holy Spirit will militate against a satisfactory expression of the eschatological dimension of Christian theology, with the result that the activity of God will tend to be located in the past rather than in the present and future." See Gunton, *Becoming and Being* (Oxford: Oxford University Press, 1978), p.163. Rosato seconds that by saying: "his (Barth's) doctrine of the Trinity in the Church Dogmatic nevertheless stresses God's origin and not His future." See Rosato, *The Spirit as Lord*, pp. 135-6.

time between the first and second *parousia* of Jesus Christ. This is the topic of section 3 of this chapter. Now we may study a response to this charge briefly. In an article, Macchia refutes this subordination with this argument:

> Barth uses pneumatology to avoid both Christomonism and anthropomonism, because the Spirit functions as the link between Jesus and the word and between Jesus Christ and the church. Due to the objective work of the Spirit creating these links, Christ cannot be dissolved into human religious imagination and the experience of the church in the Spirit cannot be collapsed into the historical Jesus, having no economy of its own in God's redemptive plan or no orientation towards an eschatological future.[33]

Different from Barth's mainly subjective understanding of the Holy Spirit, Macchia emphasizes the "objective" side of the Holy Spirit. His opinion is not incompatible with Barth's, since for Barth the work of the Holy Spirit also has an ontic function as mentioned above. Actually the difference between Vondey and Macchia lies in whether the Holy Spirit is under or supra history. At this point we must go with Macchia for certainly the Holy Spirit acts in human history, but this does not necessarily mean that he is subject to the history, otherwise the incarnate Son is surely subsumed under human history in the same way. Had the lordship of the Holy Spirit over history been denied, the coherence of triune God's pre- supra- and post-temporality would not stand. That is Macchia's insight into Barth's pneumatology.

---

33. Frank D. Macchia, "The Spirit of God and the Spirit of Life: An Evangelical Response to Karl Barth's Pneumatology," in Sung Wook Chung eds. *Karl Barth and Evangelical Theology: Convergences and Divergences* (Grand Rapids: Baker Academic, 2006), p. 159.

Section 2:
Holy Spirit the Eternal Creator

2.1 Eternal Concrete Creator

Although the creation is eminently the work of the eternal Father, Barth does not neglect the role of the Holy Spirit at all. As Gabriel says, "although Barth does not discuss the Holy Spirit explicitly to any great extent within his doctrine of creation, the ideas are certainly there, as expressed in divine action, and Barth has much to say regarding the Holy Spirit in later volumes of *Church Dogmatics*."[34] Since the creation is exclusively the work of triune God, the Holy Spirit eternally posits himself as the Creator together with the Father and the Son. In accordance with Barth's doctrine of the Trinity, God the Holy Spirit participates in the work of creation. The Holy Spirit is revealed as the spirit of the Creator also, not the spirit of the creature, so we need to discern the Holy Spirit and human spirit in light of the Creator and the creature. The latter cannot be confused with the former. The Holy Spirit is the creator "in fullness of Deity,"[35] whereas human spirit is created spirit. The difference lies in two facts:

Firstly, the Holy Spirit is eternal. As the third person of the Holy Trinity, the Holy Spirit is no less in divinity than the Father and the Son. The Holy Spirit exists in the beginning with the eternal Father and the eternal Son as the eternal love, which unites the Father and the Son, as Barth says:

> As God is in himself Father from all eternity, he begets himself as the Son from all eternity. As he is the Son from all eternity, he is begotten of himself as the Father from all eternity. In this eternal begetting of himself and being begotten of himself, he posits himself a third time as the Holy Spirit, i.e., as the love which unites him in himself.[36]

---

34. Gabriel, "A Trinitarian Doctrine of Creation?" p. 41.
35. Barth, *The Holy Spirit and the Christian Life*, p. 3.
36. *CD* I/1, p. 483.

Obviously, Barth follows Augustine by regarding the Holy Spirit as the bond of love between the Father and the Son and emphasizes the western *Filioque*: "If the rule holds good that God in is eternity is none other than the One who discloses himself to us in his revelation, then in the one case as in the other the Holy Spirit is the Spirit of the love of the Father and the Son, and so *procedens ex Patre Filioque*."[37]

Yet Barth is also aware of Augustinian depersonalizing the Spirit as *merely* a love relation and tries to ease this tendency by arguing that the Holy Spirit is "together with," "in and with," or "like" the Father and the Son.[38] However, in order to understand the independent personality of the Holy Spirit, we must study the person and work of the Holy Spirit in economy Trinity "together with" those in immanent Trinity, as McIntyre points out: "the whole burden of the theology of the Spirit in Augustine and Barth is that the Spirit is of the Godhead *ex se* from eternity, and is not constituted divine by being designated 'love.'"[39] To avoid the Augustinian depersonalizing approach to the Holy Spirit, we ought to keep in mind that the third person of the eternal Trinity also "dwells in us" and thus establishes the "consummation of the fellowship between God and man."[40]

Secondly, the Holy Spirit is concrete. He reveals the subjective aspect of God the Father by indwelling in us. The Holy Spirit is the uncreated spirit whose presence in our spirits gives us sanctifying grace. Whatever we know by faith, we have received by the power of the Spirit. This is what Jesus meant when he promised "the Advocate, the Holy Spirit, whom the Father will send in my name, will teach you everything, and remind you of all that I have said to you" (John 14:26). In this sense, Jesus Christ is the first advocate who revealed the words of God, whereas the Holy Spirit is the second advocate who enables us to understand what Jesus Christ has revealed. The subjective "in Spirit" is the counterpart to the objective

---

37. *CD* I/1, p. 483. Cf. Hunsinger, "The Mediator of Communion," pp. 154-5; David Guretzki, *Karl Barth on the Filioque* (Farnham and Burlington: Ashgate Publishing Limited, 2009), pp. 91-134.
38. Cf. *CD* I/1, p. 487; Macchia, "The Spirit of God and the Spirit of Life," pp. 156-7.
39. John McIntyre, *The Shape of Pneumatology: Studies in the Doctrine of the Holy Spirit* (Edinburgh: T&T Clark, 1997), p. 168.
40. *CD* I/1, p. 488.

"in Christ." The Father's eternal redemptive plan is manifested both in the objective revelation in the Son and human's subjective appropriation of this revelation through the Holy Spirit. As the third person of the eternal Trinity, the Holy Spirit creates the God-man relation and gives life to the creature together with the Son:

> In both the Old Testament and the New the Spirit of God, the Holy Spirit, is very generally God himself to the degree that in an incomprehensibly real way, without on this account being any the less God, he can be present to the creature, and in virtue of this presence of his effect the relation of the creature to himself, and in virtue of this relation to himself grant the creature life. The creature needs the Creator to be able to live. It thus needs the relation to Him. But it cannot create this relation. God creates it by his own presence in the creature and therefore as a relation of himself to himself. The Spirit of God is God in his freedom to be present to the creature, and therefore to create this relation, and therefore to be the life of the creature.[41]

However, G. S. Hendry criticizes that Barth identifies the Spirit, who is subjectively the principle of our renewal, with the Spirit as the principle of our creaturely reality thus evacuating the former of its specific subjective role. The two cannot be properly combined.[42] Thompson admits that "this again is doubtful since the Spirit is not only the subjective reality of reconciliation but also one with the Father and the Son in creation and preservation and so has an ontic role."[43] However, in the last section we saw that the double role of the Holy Spirit, i.e., both noetic and ontic, could strengthen each other and by no means "evacuating" either of the two. As Weinrich argues:

---

41. *CD* I/1, p. 450.
42. Cf. G. S. Hendry, *The Holy Spirit in Christian Theology* (London: S. C. M., 1957), p. 50. Also Thompson, *The Holy Spirit in the Theology of Karl Barth*, p. 170.
43. Thompson, *The Holy Spirit in the Theology of Karl Barth*, p. 171.

> When Barth speaks of the Holy Spirit as the subjective reality of the revelation, he simply has this in mind: Revelation is not only a disclosure through which we view the condition of our life in a slightly different way, but revelation is a real event that can bring about change whose subject is God himself.[44]

Apart from reveling God's eternal will to us, the Holy Spirit also establishes humanity as soul and body. "Man exists," Barth says, "because he has spirit. That he has spirit means that he is grounded, constituted and maintained by God as the soul of his body."[45] The Holy Spirit not only takes part in the *creation* of the human as body and soul, but also communicates to the soul and through the soul to the body.[46] Thompson summarizes Barth's opinions on the Spirit as basis of body and soul as such:

a) God is there for us in free grace as Creator; humanity has no divine part but is wholly creaturely;

b) To have Spirit is what makes us human, the decisive determination of our being;

c) The Spirit is in humanity in the most intimate way as principle of its existence but is not identical with it;

d) The Spirit acts on the soul and through it on the body.[47]

Our humanity is based on God's divinity and our spirit is also imparted by the Holy Spirit. The time-eternity relationship can be deduced from this

---

44. [Wenn K. Barth vom Heiligen Geist als der subjektiven Wirklichkeit der Offenbarung spricht, dann hat er eben dies im Blick: Offenbarung ist nicht nur eine Mitteilung, durch die wir die Voraussetzungen unseres Lebens nun vieleicht ein wenig anders sehen, sondern Offenbarung ist veränderndes wirkliches Geschehen, dessen Subjekt Gott selbst ist.] Michael Weinrich, *Kirche glauben* (Wuppertal: Foedus, 1998), p. 135.

45. *CD* III/2, p. 344.

46. In Barth's words, "The Holy Spirit is immediate to the soul, but through the soul he is also mediate to the body, and he is thus the basis and maintenance of the whole Christian and therefore of the man who does not belong to himself." See *CD* III/2, p. 366.

47. Thompson, *The Holy Spirit in the Theology of Karl Barth*, p. 167. Cf. also Marc Cortez, "Body, Soul, and (Holy) Spirit: Karl Barth's Theological Framework for Understanding Human Ontology," *IJST* 10:3 (July 2008): pp. 328-45. On this issue, Rosato says: "The Spirit enjoys an ontic role in man's very being to the extent that he constitutes the human person as body and soul and makes him ontically disposed to accept the covenant." See Rosato, *The Spirit as Lord*, p. 184.

creature-Creator relationship: as humanity must be based on divinity, time cannot be understood apart from eternity, because time is no other than the existential form of the creature, whereas eternity is God himself. "Time is," Barth observes, "the form of the created world by which the world is ordained to be the field for the acts of God and for the corresponding reactions of his creatures, or, in more general terms, for creaturely life."[48] For Barth, time is such a concept that it can only be approached creaturely. It is created, or more exactly, "co-created,"[49] as the form of the creature. Here Barth's definition of time echoes Kant's in a different direction. Both of them treat time as a "form" which is given or created together with everything, however, whereas Kant sees time as the form of the outer world appearing in our inner sense, Barth sees time as the existential form of the creature. The difference is caused by their different aims: whereas Kant studies time in order to know how our knowledge is possible, Barth studies it in order to know how our existence (related to God) is possible. Thus whereas the Kantian concept is for cognitive service, the Barthian one is for both cognitive and ontological use. Barth achieves this by emphasizing the cooperation of the triune God and his creature, especially through the Holy Spirit in revelation:

> It is grounded from all eternity in God that no man cometh to the Father except by the Son, because the Spirit by whom the Father draws his children to himself is also from all eternity the Spirit of the Son, because by his Spirit the Father does not call anyone except to his Son. In respect of revelation the Western Church did not recognise any Spirit to be the Holy Spirit except the Spirit of Christ. But it also spoke of the God who meets us in his revelation as the eternal God.[50]

In this passage Barth makes clear that the immanent Trinity and economic Trinity are one in God's eternity. Together with the Father and the Son, the

---

48. *CD* III/2, p. 438.
49. *CD* III/2, p. 438.
50. *CD* I/2, p. 250.

Holy Spirit is the eternal Creator for us. In human history, by his concrete presence to the creature, the Holy Spirit constitutes the relation between the Creator and the creature. Thus Barth argues: "God's Spirit, the Holy Spirit, especially in revelation, is God himself to the extent that he can not only come to man but also be in man, and thus open up man and make him capable and ready for himself, and thus achieve his revelation in him."[51] In light of this creature-Creator relationship, God's eternal redemptive plan is realized objectively by the Son and subjectively by the Holy Spirit in our concrete time. As Barth writes:

> There can be no doubt that the work of the Holy Spirit is merely to "realize subjectively" the election of Jesus Christ and his work as done and proclaimed in time, to reveal and bring it to men and women. By the work of the Holy Spirit the body of Christ, as it is by God's decree from all eternity and as it has become in virtue of his act in time, acquires in all its hiddenness historical dimensions. The Holy Spirit awakens the "poor praise on earth" appropriate to that eternal-temporal occurrence, the answer to the Easter message in the hearts and on the lips of individual men, faiths and the one and varied recognition of obedience to the Son of God as the Head of all men.

Thus Barth makes clear that the role of the Holy Spirit can be understood as the creative, concrete and dynamic communion between God and human. By the Son and through the Spirit, God himself actualizes his eternal will in our earthly time. As Thompson puts it, "[h]ence creation and we as creatures are both willed by God from all eternity and in time also created by him through the Word and sustained by the Holy Spirit."[52]

---

51. *CD* I/1, p. 450.
52. Thompson, *The Holy Spirit in the Theology of Karl Barth*, p. 170.

2.2 Conclusion

First, the Holy Spirit is God the Creator. That is to say, the Holy Spirit must be understood in Trinitarian terms. The doctrine of Trinity always refers to the three modes God has of being God, i.e., we can never speak of one without keeping the other two in mind. This means that our experience of God as Holy Spirit always involves also our relation to God as the Father to God as the Son. Barth's doctrine of creation is also Trinitarian in character: the universe and human beings are created by the Trinitarian Creator. In eternal Trinity, Jesus Christ is the Creator in an objective way, whereas the Holy Spirit is the Creator eminently in a subjective way. Together with the Son's objective work in creation, the subjective work of the Holy Spirit by no means should be ignored.

Second, the Holy Spirit presents to the creature. This presence is really omnipresence since the Holy Spirit is both transcendent and immanent to any specific time and space. And, "[b]y bringing the eschata into history, the Spirit does not vivify a preexisting structure; he *creates* one; he changes linear historicity into a *presence*."[53] However, in this presence, Holy Spirit the Creator differentiates himself from the creature: there is no loss of identity in the union of Holy Spirit and human spirit. Human beings can have the Holy Spirit but by no means can human spirit become or be confused with the Holy Spirit.

Third, the Holy Spirit determines the existence of human beings both noetically and ontically. Noetically, the Holy Spirit enlightens our minds, imparting the redemptive work of Jesus Christ to us; ontically, the Holy Spirit constitutes the twofold existence of humanity as body and soul and changes human life into Christian life. This twofold determination appropriates the role of the Holy Spirit as our eternal Creator.

Fourth, by imparting Jesus' redemptive grace to us subjectively, the Holy Spirit also brings the Father's eternal salvation to our time. As the creative agent between God and human, the Holy Spirit bridges the eternity of Trinitarian Creator and the temporality of creature. By the power of the Holy Spirit, our time is created, renewed and sustained in God's eternity.

---

53. Zizioulas, *Being as Communion*, p. 180.

Section 3:
Holy Spirit the Reconciler in "Time Between"

3.1 The Reconciler in the Time of Community

In the last section we learned from Barth that the Holy Spirit as Creator is simultaneous with all creatures. Out of his divine freedom, he creates the God-man relation and chooses to be present to all creatures. In this relation, the Holy Spirit makes an invitation to all of temporal humanity to partake divine eternity. The Father's eternal will in his Holy Spirit calls for our response in time, but by no means such a communicational work should be regarded as a kind of predestined necessity, as Barth observes: "Even though salvific reception is totally enabled by God, it is not given without the temporal response of us. It may be called a paradox of grace that all are justified of God and yet justification is a human response, albeit passive, this paradox is then a miracle."[54]

However, our temporal response may neglect, distort or even rebel against the eternal calling. Out of our sinful nature, we always set ourselves in opposition to the Creator and resist his grace. As creatures, "we do not allow the work of the Word and of the Spirit to befall us."[55] We always, like the prophet Jonah, try to escape from God's calling. In a recent article, Ables gives a clear exposition of this situation:

> Humanity will always seek to find some other way, some other means, of reconciliation apart from Jesus Christ, even at the expense of multiplying the works of God, so that the Spirit might have some gift to give other than Jesus Christ. But if the election of Jesus Christ is the eternal beginning of all the ways and works of God, what other gift could there possibly be? The problem with the Spirit is not, then, Barth (or Augustine, Aquinas or Rahner): it is we ourselves, wanting to secure a

---

54. *CD* I/2, p. 278. In *The Holy Spirit and the Christian Life*, Barth also says: "Although faith can only be understood as the work of the Holy Spirit, and in the secrecy of faith is characterized as repentance and trust, it is still *our own* faith" (p. 32).

55. Barth, *The Holy Spirit and the Christian Life*, p. 19.

place of autonomy and reciprocity at the event of revelation, something which Barth will not allow.[56]

In this sense we are no other than rebellious sinners before God. However, since the Holy Spirit is not just some sort of spirit, "like the spirit of the true, the good, the beautiful,"[57] but is the Holy Spirit, he is strong enough to conquer our enmity toward himself. It is only by the Holy Spirit that we can go exit ourselves and enter the relationship with the Father, thus the Holy Spirit is always in our time the mediator between the triune God and us. Together with the Father and the Son, the Holy Spirit comes from eternity to our time as Creator, Reconciler and Redeemer alike.[58] By the agential work of the Holy Spirit, we have the opportunity to carry the message of reconciliation and redemption to the temporal world, to be inspired by the Spirit to bring people to eternity. For Barth, the Holy Spirit is not only the mediator of Jesus' reconciling work to us but also mediator of our temporality to God's eternity. Hunsinger thus explains the Holy Spirit as a mediator of communion:

> The mediation of the Spirit thus moves in two directions at once: from the eternal Trinity through Jesus Christ to humankind, and from humankind through Jesus Christ to the eternal Trinity. It is a mediation of communion – of love in knowledge, and of knowledge in love – as the origin and goal of all things, made possible by the saving work of Christ.[59]

As the mediator, the Spirit does not work alone, indeed, "the only content of the Holy Spirit is Jesus; his only work is his provisional revelation; his only effect the human knowledge which has him as its object."[60] In Jesus' lifetime, the Holy Spirit reveals the knowledge of his community with us

---

56. Travis Ables, "The Grammar of Pneumatology in Barth and Rahner: A Reconsideration," *IJST* 11: 2 (April 2009): p. 215.
57. Barth, *The Holy Spirit and the Christian Life*, p. 20.
58. Cf. *CD* I/2, pp. 203-79.
59. Hunsinger, "The Mediator of Communion," p. 151.
60. *CD* IV/2, p. 654.

and our community with him. In this revealed knowledge we know that he is with us in our time, and therefore we are at unity with one another. "It is in this way, by this self-attestation, self-presentation and self-impartation, that he founds and quickens the community, which is the mighty work of the Holy Spirit."[61] In this community, by the objective work of the Son and the subjective work of the Holy Spirit, all humanity is reconciled to God and our old time has been changed into a new eon, as Trowitzsch writes: "Christ implants a transition and turning point in our days, in every moment, in light and dark hours: a transition from the old silhouette to the bright future-proof contour of the new eon."[62]

However, after Jesus' lifespan on earth, before his glorious second coming, we live. Our time thus beomes the "time between," i.e., the time between the first and second *parousia* of Jesus Christ. From our temporal point of view, Jesus died about two thousand years ago. Although his story and his words are preached every Sunday in every church in our time, he is not a living man as the one in his incarnate time. However, Barth reminds us that the invisible Jesus does not mean the non-existent Jesus. In our time, the time between his two *parousia*, we are not alone. The triune Creator never creates us as orphans on earth and divine eternity never lets any moment of our time go. During the time that the Son does not live among us empirically, it is the Holy Spirit who is present to us as our covenant-partner. Barth thus defines the "time between":

> The time of the community is the time between the first *parousia* of Jesus Christ and the second. "Parousia" means the immediate visible presence and action of the living Jesus Christ himself. His first immediate visible presence and action was that in which he encountered the disciples in the forty days after Easter as the Judge who was judged for the unjust. His

---

61. *CD* IV/2, p. 654.
62. [Christus pflanzt *Übergang und Wende* in meine Lebenstage, in die Augenblicke, in die leichten und in die dunklen Stunden: den Übergang vom Schattenriß des alten zur hellen zukunftssicheren Kontur der neuen Äon.] Michael Trowitzsch, "Die Zeit Jesu Christi. Bemerkungen zum Zeitverständnis Karl Barth, " *Zeitschrift für dialektische Theologie* 16 (2000): p. 147.

second presence and action will be his final coming in his revelation as the Judge of the quick and the dead. The community exists between his coming then as the risen One and this final coming. Its time is, therefore, this time between. Its movement is from direct vision to direct vision; and in this movement by his Holy Spirit he himself is invisibly present as the living Head in the midst of it as his body.[63]

Barth views the interim period, which sustains hope, as the time of the eschatological Spirit between the first and second *parousia* of Jesus Christ. The "time between" has both strength and weakness.[64] Its strength lies in the resurrection of Jesus Christ, i.e., the Easter event. That event is not a mere event and Jesus history is not a dead history. In the time between, it is the Holy Spirit who renews this reconciling message again and again in Christian community. The Easter event fulfils all times and thus unites the beginning and the end as one whole duration. And, the message of Easter is bestowed to us by the Holy Spirit, as Barth says: "By the awakening power of the Holy Spirit it is gathered in the unity of the faith to this message, i.e., to the One who, according to this message, is the living Lord."[65]

In *CD* III/2, Barth has already made clear that there is no separation between the first and second of Jesus' *parousia*:

> We refer to the lordship of Jesus in the time between the resurrection and the *parousia* and therefore between the commencement and the completion of his final revelation. That it has the form of the Spirit means that the community not only derives temporality from this commencement and moves

---

63. *CD* IV/1, p. 725. Cf. also *CD* IV/1, pp. 327-33. Bromiley explains the "time between" this way: "This is the time of the advance of Jesus' prophecy. It is the time of our human freedom under the condition of our effected but not yet fully manifested reconciliation. It is the time of the solidarity of Christians with non-Christians in ignorance and imperfection but also the time when Christians see Christ's prophecy in the light of the Easter event and live in the tension of movement from the first form of the *parousia* to the last." See Bromiley, *An Introduction to the Theology of Karl Barth*, p. 224.
64. For the strength and weakness of the time of the community, Cf. also Anderson, "Living in the Spirit," pp. 327-9; Dawson, *The Resurrection in Karl Barth*, pp. 191-4.
65. *CD* IV/1, p. 725. Cf. also p. 727.

towards this consummation but that it is effectively established and gathered by the One who was and who comes, being not only ruled but continually nourished and quickened by him. That is why it lives always in expectation and even in imminent expectation.[66]

Since the expectation is so "imminent," it is by no means an empty longing or desire. Because what we expect has already been given in the Easter event and the end is already coming to our aid in this time between, there is no separation between the past and the future. The time of the community, albeit provisional,[67] is not contradictory, for "[t]here can be posed no fundamental antithesis between this time, between the times and the future final time."[68] In his resurrection Jesus shows that he is the Lord of time and thus knows time like the shepherd knows his sheep. In this sense Barth summarizes the strength of the time between: "it is strong because it knows what time is – time which begins and ends, but for that reason the filled-out present of every time, between every yesterday and tomorrow."[69]

The weakness of the time of the community lies in the fact that the Easter event is after all a "past" event for us. What we could have toward this event is only an invisible faith which is inspired by the power of the Holy Spirit alone. Without the work of the Holy Spirit, "this weakness," Barth confesses, "will be fatal."[70] In Jesus' lifetime, "the Word became flesh

---

66. *CD* III/2, p. 505.

67. "It is provisional," Barth explains, "because it has not yet achieved it, nor will it do so. It can only attest it 'in the puzzling form of a reflection' (1 Cor 13:12). And it is provisional because, although it comes from the resurrection of Jesus Christ, it is only on the way with others to his return, and therefore to the direct and universal and definitive revelation of his work as it has been accomplished for them and for all men. The fact that it is provisional means that it is fragmentary and incomplete and insecure and questionable for even the community still participates in the darkness which cannot apprehend, if it also cannot overcome, the light (John 1:5). But the fact that it is provisional means also – for in this provisional way it represents the sanctification of humanity as it has taken place in Jesus Christ – that divine work is done within it truly and effectively, genuinely and invincibly, and in all its totality, so that even though it is concealed in many different ways it continually emerges and shines out from this concealment in the form of God's people." See *CD* IV/2, pp. 620-1.

68. Dawson, *The Resurrection in Karl Barth*, pp. 193.

69. *CD* IV/1, p. 727.

70. *CD* IV/1, p. 728. Cf. Colwell, *Actuality and Provisionality*, pp. 159-60.

and lived among us" (John 1:14); however in the time between, "it must be content to move in faith and without any kind of sight from the first to the second and last *parousia* of Jesus Christ."[71] For this very reason the Holy Spirit is crucial for us in this time between: without the imparting work of the Holy Spirit, the Easter event would only be an ordinary event in our time. We cannot understand that this event "terminates time and includes all times."[72] What was objectively fulfilled by Jesus Christ must be imparted to us subjectively by the Holy Spirit. Only by the power of the Holy Spirit does the fulfilled time, the time between, become "our time."[73] Awakened by the Holy Spirit, our faith becomes concrete and is molded as obedience in our time, and thus even constitutes the existence of the community. As Barth puts it: "It is in this way that the whole truth of the occurrence of growing fellowship, in the reconciliation through Christ, between God and man, on its subjective side, therefore becomes concrete. It becomes concrete as the gift of the Holy Spirit, in the reality of sanctification."[74]

The time of the community is our real time which has been touched by the incarnation of the Son and fulfilled by his reconciling work, thus "the meaning and content of our time – the last time – is the fulfillment of this provisional representation as the task of the community of Jesus Christ."[75] After the Easter event, we do exist between the first and second *parousia* thus the time between is exactly our "present" time, our "now." However we are not left alone between these two events since the Holy Spirit is standing between God and us in this time. By the power of the Holy Spirit, this time between puts on some eternity-like characters: from

---

71. *CD* IV/1, p. 728. In this sense Burgess calls the time between "the time of Jesus' 'absence', of his *invisible* presence in the church." See Andrew R. Burgess, *The Ascension in Karl Barth* (Aldershot: Ashgate, 2004), p. 68.

72. *CD* IV/1, p. 731.

73. Cf. *CD* IV/1, p. 735. Although this is time that will end with all time, yet "there is still time. And the time which is now is its time, and the time of its service. It renders it in the strength and weakness which both have their basis in the nature of this time. But in strength or in weakness it can render it gladly because it knows why we still have time, and it can do the decisive thing which gives meaning, real meaning, to the time which is given us." See *CD* IV/1, p. 739.

74. Barth, *The Holy Spirit and the Christian Life*, p. 33.

75. *CD* IV/2, p. 621.

our point of view, it is time in which the past, present and future are not separate, thus it becomes a coherent duration and this duration is exactly what Barth employs to describe God's eternity in the section under the title of "The Eternity and Glory of God" (*CD* II/1); from God's point of view, like the Son is eternally begetting by the Father for us, the Holy Spirit is eternally proceeding from the Father and the Son for us,[76] thus becoming the mediator in time between the two *parousia*, as Matczak observes:

> The Holy Spirit, then, is the turning (*Zuwendung*) of God towards us. This turning is manifested on earth in the activity and life of the church and her members. This activity is the temporal (*zeitlich*) abiding on earth of that which is eternal (*des ewig Gegenwärtigen*). Here Barth displays the vertical union of the temporal with eternal, the contact of time with eternity, which is the work of the Holy Spirit. This contact is nothing more than the unity of the Trinity in its temporal form, the unity manifested to us who, as such, are against God, but not against him in Jesus Christ.[77]

Indeed the Holy Spirit is both the turning of God towards us and the turning of us towards God. Both turnings are for our sake, not for God's sake. In the time of communion, it is the Holy Spirit who imparts triune God's eternity to us, therefore turning our enmity into faith, making our time concrete and coherent. Without the Holy Spirit's subjective reconciling and sustaining work, what Jesus achieved for us in his resurrection and

---

76. Interestingly, McCormack infers the movement of the Holy Spirit in eternity from the movement of the Son in eternity: "the condition of the possibility of the incarnation in time is to be found in the eternal generation of the Son. The condition of the possibility of the outpouring of the Holy Spirit in time is to be found in the eternal procession of the Holy Spirit from the Father and the Son. To the movement (the lived history) of the Son in time, there corresponds a movement in eternity. And so also with the Spirit." See Bruce McCormack, "The Ontological Presuppositions of Barth's Doctrine of the Atonement," in Charles Hill and Frank James III eds. *The Glory of the Atonement: Biblical, Theological, and Practical Perspectives* (Downers Grove: InterVarsity Press, 2004), pp. 358-9.

77. Sebastian A. Matczak, *Karl Barth on God: The Knowledge of the Divine Existence* (New York: St. Paul Publications, 1962), pp. 116-7.

Easter history, would remain alien to us, therefore our past, present and future would still be discontinuous and fragmental.

3.2 Conclusion

Firstly, the work of the Holy Spirit in the time between is based on the Easter event. The Holy Spirit enlightens church history after the death and resurrection of the Son. When the incarnate Son is no longer among us by incarnation, the Holy Spirit sustains our present time that has been fulfilled by the Easter event.

Secondly, the strength of the time between lies in the fact that the Easter event has already accomplished our salvation. The weakness in this lies in the fact that Jesus has left us as the incarnate Son. In the time between the first and second *parousia*, Jesus is invisible, thus the Christian communion can only rely on the Holy Spirit as the Reconciler.

Thirdly, in the time between, the Holy Spirit links the beginning (Jesus' resurrection) and the end (Jesus' final return) of our salvation history, thus making our past, present and future a coherent, eternity-like duration, although not eternity in itself. Without the sustaining power of the Holy Spirit, our time would inevitably fall into fragments and become nothing.

Section 4: Holy Spirit the Eschatological Redeemer

4.1 The Promise of the Holy Spirit

Although Volume V of the *CD* – The Doctrine of Redemption, which should have been developed in a pneumatic frame, was never written – we may still find Barth's insights on this doctrine in other parts of *CD* and his other works. In *The Holy Spirit and the Christian Life*, Barth shows that the Holy Spirit for us is also the Redeemer in an eschatological sense.[78] The eternal Creator and the Reconciler in time between, in the third place, presents to us as the realization of the *eschaton*. The eschatological existence of the

---

78. In Barth's word, "the holiness of the Holy Spirit consists, above all, in the fact that in the revelation of God to the human spirit he is not present in any other guise than the *eschatological* one." See *The Holy Spirit and the Christian Life*, p. 59.

Holy Spirit means that, "in his revelation he promises us something that is ultimate and future, something that is his characteristic purpose with us. It is a something that is 'absolutely final': a future that is a starting point."[79] We have no future without God. Apart from God's eternity, our future being is time enclosed by uncertainty, and our end results nothing other than a catastrophe. "We do not seize the future; it seizes us and overpowers us."[80] The "not yet" in future threatens us just like the "no longer" in the past does.[81] However, God has ordained our future in his eternal redemptive plan. In his eternity the triune God himself is our future. Coherent with God's pre- and supra- temporality, Barth thus describes God as our future:

> For God there is no "not yet" which might possibly be a threatening "never." But as he was and is he also will be. As he was, is and will be simultaneously without limit or separation, his eternity is original, authentic and creative time. But this eternal God will guarantee the reality of our future too (however long or short it may be), just as he guarantees it even now and has always done so. He will give it to us as the dimension of the life which he has appointed for us. He will do this because his eternity is the eternity of his will which has as its goal that we should live as his creatures and not have to perish, and therefore have our time. This is what God will also will for us in our long or short future. We can know this for a fact because he wills it now, always willed it, and never did not will it. Never did not do it – we must say even more strongly. For he was never not our Creator, Father and Redeemer. He never did not do what had to be done for us to have time for life. He did it as he initiated our particular time, and before he initiated it, as he initiated all time and before he initiated it in his eternal counsel. And with the same definiteness he will do it in our particular future in all the future, and beyond the

---

79. Barth, *The Holy Spirit and the Christian Life*, p. 59.
80. *CD* III/2, p. 543.
81. Cf. *CD* III/2, pp. 541-2.

end of all time in his eternity. Thus he will be over us, for and with us, as we shall also be in all the uncertainty of our future being.[82]

In human history, our future is concretely safeguarded by the Son and the Holy Spirit. The Holy Spirit is the guarantee that what has already been received initially in Jesus' first *parousia* will be received in its fullness at the second. The work of the Holy Spirit provides the provisional experience of the eschatological expectation to be accomplished completely in the return of Jesus Christ. "In this eschatological sense," Barth writes, "he is thus present as the Spirit of God the Creator and Reconciler."[83] In this eschatological expectation, our future has already begun in Easter event. As Cho puts it: "Our future has already begun from the Easter event. The eternal life has already been a present reality and a present event as the border between past, present and future fades in Jesus Christ."[84] The resurrection of Jesus Christ constitutes our salvation objectively. Thanks to this salvific event, those united with Jesus Christ through faith are endowed with life by the Holy Spirit that reaches beyond their life's limitation. Still the believers continue to live in the time between being already saved but not yet fully redeemed.

As the Redeemer, the Holy Spirit also works together with the Son. In the Easter event, the Son finishes his earthly life and dies for us. However that is not the end of salvation history. On the contrary, it is a new beginning and the Holy Spirit continues to work on this stage. Hunsinger rightly points out that "Barth does not see the Spirit merely as epiphany of an eternal present. Through the proclamation of God's Word, the Spirit acts to make contemporary, to reveal, and to impart the reconciliation wrought and embodied by Jesus Christ – a living salvation that is all-emcompassing,

---

82. *CD* III/2, p. 545.
83. Barth, *The Holy Spirit and the Christian Life*, p. 59.
84. [Unsere Zukunft hat also im Ostergeschehen bereits begonnen. Das ewige Leben ist auch eine gegenwärtige Realität und ein gegenwärtiges Geschehen, weil in Jesus Christus die Grenze zwischen Vergangenheit Gegenwart und Zukuft schwindet.] Hyun-Chul Cho, *Der theologische Zeitbegriff bei Karl Barth* (Erlangen: Th. D. Dissertation, 2000), p. 211.

differentiated and unity in itself."[85] Since the Holy Spirit eternally proceeds from the Father and Son to humanity, the Holy Spirit who raised Jesus from the dead is the same Spirit who brings us the Gospel of Jesus Christ and shapes our lives into his.[86] We should not have the impression that the Son and the Holy Spirit work in different stages of salvation history, as Zizioulas says:

> If the Son dies on the cross, thus succumbing to the bondage of history of historical existence, it is the Spirit that raises him from the dead. The Spirit is the *beyond* history, and when he acts in history he does so in order to bring into history the last days, the *eschaton*.[87]

We must insist that even if the Holy Spirit is the beyond history, he is only beyond the earthly history of Jesus' lifespan, not beyond the entire expression of salvation history. The Holy Spirit does not work as a new agent between God and us in the time between the resurrection and final redemption. The Holy Spirit remains as the Spirit of Jesus Christ. In this sense, Barth argues, "He is not to be regarded, then, as a revelation of independent content, as a new instruction, illumination and stimulation of man that goes beyond Christ, beyond the Word, but in every sense as the instruction, illumination and stimulation of man through the Word and for the Word."[88] Hunsinger argues that for Barth the salvation accomplished on the cross, the consummation toward which this work is moving and the sending of the Spirit through whom the work is contemporized and imparted to us, are not three different events, but three forms of one single event.[89] This "single-event in multiform" interpretation ensures the coherence and continuity of three dimensions of time from our point of

---

85. Hunsinger, "The Mediator of Communion," p. 173.
86. "The Spirit is also conceived as the Spirit of God insofar as the Spirit who leads believers through the Son to the Father is the Spirit who from the beginning energizes God's creation by bringing it to its eschatological fulfilment." See Schwöbel, "Christology and Trinitarian Thought," p. 125.
87. Zizioulas, *Being as Communion*, p. 130.
88. *CD* I/1, pp. 452-3.
89. Cf. Hunsinger, "The Mediator of Communion," pp. 173-9.

view: for us Easter event is a *past* event and the final redemption a *future* event; we live in a time between times, at *present*. However in such an indivisible procession there is no development or novelty in "God for us," since the resurrection of Christ has accomplished our final redemption once for all. There is nothing left to be completed between the first and second *parousia*, although from our temporary stand, the final redemption is yet to come. Comparatively, Buckley's "resurrection-dominant" interpretation over-stresses the "unsurpassable novelty" of the resurrection, thus collapses the time of community into Easter event when he says this:

> Barth's grammatical and ontological claims about the church as 'event' must be read against the background of his *narratio* of Jesus Christ as the judge judged for us and raised by the verdict of the Father. The being (as an event) which the church is, is the being of Jesus Christ as his history 'transition' from resurrection to coming again.[90]

Indeed Jesus' resurrection opens all times for us. As McIntyre says: "That triumph, which happened in the temporal and spatial history of Jesus Christ, in fact showed itself in its totality to be history present for all time to come and for all time past as well."[91] However if we over emphasize the resurrection of Jesus Christ, the first *parousia*, we cannot avoid the first one-sidedness that Barth depicts, i.e., making the pre-temporality prior to the supra-temporality and post-temporality.[92] After all in our temporality the resurrection is a past event, whereas the "time between" is present and the redemption is future. In the first volume of *CD*, Barth even makes an opposite acclamation:

> The New Testament speaks eschatologically when it speaks of man's being called, reconciled, justified, sanctified and redeemed. In speaking thus it speaks really and properly. One

---

90. James J. Buckley, "A Field of Living Fire: Karl Barth on the Spirit and the Church," *Modern Theology* 10: 1 (January 1994): p. 89.
91. McIntyre, *The Shape of Pneumatology*, p. 160.
92. Cf. *Chapter Three*.

has to realize that God is the measure of all that is real and proper, that eternity comes first and then time, and therefore the future comes first and then the present.[93]

In this sense, do we understand Barth's eschatology as a "Theology of Hope"? Not so quickly. In the theology of Pannenberg, that is the case. Pannenberg's teaching on the relationship between the Holy Spirit and time is penetrated by his omnipotent "absolute future." According to him, the future of the Holy Spirit embraces the origin and consummation in such an all-powerful way:

> We can thus to think of the dynamic of the divine Spirit as a working field linked to time and space – to time by the power of the future that gives creatures their own present and duration, and to space by the simultaneity of creatures in their duration. From the standpoint of the creature, origin from the future of the Spirit has the appearance of the past. But the working of the Spirit constantly encounters the creature as its future, which embraces its origin and its possible fulfillment.[94]

Apparently Pannenberg's futurism is similar to Barth's earlier thought. However Pannenberg's future is all-determining, whereas Barth always stresses the balance of the past, present and future in his later works. On Pannenberg's teaching about ontological priority of the future, Watts has an illuminating interpretation:

> Each event which occurs in the present is contingently derived from the possible field of future events. This field of possibility "may be seen as a field of force with a specific temporal structure." The dynamic of the Spirit thus establishes

---

93. *CD* I/1, p. 464. Hunsinger says that this expresses the "ontological priority of eternity." Cf. Hunsinger, *Disruptive Grace*, p. 174.
94. Pannenberg, *Systematic Theology* volume 2, p. 102.

the contingency of all individual events while also giving the processes of natural occurrence reliability and predictability.[95]

Comparatively, although Barth allows a priority to the future dimension, he never makes any strong acclamation that the future may decide the past and the present. In other words, Barth is not a strong futurist from the beginning.[96] As time goes by, Barth's futurist stand is more and more counterbalanced by the coherence of the pre-, supra- and post-temporality. In his later years, Barth confesses his earlier eschatologically dominated theology with regret:

> Even I began with eschatology and ascribed to it a decisive role for theology. I gave the future priority – but over years I was forced to realize that I could not maintain this. The more time passed on, the more I became aware that I could not remain standing where I was. Present and past are equally important for theology if theology allows itself to be oriented by God's time. And theology must not confuse this time with one of the dimensions of the human experience of time.[97]

Barth corrects the one-sidedness of his exposition of over-emphasizing the post-temporality in relation to that of pre-temporality and supra-temporality.[98] To avoid this one-sidedness, we must, once again, see the three dimensions of human time from an eternal angle, i.e., for us the three dimensions are separate, however for God they are three aspects of the one and same event. In this sense Barth points out:

---

95. Watts, *Revelation and the Spirit*, p. 131. Cf. also Christiaan Mostert, *God and the Future*.
96. Cf. Gerhard Sauter, "Why is Karl Barth's Church Dogmatics not a 'Theology of Hope'? Some Observations on Barth's Understanding of Eschatology," trans. Arnold Neufelde-Fast, *SJT* 52: 4 (2000): pp. 407-29.
97. In a dialogue between Barth and Gerhard Sauter in 1968. See Sauter, "Why is Karl Barth's Church Dogmatics not a 'Theology of Hope'?" p. 407.
98. Cf. *Chapter Three* and Sauter, "Why is Karl Barth's Church Dogmatics not a 'Theology of Hope'? " p. 409.

> According to the New Testament, the return of Jesus Christ in the Easter event is not yet as such his return in the Holy Ghost and certainly not his return at the end of the days. Similarly, his return in the Easter event and at the end of the days cannot be dissolved into his return in the Holy Ghost, nor the Easter event and the outpouring of the Holy Spirit into his last coming. In all these we have to do with the one new coming of him who came before.[99]

Actually, the threefold *parousia* of Jesus Christ[100] comes to us *simultaneously* by the power of the Holy Spirit. This is what "the Spirit of Promise" means, as Hunsinger describes:

> Contemporaneity with Christ in the Spirit embraces the full range of the eschatological complexity. Since those to whom the Lord comes have died and risen with him, what this contemporaneity imparts is something accomplished and fulfilled. Since their new reality in him is still hidden, what it imparts is yet to come. Since they actively partake of it by faith, what it imparts is present even now.[101]

In this contemporaneity the end-time power has its impact on us. Nowhere can we escape from God's face since the Spirit brings us into the eschatological life of the finality, thus "the dynamic of the Spirit in creation can be viewed as the anticipatory presence of the coming consummation."[102] What God promises us in eternity is brought to our expectation by the Holy Spirit here and now. God's promise is that through the Holy Spirit the Son will be with us in every age, till the end of time.[103] While the future

---

99. *CD* IV/3, p. 294.
100. Cf. Sauter, "Why is Karl Barth's Church Dogmatics not a 'Theology of Hope'?" p. 407.
101. Hunsinger, *Disruptive Grace*, p. 178. Barth also says that "the Holy Spirit is actually *present*: present in the eschatological sense, present, we will say, as the Spirit of Promise." See Barth, *The Holy Spirit and the Christian Life*, p. 61.
102. Watts, *Revelation and the Spirit*, p. 131.
103. On Barth's eschatological promise, Williams comments: "All that can be said of

cannot be predicted by any person, it only comes to us in divine promise: "Finality and futurity from the Beyond of our existence is the peculiar quality of God's purpose with us, imparting a quality to our redemption, to the resurrection and to eternal life. In the fact that God promises us our resurrection he is present with us."[104] This continues to be the stance of the believers in Christ who, grateful for the final redemption he has brought, look forward to his return in glory. This very expectation is enhanced by the presence of the Holy Spirit who is none other than the Spirit of Jesus, making us leave our sins behind and anticipate forward to his final coming. In this eschatological expectation in the Holy Spirit we have been changed ontologically as well, as Braun observes: "The Holy Spirit is God's end-time power. As the dynamic force in the creation, it vouches for a double purpose: the victory over the power of sin and death and the ground of the hope of the expected, but still hidden new being of the world."[105]

Thus Jüngel depicts the Holy Spirit as "the creative power of renewal"[106] which not only effects the economic Trinity, but also works in the immanent Trinity: "in God's own life the Spirit – as the third person or mode of being of the Trinitarian God – binds the end with the origin in such a way that even at the end of his ways, God is never at an end but is, precisely at the end, the one who begins anew."[107] In other words, the Holy Spirit makes the beginning and the end of God's time penetrate each other, and thus becomes the touching point of the economic Trinity and the immanent Trinity, as well as time and eternity. As Peters puts it:

---

man's relation to God in the Spirit has to do with promise, it is eschatological. If this were not so, God would not remain the Lord, our security would be in ourselves, not in him. The deity of the Spirit, as that of Father and Son, is always to be understood as radical freedom – in this case, the freedom of 'God's future.'" See R. D. Williams, "Barth on the Triune God," in S. W. Sykes eds. *Karl Barth: Studies of His Theological Method* (Oxford: Clarendon Press, 1979), p. 165.

104. Barth, *The Holy Spirit and the Christian Life*, p. 60.
105. [Als dynamische Kraft in der Schöpfung ist er (sc. der Heilige Geist) Gottes endzeitliche Macht, die beides verbürgt: den Sieg über die Macht der Sünder und der Todes und den Grund der Hoffnung auf das erwartete, aber noch verborgene neue Sein der Welt.] Dietrich Braun, *Arbeiten zu Karl Barth* (Rheinfelden: Schäuble Verlag, 1993), p. 37.
106. Jüngel, "The Emergence of the New," p. 55.
107. Jüngel, "The Emergence of the New," p. 56.

As trinity, God is both eternal and temporal. God is the transcendent and hence eternal source of the created world. God is also immanent to the world as one finite being among other beings, as incarnate in Jesus of Nazareth, as a single objectifiable person in a single temporal-spatial frame of reference. God is also paradoxically immanent and transcendent as the Spirit, which ties times together and which promises the consummate unity of the whole of time in the eschatological kingdom of God.[108]

The work and activities of the Holy Spirit join our time with God's eternity in a concrete way. A close study of the eschatological movement of the Spirit in Barth may show that the future does not come to us in an ideal way, but as a promise of the complete redemption that will be effected concretely not only in the new creation and the resurrection, but also in our ordinary life here and now. For Barth, the future is a powerful dimension of the "already" of the end time of God that has invaded the present. As Jüngel puts it:

> The future opened up by the Holy Spirit is not empty but instead concretely and sharply contoured by the person of Jesus Christ. ... The Spirit of God, powerfully present in proclamation and confession, implements the fact that God in Jesus Christ has *reached* this, his goal. The Spirit of God, through his inexpressible groaning, makes us understand that we have not yet reached that goal; that God then will still come with his goal. Thus the Spirit with his gifts enters into the moved and moving state of anticipation of faith, in which we for our part oriented to the future out of which God is coming.[109]

---

108. Ted Peters, *God as Trinity: Relationality and Temporality in Divine Life* (Louisville: Westminster/John Knox Press, 1993), p. 171.
109. Jüngel, *God as the Mystery of the World*, p. 389.

Thus far, it appears that salvation is totally accomplished for us by Jesus Christ (objectively) and the Holy Spirit (subjectively). Both the Son and the Holy Spirit bring the future to us positively and we accept it passively. However, one cannot help asking such questions: Can we really find "us" in Barth's Christology or pneumatology? Does the triune God really need our response in his eternal redemptive plan? Actually both Bouillard and Rosato charge Barth for the lacking of human cooperation and human freedom in salvation history.[110] Rosato argues that, "Barth means to present the being of God as relevant for the entire scope of history; what results, however, is a conception of the Trinity as a closed triangle in a timeless realm, and not as an open circle in which man constantly participates through grace."[111] Within such a closed system, there is no place for human actions. As for the role of the Holy Spirit, Rosato critically comments that since "Barth allows the Spirit himself, God's eternal mediating principle, to become the sole point of contact between God and man in time as well, so that autonomous human actions lose their right to play even a subordinate part in divine-human interaction."[112] Webster calls this the collapse of "*Spiritus Creator* into *Spiritus Redemptor.*"[113]

Rosato's charge will stand or fall on two counts. The first concerns a fact: is there real human cooperation in salvation history? The answer is quite simple since, in Barth, the supporting issues of real human response enabled by the Holy Spirit are too many to be quoted.[114] Further, although Barth allows real human experience in salvation history, he does not give it a prior position – and for a good reason: no real human experience can be counted as "real" from an eschatological view. In other words, from a temporal view, our experience is "real"; from an eternal view, it is unreal, abstract and easy to collapse into nothingness. As Dalferth reminds us:

---

110. Cf. Henri Bouillard, *Karl Barth III: Parole de Dieu et Existence Humaine* (Paris: Aubier, 1957), p. 291; Rosato, *The Spirit as Lord*, pp. 135-6.
111. Rosato, *The Spirit as Lord*, p. 136. Cf. John Webster, *Barth's Ethics of Reconciliation* (Cambridge: Cambridge University Press, 1995), p. 134.
112. Rosato, *The Spirit as Lord*, p. 139.
113. Webster, *Barth's Ethics of Reconciliation*, p. 134.
114. Cf. *CD* IV/2, p. 361; *CD* IV/4, p. 3, 27. Also Dawson, *The Resurrection in Karl Barth*, pp. 167-8; Webster, *Barth's Ethics of Reconciliation*, pp. 134-5.

> Taken by itself it is nothing but an abstraction of the only concrete reality there is: God's self-realization in the life, death and resurrection of Christ, the foundation of all this in the eternal will of God and its consequences in and for our world. It does not follow from this that what we experience as real is not real or only seems to be so. Rather it is a preliminary, penultimate, abstract reality which as such is in permanent danger of relapsing into non-existence. In short, our world of common experience is an *enhypostatic reality* which exists only in so far as it is incorporated into the concrete reality of God's saving self-realization in Christ.[115]

The second concerns theological logic: in the relation between time and eternity, shall we derive the former from the latter? Or do we derive the latter from the former? Obviously, Rosato derives eternity from time: God's eternity is timeless when it is closed to itself and not open to our history. On the contrary, Barth reminds us again and again that time must be defined in light of eternity and not vice versa. In this paragraph Jüngel illustrates this logic in eschatology very well:

> The eschaton is distinct from everything which occurs in time and from time as the mode of all creaturely occurrences in that it *determines* everything which occurs in time. The eschaton determines whether that which occurs in time will not only pass away in time…or whether it will pass away *eternally*.… The eschaton determines whether that which occurs in time has not merely a temporal future, but rather an eternal future. In this we presuppose that the concept of an *eternal future* is not a mere paradox but rather an indication that there is not only a *temporal succession* of the modes of time, but also an *eternal interpenetration* of the modes of time.[116]

---

115. Dalferth, "Karl Barth's Eschatological Realism," p. 29.
116. Eberhard Jüngel, "The Emergence of the New," in J. B. Webster eds. *Eberhard Jüngel: Theological Essays II*, trans. Arnold Neufeldt-Fast and J. B. Webster (Edinburgh: T&T Clark, 1995), p. 54.

4.2 Conclusion

First, the eschatological promise is literally Christocentric. The future revealed by the Holy Spirit has no other basis than the resurrection of Jesus Christ and the content of our expectation is no other than the consummation of our salvation in the final return of Jesus Christ. Christocentrism does not necessarily lead to Christomonism or the subordination of the Holy Spirit to the Son.[117]

Second, the Holy Spirit as Redeemer cannot be understood apart from the fact that he is also the Creator and Reconciler.[118] The Holy Spirit does not have these three identities alternatively in three different ages. Rather the Spirit is the same Spirit in three different relations between God and human. "Now there are varieties of gifts, but the same Spirit" (1 Cor 12:4). The beginning of time, the time between, and the future the Holy Spirit presents to us, are different gifts from the same eternal concrete Holy Spirit.

Third, the Holy Spirit presents the future consummation of God's salvation to us in our time, linking time and eternity as the Redeemer of the former. In contemporaneity with Christ in the Spirit our time is embraced by end-time, thus our time cannot remain as closed personal history but is construed as open to God's eternity.[119] Our future will not simply die away and result in nothingness, rather, what the Holy Spirit promises is that all our past, present and future will be reunited in God's eschatological presence. In this way our time is penetrated by God's eternity.

---

117. Cf. Webster, *Barth's Ethics of Reconciliation*, pp. 137-8.

118. As Lovin points out: "We cannot know God's spirit with us as a source of hope and promise (the Holy Spirit as Redeemer) except as we also grasp the divine initiative that sets the terms for our lives apart from what we choose and know (the Holy Spirit as Creator) and at the same time overcomes our hostility and resistance to this power which undoes all our attempts to control our lives and to justify ourselves (the Holy Spirit as Reconciler)." See Robin W. Lovin, "Foreword," in *The Holy Spirit and the Christian Life*, p. xv.

119. At the end of Shults and Hollingsworth's book, *The Holy Spirit*, they sketch out three articles for the future pneumatology (all are time-related) and the last one is: "a pneumatology in which the divine Spirit is understood as the promising presence of Eternity to time, constituting the creaturely experience of temporality precisely by calling all things to share in the absolute Beauty of God, invites the exploration of forms of spiritual life in which the opening up of the future is interpreted as pure gift, liberating persons as agents of hope in the world." See F. LeRon Shults and Andrea Hollingsworth, *The Holy Spirit* (Grand Rapids: William B. Eerdmans Publishing Co., 2008), p. 94. Although they may not specifically have Barth in mind, this is exactly the character of Barth's doctrine of time and eternity in light of pneumatology.

CHAPTER 5

Conclusion

Section 1: A Concrete Trinitarian Understanding of Time and Eternity

1.1 Relational in Ontology

From the last three chapters, we may draw the conclusion that Barth takes a relational view[1] of time and eternity. There are no such things as independent human time without God's eternity and divine eternity confined in God himself. If we talk about human time *itself*, we can never approach time as one of the Kantian "things of themselves." For Barth, our past and future only exist in an Augustinian psychological way: the past exists in recollection and the future in anticipation; both recollection and anticipation are incomplete and unreliable, hence are to some extent "unreal." The present is even less real than the past and the future. The present is nothing other than a boundary between the past and the future, hence possesses no duration at all. Our "perception" to the present is also less reliable than our memory and expectation. To sum up, human temporality itself is discontinuous and uncertain. Every moment of our lifespan is not only under

---

1. Barth's relational stand is different from Leibniz's. Leibniz regards time as a relation of "successive order of things." Time has no reality when considered in abstraction from the things that stand in this successive relation (Cf. the subsection about Kant in chapter 1). Barth reminds us that time can be only understood when it is related to God's eternity. Apart from this time-eternity relationship there are no time and no eternity at all.

the threat of nothingness, but also moves toward nothingness.[2] Since our time is nothing by itself, it is impossible to take a substantial stand on it. The reality of human time lies totally in its relationship with God's eternity.

Once human temporality is embraced by God's eternity, like a baby in its mother's arms, its ontological situation changes. From an inside view of temporality, all three dimensions of time are confronted with us anew when they are related to God's eternity. Firstly, our past does not fade and disappear into the abyss for we are delivered from the dead memory of the past.[3] The oblivion of the past has been smoothed by God's eternal renewing power. In God's providence our past not only was real but is real and will be real forever. Secondly, "it is not we who are now but God who is now."[4] Our created time is being sustained and preserved by God now, therefore the present is no longer merely a boundary between the past and the future, rather, it is a turning point which is sincere to the past and ready for the future. Thirdly, our future does not come to us as a series of unpredictable and uncertain events.[5] There is no "not yet" in God's future for he is simultaneous with all times. God's eschatological promise of eternal life constitutes our future and changes our past and present ontologically as well.

From an outside view of our temporality, our limited lifespan is a blessing rather than a curse. We are created in the allotted time and space so there was a time before which we were not and there will be a time after which we shall be no longer. Human life as such desires extension and duration outside of this allotted time. However Barth reminds us that only in this time span which God has allotted to us in his creation, can we confront him and rely on him alone concretely.[6] Otherwise, had we had an infinite life on this earth, we would have been drowned in our everlasting temporality and confined in our self-contained humanity forever, never minding the divinity above us, even uplifting ourselves as gods. That is really a curse.

---

2. This point is made clear especially in the section "Man in His Time" in *CD* III/2, pp. 511-53.
3. Cf. *CD* III/2, pp. 527-32.
4. *CD* III/2, p. 529.
5. Cf. *CD* III/2, pp. 541-50.
6. Cf. *CD* III/2, pp. 553-72.

On the other hand, there is no such a thing as an absolute and isolated divine eternity. According to Barth, a god who is self-contained in his eternity is a pagan god, a god who only dominates and threatens us from above.[7] Thinking of God in such an absolute transcendental way may lead to abstraction and nothingness only. God's immanent side must not be ignored for the God revealed in Jesus Christ is eternally "God for us." Our God is not a God without human partner; his eternity is not a kind of eternity without temporality. Barth sums up God's "eternity for us" thus:

> We have been speaking of a God who is not without man or against him, but for him. He is the God who far from thinking it beneath him made it his glory eternally to elect himself for man and man for himself. He is the eternal self-grounded and self-satisfying majesty, but in the full freedom and sovereignty of his work as Creator, Reconciler and Redeemer addressed wholly to another, to man who cannot do anything for it, who cannot merit the divine address, or correspond to it, but can only receive it as a gift, the gift to which he owes everything.[8]

In conclusion, there are no such things as "time of itself" or "eternity not for us"; there is only a time-eternity continuum in God's salvation history which is initiated, executed and completed by triune God for us. However, our human history by no means collapses into God's eternity, rather, it is created, preserved and fulfilled by God's eternal redemptive plan. In this sense we confirm that in Barth's doctrine of time and eternity, eternal immanent Trinity and temporal economic Trinity are the same concrete eternal-temporal Trinity. Although there are differences between time and eternity, e.g., time's passivity and eternity's positivity; time's finiteness and eternity's infinity; time's humanity and eternity's divinity..., we can still maintain that ontologically time and eternity are a relational pair.

---

7. Cf. *CD* IV/1, p. 112.
8. *CD* III/2, p. 567.

1.2 Trinitarian in Background

That time and eternity must be held together does not mean there is no difference between the two. In this co-existent pair, time is always passive and eternity is always positive; time must be understood in light of eternity and not vice versa.[9] In eternity, the triune God approaches time in a Trinitarian way: in the immanent Trinity, God the Father begets God the Son eternally; God the Holy Spirit proceeds from the Father and the Son eternally. Likewise, in the economic Trinity, God creates us as creatures in the form of time from his eternity; God eternally elects us as his covenant-partners, reconciling our time with his eternity; God eternally sends the Son and the Holy Spirit to our time, achieving the eschatological redemption.[10]

The three persons in Godhead relate themselves to our time in three coherent but distinctive ways. God the Father, eminently the eternal Creator who initiates the deity in eternity, also creates time as our existential form. In our history, God the Creator is also God the Preserver, who sustains our time before our birth, throughout our lifetime and after our death. Nothing is lost in this eternal preservation and only in the time allotted to us we confront God concretely. At the end of all times, the Father creates everything anew by granting the eternal life to his creatures. This eschatological promise is nothing other than God's original good will in his creation.[11]

The Son is eternally begotten by the Father, which means he is coeternal with the Father. He preexists in a concrete way for us. In the due time, he enters our time in humanity. Among the three eternal persons of the Godhead, only the Son becomes history, therefore in him, this very man and very God, the immanent relation of time and eternity consummates. The Father's eternal will is revealed most concretely in the incarnate Son. Both his death and resurrection are also historic events, which open the door of eternity for us in our space and time. By defeating the power of death, the risen Son shows his lordship over time and becomes

---

9. This kind of relationship between time and eternity is made clear in the paragraph about "God is supra-temporal" in *CD* II/1, pp. 623-9.
10. Cf. *CD* II/2, pp. 615-7.
11. Cf. Barth, *The Holy Spirit and the Christian Life*, pp. 59-60.

the "contemporary of all men."[12] This contemporary of all men in all times makes clear that the Son is eternal rather than everlasting.

The Holy Spirit eternally posits himself as the Creator together with the Father and the Son. In eternal Trinity, Jesus Christ is the Creator in an objective way, whereas the Holy Spirit is the Creator eminently in a subjective way. The Holy Spirit also establishes humanity as soul and body and presents himself to our soul, then through the soul to communicate with the body as well. In human history, the Holy Spirit sustains our time in the time between the first and second *parousia* in two ways: by continuously imparting what the Son achieved in his first *parousia* (resurrection) to us, the Holy Spirit reconciles our creaturely time with God's eternal good will in creation; by presenting the future consummation of God's salvation in the Son's second *parousia* to us, the Holy Spirit redeems our time in an eschatological way.

To sum up, in a Trinitarian background, the three persons of the one Godhead reveal divine eternity in our concrete time. All three modes of the holy Trinity are pre-, supra- and post- to human temporality. In this threefold relationship of time and eternity, Barth makes clear that God's eternity is both transcendental and immanent to our time: transcendental because the triune Creator's infinite deity cannot be confused with creature's limited humanity; immanent because God elects us in the Son through the Holy Spirit as his covenant partner.

1.3 Concrete in Character

For Barth, the relationship of time and eternity must be understood in a concrete way. Time, as the form of God's creature (especially the form of human beings), is eternally created, elected and reconciled by the triune God himself. There is no other time outside the triune God. Apart from the eternal concrete God, time is only an abstract concept, even nothingness. For example, Mouroux approaches time and eternity this way:

> Here, through the human mind of the Son of God, the mystery of time and eternity is expressed. They are two realities

---

12. *CD* III/2, p. 440. Cf. also Dawson, *The Resurrection in Karl Barth*, p. 67.

necessarily linked together. They imply and yet exclude each other; they oppose and yet complement each other, they must be viewed together in permanent dialectical action if we wish to account for both. To be sure, we start with time and come to a knowledge of eternity by a process of negation and purification; but, on the other hand, eternity is the foundation and the explanation of time. That is why, since the time of Plotinus and St. Augustine, theologians quite naturally begin a consideration of time with a meditation on eternity.[13]

Although Mouroux refers to the Son of God, nevertheless, we may approach time and eternity only through the Son's "human mind." In that case the negation, purification and meditation are only a development in conceptions. This method can lead us to no other place than to abstraction and nothingness. However, Barth's doctrine of time and eternity itself is also criticized for leading to abstraction. For example, Balthasar charges Barth: "Too much in Barth gives the impression that nothing much really happens in his theology of event and history, because everything has already happened in eternity."[14] Horton seconds the charge by saying that "the actual history is not really decisive: it is the eternal truth of that to which they gave witness. The temporal events in history are simply manifestations of what has decisively taken place already in eternity."[15] These opinions are difficult to maintain due to the concreteness of Barth's relational ontology of the doctrine of time and eternity. Although "the grace of the Lord Jesus Christ, the love of God, and the communion of the Holy Spirit" (2 Cor 13:13) appear irresistible and overwhelming in Barth, he never denies the autonomy of human beings. Instead of being absorbed or cancelled in this time-eternity relationship, the reality of human history is constituted by this relationship, as Macken points out: "Humanity exists in relationship with God, not in isolation. Concretely, that relationship is es-

---

13. Jean Mouroux, *The Mystery of Time*, trans. John Drury (New York-Tournai-Paris-Rome: Desclee Company, 1964), p. 10.
14. Hans Urs von Balthasar, *The Theology of Karl Barth*, trans. Edward T. Oaks (Edinburgh: T & T Clark, 1992), p. 94.
15. Horton, "A Stony Jar," pp. 359-60.

tablished by the call of God who reveals himself in Jesus Christ. Within the framework of that relationship, autonomy can be affirmed."[16] The triune God is eternally "God for us": the Creator is the Creator for the creature; the Reconciler and Redeemer are two mediators (objective and subjective) between God and us. The authenticity of human time, albeit passive, is not nullified by God's eternal positive intention to us.

Section 2:
The Significance of Barth's Contribution

2.1 It transcends the Temporal and Atemporal Debate

Now we have the entire picture of the Trinitarian time-eternity in front of us. At the end, we need to go back to the beginning in order to see what Barth contributes to our understanding of time and eternity.

Most of all, Barth's doctrine transcends the traditional temporal-atemporal dilemma of God's eternity. Since Augustine understands time psychologically and Boethius approaches God's eternity abstractly, they can only get an atemporal picture of God's eternity: God is simultaneous with all times; there is no beginning, duration and end in eternity. This atemporal understanding of eternity excludes God out of time. The difficulty caused by this approach lies in the relationship between God and human: How could a God outside of time interact with human beings? Had there been any communication between them, either human beings would have gone out of their time from inside or God would have entered time from outside. Both ways are impossible according to this atemporal understanding. Any temporal or processional view emphasizes the immanent side God's eternity.[17] God is, it is proposed, not outside of time but inside of it. God's eternity is distinct from time but not separate from it. Eternity in this sense is merely everlasting or endless time. This view may resolve the problem of communication between God and his creature. However

---

16. John Macken, *The Autonomy Theme in the Church Dogmatics: Karl Barth and His Critics* (Cambridge: Cambridge University Press, 1990), p. 181.
17. Cf. Hunsinger, *Disruptive Grace*. p. 188.

the price paid is that it invites changes and innovations in God, which is apparently contradictory with the God in the Holy Scripture.[18] Barth's conception of eternity, according to Hunsinger, "overlaps elements of each while transcending both."[19]

There is no difficulty in understanding how Barth's doctrine transcends the traditional atemporal approach. In chapter 1 we see that the temporal factors of God's eternity become more and more obvious throughout the course of the history of theology. However, we do not have a fully developed Trinitarian understanding of God's eternity until Karl Barth who establishes, on Trinitarian ground, both temporal eternity and eternal time concretely, transcending the temporal-atemporal dilemma in a temporal way. For Barth, God's eternity must be temporal, otherwise it is no more than an abstract speculation. However, Barth accepts Boethius' classical atemporal definition with admiration. What he does with this definition, according to Hunsinger, "is to relocate it within an explicit doctrine of Trinity."[20] This relocation is revolutionary for it changes the conception of eternity reversely, i.e., from timeless to temporal. It is not an abstract omnipresent God who possesses past, present and future simultaneously and perfectly, but a concrete Trinitarian God who embraces our temporality with his eternity. From eternity God creates time for us, sends the Son and the Holy Spirit into our time to reconcile and redeem us from our limited temporality. By positing himself in a threefold relationship with time, i.e., pre-, supra- and post- temporality, God reveals his eternity as temporal.

If so, how does Barth differentiate himself from other interpreters who hold a temporal or processional view on God's eternity? How does he insist on a temporal understanding without recommending development or self-realization in God's perfect divinity? The processional view of eternity,

---

18. "Does God change according to the Bible?" is a highly controversial issue. For the detailed discussion, Cf. John Sanders, *The God Who Risks: A Theology of Divine Providence* (Downers Grove: InterVarsity press, 2007), pp. 72-84; Nicholas Wolterstorff, "Unqualified Divine Temporality," in Gregory G. Ganssle eds. *God & Time: Four Views* (Downers Grove: InterVarsity Press, 2001), 210-3. Both authors think the God in the biblical narrative implicitly or explicitly attains changes. Paul Helm disagrees with them and defends a timeless and changeless God in the Scripture, Cf. Paul Helm, "Divine Timeless Eternity," in *God & Time: Four Views*, p. 46.

19. Hunsinger, *Disruptive Grace*. p. 188.

20. Hunsinger, *Disruptive Grace*. p. 199.

as George Hunsinger points out, regards that God is more fully actualized at the end of this process than at the beginning.[21] But from a Barthian point of view, although "God's being is in becoming," God just moves from perfection to perfection. The redemption and fulfillment of time does not add anything to eternity in order to make it better. Everything is created perfectly in creation; everything is completed in the Easter event; everything is promised to us in the Holy Spirit. From the beginning to the end, the redemption and fulfillment of time is for time's sake, not for eternity's sake. The triune God does not develop himself or become something new in time. That is to say, there is no development of the immanent Trinity in the economic Trinity. Furthermore, owing to eternal God's revelation in time, human time has been bestowed with authenticity and continuity in Jesus Christ through the Holy Spirit. In our time, the past, present and future are not separate like before, instead they penetrate each other since they are united and fulfilled by eternity.

On this issue, Barth is criticized for suggesting a fusion of the beginning and end, or the before and after. It appears that Barth makes the entire salvation history a closed and empty circle: in the beginning, God creates the heavens and the earth; then the Son and the Holy Spirit reconcile and redeem the creature back to the triune God; at the end, God creates the new heavens and the new earth. Thus, both time and eternity appear circular rather than linear. Nothing is really lost in the whole process. Horton accuses Barth that "he is wary of any notion of 'before' and 'after' in relation to the cross and resurrection: so thoroughly is history assimilated to eternity. Revelation, for Barth, occurs in an 'eternal Moment' with no extension in time."[22] Or, in Helm's words, "it is McCormack (and Barth) who countenance a 'before' and 'after' in the discussion: 'before' there is God who is sovereign over his own being, and 'after' there is the God whom he freely decides to be."[23]

---

21. Cf. Hunsinger, *Disruptive Grace*. p. 188. Cf. also Alan G. Padgett, "Eternity as Relative Timelessness," in *God & Time: Four Views*, pp. 95-100.
22. Horton, "A Stony Jar," p. 351.
23. Helm, "Karl Barth and the Visibility of God," in *Engaging with Barth*, p. 285. Cf. also Bruce McCormack, "Christ and the Decree: An Unsettled Question for the Reformed Churches Today," in L. Quigley eds. *Reformed Theology in Contemporary Perspective* (Edinburgh: Rutherford House, 2006), pp. 140-1.

These accusations neglect the temporality of eternity. Certainly from the eternal view, there is no before and after since the past, present and the future are simultaneous in God's sight. Even for the earlier Barthian term – the "eternal now" – there is no before and after since it means that eternity breaks into time. However, from the temporal view, everything has its beginning and end; everyone has his or her birth and death. Although the Son and Holy Spirit confront the created beginning and eschatological end to us here and now, we will not confuse the beginning and end with our lifespan. Actually, they make this mistake through over-emphasizing the supra-temporality dimension of the time – the second one-sidedness warned by Barth.

2.2 It transcends the A-series and B-series Dilemma

Similarly, Barth's doctrine of time and eternity also transcends McTaggart's A-series and B-series dilemma.[24] A-series and B-series are similar to the traditional temporal and timeless perspectives. The A-series of time is the tensed, dynamic view of time, whereas the B-series views time as a static four-dimensional container in which every event in the universe possesses a spatio-temporal slice. It appears paradoxical when we make "a hybrid A-B-theory" statement like "Nixon is apparently both alive and dead at once in the eternal present"; however, if we replace Nixon with Jesus Christ, and state that "Jesus is both alive and dead at once in the eternal present," somehow we may smooth over the absurdity of Schrödinger's cat in McTaggart's paradox. One obvious illustration is in Revelation 5:6 – "I saw a lamb, looking as if it had been slain." Here indeed Jesus shows himself *at once* in a superposition of two states – the Lamb slain and alive. Also we may recall Jesus presenting his deathly body to Thomas in John 20:26-27. Thus, imitating Heidegger, we could say "what is decisive is not to get out of the paradox but to perceive it in a right way."

We human beings begin and cease to live. Our lives are confined within our lifespans. Although many people have had the so-called "near-death experience," we understand it as a middle state of life and death rather than

---

24. For an A-series and B-series analysis of Barth's doctrine of time and eternity, Cf. Dalferth, "Der Mensch in seiner Zeit."

the superposition of the two states. However, when the paradox is looked from a Trinitarian eternal perspective, it cannot remain the same. Let us consider the resurrection of the Son and the outpouring of the Holy Spirit. From an A-series perspective, the resurrection is a future event for Jesus on the cross and a past event for the Holy Spirit on the day of Pentecost. The Son conquers his past death on the cross and opens a new future for us in the Holy Spirit. From a B-series point of view, death on the cross, resurrection and the outpouring of the Holy Spirit are three independent events which locate in their respective spatio-temporal slices. We can calculate the distance between these events in the spatio-temporal continuum but there is no internal connection between them. However, from a Trinitarian view, the mere B-series view cannot stand, for all these three events are parts of God's eternal salvation plan. They happen in a tensed order in time in an A-series sense, and at the same time, they are ET-simultaneous[25] with the Father's eternal will in a B-series sense. In a Trinitarian background, God's eternity is both transcendental and immanent to our time: transcendental because the triune Creator's infinite deity cannot be confused with creature's limited humanity; immanent because God elects us in the Son through the Holy Spirit as his covenant partner.

Therefore, through the resurrection of Jesus Chris and the outpouring of the Holy Spirit, our life and death (of course, Nixon is among us) get connected with triune God's eternity, as evidenced by Galatians 2:12 and 1 Corinthians 15: 20-26. The superposition of Nixon's life and death remains irresolvable from either a mere A-series side or a mere B-series side. Only after both sides have transformed into a concrete Trinitarian time-eternity continuum could the apparent paradox of ET-simultaneity be avoided. That is to say, the A-series and B-series dilemma could be transcended by assigning the B-series-like eternity a total temporal nature through the work of the Son and the Holy Spirit in the concrete salvation history. The A-series-like human time is also reconciled into the triune God's eternity.

---

25. Cf. Padgett, 'Eternity as Relative Timelessness', in Gregory G. Ganssle (ed), *God & Time: Four Views* (Downers Grove: InterVarsity Press, 2001), pp. 100-1.

2.3 It transcends the Absolute and Relative Controversy

When we reflect on Barth's contribution to any scientific understanding of time, we must not exaggerate that Barth's doctrine of time and eternity is a "theory of everything." Compared with Newtonian and Einsteinian theories of time, Barth's doctrine does show some weaknesses. For instance, Barth rarely bothers himself with the nature of time itself. Since time can only be understood in light of God's eternity, there is no such notion as "time in itself" and thus there is no theological necessity of studying the nature of time itself.[26] For similar reasons, Barth often neglects the physical and cosmological dimension of time and confines his discussion of time within human history or individual life. However, if only we keep in mind that our effort in bringing Barth into such a conversation remains tentative, perhaps we may gain some new perspectives on the relationship of time and eternity.

Does Barth have anything to say to Newton and Einstein on the issue of time? As mentioned before, the Newtonian notion of absolute time is no more than a metaphysical speculation which is isolated from any physical motion and measurement. Definitely Barth would admit eternity is absolute in the sense of infinite, but not in the sense of isolation, i.e. there is no limit in God's temporality and God never chooses to live without us.[27] In other words, Newtonian absolute time is something too transcendental, too ideal and too abstract, so its acknowledgement and actualization could only appeal to a God – an abstract God. When we turn to the Barthian approach, by emphasizing both transcendental and immanent relationship between eternity and time, the Newtonian difficulty disappears in this Trinitarian perspective: from an eternal point of view, three coeternal persons of the triune God transcend all human time absolutely; from a temporal point of view, three temporal persons of the triune God interact with our time – a Newtonian temporal container in this sense – in different ways and not conditioned by human time at all.

---

26. Cf. Pannenberg, *Systematic Theology*, volume 1, pp. 405-7.
27. According to Busch, the concept of "absolute time" is rooted theologically in an "absolute" eternity, eternity cut loose from creaturely time. Cf. Busch, *The Great Passion*, p. 268.

In Einstein's theory of relativity, time is intrinsic to the speed of movement and the field of gravity, but relative to the inertial frames. The crucial distinction between Newtonian time and Einsteinian time lies in the question: is there a privileged reference system? If there is one, we can save the notion of Newtonian absolute time and maintain the concept of "present"; if there is no such system, we must choose Einsteinian relative time and embrace a B-theory like universe.[28] In Barthian pre-, supra- and post-temporality, the perspective of the triune God might be such a privileged system since time, energy and movement are all created and sustained by one same God. Whatever the speed of a moving body is (even at the speed of light), whichever reference system it locates, it is ET-simultaneous with God's eternity, for in his eternity the triune God simultaneously possesses all time (of course not in an atemporal way).

Another potential contribution which Barth's doctrine could make for scientific theory of time is that the Trinitarian transcend-immanent temporality may smooth over the atemporal character in both Newtonian and Einsteinian perspectives of time. Although Newton holds to the opinion that absolute time is temporal and dynamic, actually he has to share the same difficulty with those atemporal God advocators. In Einstein's case, the situation is even worse, because in an Einsteinian fixed universe the complete history of the universe is depicted. Every event in this four-dimensional entity is posited as a spacetime slice, thus there is no ontological difference between them at all. Since all events are independent and there is no communion among them, continuity and becoming are beyond imagination. However, in Barth's Trinitarian opinion, although all events in history could be simultaneously present in God's eternity, there are still ontological distinctions among them. Such "highlighted" events as the creation of heavens and earth, the Easter event and the Pentecostal experience etc. are ontologically superior to other ordinary events in human history because they do change our temporality in an absolute way: such historic events make a historic man – Jesus Christ – and the concrete Holy Spirit become the contemporary of all humans and all events in a fixed

---

28. Cf. John Lucas, "The Special Theory and Absolute Simultaneity," in William Lane Craig and Quentin Smith eds. *Einstein, Relativity and Absolute Simultaneity* (London and New York: Routledge, 2008), p. 280.

space-time continuum. Penetrated by the Trinitarian eternity, those discrete space-time slices also become communicable and hence take genuine temporal characteristics, i.e., the past, present and future.

To sum up, we have enough reason to believe that Barth's Trinitarian understanding of time and eternity may also shed some light on our scientific knowledge of time.

Bibliography

Primary Sources

———, *Church Dogmatics*, 13 part volumes, (eds.), G. W. Bromiley and T. F. Torrance, Edinburgh: T & T Clark, 1956-75.

———, *The Epistle to the Romans*, trans. Sir Edwyn Hoskyns, London: Oxford University Press, 1980.

———, *Come Holy Spirit*, trans. Richard Ernst and Honrighausen, New York: Round Table Press, 1939.

———, *The Holy Spirit and the Christian Life*, trans. R. Birch Hoyle, Louisville: Westminster/John Knox Press, 1993.

———, *Dogmatics in Outline*, trans. G. T. Thomson, London: S. C. M. Press, 1949.

———, *The Resurrection of the Dead*, trans. H. J. Stenning, London: Hodder & Stoughton, 1933.

Secondary Sources

Ables, T., "The Grammar of Pneumatology in Barth and Rahner: A Reconsideration," *IJST* 11: 2 (2009): pp. 208-24.

Achtner, W., Kunz, S., and Walter, T., *Dimensions of Time*, trans. Arthur H. Williams, Jr., Grand Rapids and Cambridge: William B. Eerdmans Publishing Company, 2002.

Allais, L., "Kant's One World: Interpreting 'Transcendental Idealism'," *British Journal for the History of Philosophy* 12: 4 (2004): pp. 655 – 84.

Althaus, P., *The Theology of Martin Luther*, trans. Robert C. Schultz, Philadelphia: Fortress Press, 1966.

Ameriks, K., "The Critique of Metaphysics: Kant and Traditional Ontology," in Paul Guyer (eds.), *The Cambridge Companion to Kant*, Cambridge: Cambridge University Press, 1992, pp.249-79.

Anderson, R.S., "Living in the Spirit," in Ray S. Anderson (eds.), *Theological Foundations for Ministry: Selected Readings for a Theology of the Church in Ministry*, Edinburgh: T & T Clark, 1999, pp. 302-29.

Anselm, *Saint Anselm: Basic Writings*, trans. and eds. S.N. Deane, La Salle: Open Court Publishing Company, 1968.

———, On the Harmony of the Foreknowledge, the Predestination and Grace of God with Free Choice, in *Anselm of Canterbury*, vol. 2, trans. and eds. Hopkins and Richardson, London: S. C. M. Press, 1976.

Augustine, *Confessions*, trans. R.S. Pine-Coffin, London: Penguin Books, 1961.

———, *Confessions*, trans. Henry Chadwick, Oxford: Oxford University Press, 1991.

———, *The Trinity*, trans. Edmund Hill, New York: New City Press, 1991.

Balthasar, H.U., *The Theology of Karl Barth*, trans. Edward T. Oaks, Edinburgh: T & T Clark, 1992.

Barbour, I.G., *Religion and Science*, London: S. C. M. Press, 1998.

Bauckham, R. and Hart, T., "The Shape of Time," in David Fergusson and Marcel Sarot (eds.), *The Future as God's Gift*, Edinburgh: T & T Clark, 2000, pp. 41-72.

Berkouwer, G.C., *The Triumph of Grace in the Theology of Karl Barth*, Grand Rapids: Wm. B. Eerdmans, 1956.

Bloesch, D.G., *The Holy Spirit: Works and Gifts*, Downers Grove: InterVarsity press, 2000.

Blumhardt, C.F. and Blumhardt, J.C., *Thy Kingdom Come: A Blumhardt Reader*, eds. Vernard Eller, Farmington: Plough Publishing House, 2007.

Boethius, *The Consolation of Philosophy*, trans. S. J. Tester, Cambridge: Harvard University Press, 1973.

Bouillard, H., *Karl Barth III: Parole de Dieu et Existence Humaine*, Paris: Aubier, 1957.

Bradshaw, T., "Karl Barth on the Trinity: A Family Resemblance," *SJT* 39: 2 (1986): pp. 145-64.

Braun, D., *Arbeiten zu Karl Barth*, Rheinfelden: Schäuble Verlag, 1993.

Bromiley, G.W., *An Introduction to the Theology of Karl Barth*, Grand Rapids: William B. Eerdmans Publishing Co., 1979.

Buckley, J.J., "A Field of Living Fire: Karl Barth on the Spirit and the Church," *Modern Theology* 10: 1 (January 1994): pp. 81-102.

Burgess, A.R., *The Ascension in Karl Barth*, Aldershot: Ashgate, 2004.
Busch, E., *The Great Passion: An Introduction to Karl Barth's Theology*, Grand Rapids: William B. Eerdmans Publishing Co., 2004.
Carnell, E.J., *The Burden of Kierkegaard*, Exeter: The Paternoster Press, 1965.
Caygill, H., *A Kant Dictionary*, Oxford: Blackwell Publishers Ltd, 1995.
Chadwick, H., *Boethius: The Consolations of Music, Logic, Theology, and Philosophy*, Oxford: Clarendon Press, 1981.
Chaning-Pearce, M., *The Terrible Crystal*, New York: Oxford University Press, 1941.
Cho, H.C., *Der theologische Zeitbegriff bei Karl Barth*, Erlangen: Th. D. Dissertation, 2000.
Collins, G.O., *Christology*, New York: Oxford University Press, 1995.
Colwell, J., *Actuality and Provisionality: Eternity and Election in the Theology of Karl Barth*, Edinburgh: Rutherford House Books, 1989.
Cortez, M., "Body, Soul, and (Holy) Spirit: Karl Barth's Theological Framework for Understanding Human Ontology," *IJST* 10:3 (July 2008): pp. 328-45.
Craig, W.L., *Time and Eternity*, Wheaton: Crossway Books, 2001.
———, *The Tensed Theory of Time: A Critical Examination*, Dordrecht: Kluwer Academic Publishers, 2000.
———, "The Special Theory of Relativity and Theories of Divine Eternity," *Faith and Philosophy* 11: 1(Jan 1994): pp. 19-37.
———, "Oaklander on McTaggart and Intrinsic Change," *Analysis* 59: 4 (October 1999): pp. 319-20.
———, "Relativity and the 'Elimination' of Absolute Time," in Peter Øhrstrøm (eds.), *Time, Reality, and Transcendence in Rational Perspective*, Aalborg: Aalborg University Press, 2002, pp. 91-128.
———, "McTaggart's Paradox and the Temporal Solipsism," *Australasian Journal of Philosophy* 79: 1 (March 2003): p. 32-44.
Cross, R., *Duns Scotus on God*, Aldershot: Ashgate Publishing Limited, 2005.
Cullmann, O., *Christ and Time: The Primitive Christian Conception of Time and History*, trans. Floyd V. Filson, Philadelphia: The Westminster Press, 1950.
Curtis, J.M., *Trinity and Time: An Investigation into God's Being and His Relationship with the Created Order, with Special Reference to Karl Barth and Robert W. Jenson*, Edinburgh: Ph D dissertation, 2007.
Dabney, D.L., *Die Kenosis des Geistes: Kontinuität zwischen Schöpfung und Erlösung im Werk des Heiligen Geist*, Neukirchen-Vluyn: Neukirchener, 1997.
Dalferth, I.U., "Der Mensch in seiner Zeit," *Zeitschrift für dialektische Theologie* 16 (2000): pp. 152-80.

———, "Karl Barth's Eschatological Realism," in *Karl Barth: Centenary Essays*, Cambridge: Cambridge University Press, pp. 14-45.
Davies, P., *About Time*, New York: Touchstone, 1996.
———, *God and the New Physics*, London: J. M. Dent & Sons Ltd, 1983.
Dawson, R.D., *The Resurrection in Karl Barth*, Aldershot: Ashgate, 2007.
DeWeese, G.J., *God and the Nature of Time*, Aldershot: Ashgate Publishing Limited, 2004.
Driel, E.C., "Karl Barth on the Eternal Existence of Jesus Christ," *SJT* 60: 1 (2007): pp. 45-61.
Duke, J.O., and Streetman, R.F. (eds.), *Barth and Schleiermacher: Beyond the Impasse?* Philadelphia: Fortress Press, 1988.
Dupre, L., "Of Time and Eternity in Kierkegaard's *Concept of Anxiety*," *Faith and Philosophy* 1: 2 (April 1984): pp. 160-76.
Einstein, A., *Albert Einstein-Michele Besso Correspondence: 1903-1955*, Paris: Herman, 1949.
Eitel, A., "The Resurrection of Jesus Christ: Karl Barth and the Historicization of God's Being ," *IJST* 10: 1 (Jan 2008): pp. 36-53.
Ellis, G.F.R., "Physics in the Real Universe: Time and Space-Time," in Vesselin Petkov (eds.), *Relativity and the Dimensionality of the World*, Dordrecht: Springer, 2007, pp. 49-80.
Evans, G.R., *Anselm and Talking about God*, Oxford: Clarendon Press, 1978.
Evans, C.S., *Kierkegaard's Fragments and Postscript: The Religious Philosophy of Johannes Climacus*, Atlantic Highlands: Humanities Press International, 1983.
Farrow, D., *Ascension and Ecclesia: On the Significance of the Doctrine of the Ascension for Ecclesiology and Christian Cosmology*, Edinburgh: T & T Clark, 1999.
Fagg, L.W., *The Becoming of Time*, Atlanta: Scholars Press, 1995.
Franks, C.A., "The Simplicity of Living God: Aquinas, Barth, and Some Philosophers," *Modern Theology* 21:2 (April 2005): pp. 275-300.
Freyer, T., *Zeit – Kontinuität und Unterbrechung: Studien zu Karl Barth, Wolfhart Pannenberg und Karl Rahner*, Würzburg: Echter, 1993.
Gabriel, A.K., "A Trinitarian Doctrine of Creation?: Considering Barth as a Guide," *McMaster Journal of Theology and Ministry* 6 (2003-2005): pp. 36-48.
Gale, R.M., "Introduction," in Richard M Gale (eds.), *The Philosophy of Time*, London: Macmillan, 1968, pp. 65-85.
———, *The Language of Time*, London: Routledge, 1968.

Gathercole, S., "Pre-existence, and the Freedom of the Son in Creation and Redemption: An Exposition in Dialogue with Robert Jenson," *IJST* 7: 1 (Jan 2005): pp. 38-51.

Giles, K., *The Trinity & Subordinationism*, Downers Grove: InterVarsity Press, 2002.

Gilson, E., *The Christian Philosophy of Saint Augustine*, trans. L.E.M. Lynch, London: Victor Gollancz, 1961.

Gorringe, T.J., *Karl Barth: Against Hegemony*, Oxford: Oxford University Press, 1999.

Greene, B., *The Fabric of the Cosmos: Space, Time, and the Texture of Reality*, New York: Alfred A. Knopf, 2004.

Grier, M., *Kant's Doctrine of Transcendental Illusion*, Cambridge: Cambridge University Press, 2001.

Gunton, C., *The Promise of Trinitarian Theology*, London and New York: T & T Clark, 1991.

———, *The Barth Lectures*, London and New York: T & T Clark, 2007.

———, *Father, Son & Holy Spirit*, London and New York: T & T Clark, 2003.

———, *Yesterday & Today: Study of Continuities of Christology*, London: SPCK, 1997.

———, *Christ and Creation*, Grand Rapids: Wm. B. Eerdmans, 1992.

———, *The One, The Three and The Many: God, Creation and the Culture of Modernity*, Cambridge: Cambridge University Press, 1993.

———, *Becoming and Being*, Oxford: Oxford University Press, 1978.

———, "Barth, The Trinity, and Human Freedom," *Theology Today* 43:3 (Oct 1986): pp. 316-30.

———, "Salvation," in John Webster (eds.), *The Cambridge Companion to Karl Barth*, Cambridge: Cambridge University Press, 2000, pp. 143-58.

———, "Foreword," in *Actuality and Provisionality: Eternity and Election in the Theology of Karl Barth*.

Guretzki, D., *Karl Barth on the Filioque*, Farnham and Burlington: Ashgate Publishing Limited, 2009.

Gutenson, C.E., "Time, Eternity, and Personal Identity," in Joel B. Green (eds.), *What about the Soul? Neuroscience and Christian Anthropology*, Nashville: Abingdon Press, 2004, pp. 117-32.

Guyer, P., "The Transcendental Deduction of the Categories," in Paul Guyer (eds.), *The Cambridge Companion to Kant*, Cambridge: Cambridge University Press, 1992, pp. 123-60.

———, "Introduction," in *The Cambridge Companion to Kant*, pp. 1-25.

———, *Kant and the Claims of Knowledge*, Cambridge: Cambridge University Press, 1987.

Hamerton-Kelly, R.G., *Pre-Existence, Wisdom, and the Son of Man*, Cambridge: Cambridge University Press, 1973.

Harris, C.R.S., *Duns Scotus*, vol. 2, New York: The Humanities Press, 1959.

Hauerwas, S., *Character and the Christian Life: A Study in Theological Ethics*, San Antonio: Trinity University Press, 1975.

Hawking, S., *A Brief History of Time: From the Big Bang to Black Holes*, New York: Bantam Books, 1998.

Helm, P., "Karl Barth and the Visibility of God," in David Gibson and Daniel Strange (eds.), *Engaging with Barth: Contemporary Evangelical Critiques*, Nottingham: Appolos, 2008, pp. 273-99.

———, "Divine Timeless Eternity," in Gregory G. Ganssle (eds.), *God & Time: Four Views*, Downers Grove: InterVarsity Press, 2001, pp. 28-60.

Hendry, G.S., *The Holy Spirit in Christian Theology*, London: S. C. M., 1957.

Hodgson, P.E., "Relativity and Religion: The Abuse of Einstein's Theory," *Zygon* 38: 2 (June 2003): pp. 393-409.

———, "God's Action in the World: The Relevance of Quantum Mechanics," *Zygon* 35:3 (Sep 2000): pp. 505–16.

Holt, D.C., "Timelessness and the Metaphysics of Temporal Existence," *American Philosophical Quarterly* 18: 2 (Apr 1981): pp. 149-56.

Hopkins, J., *A Companion to the Study of St. Anselm*, Minneapolis: University of Minnesota Press, 1972.

Horton, M.S., "A Stony Jar: The Legacy of Karl Barth for Evangelical Theology," in *Engaging with Barth*, pp. 346-81.

Hunsinger G., "The Mediator of Communion: Karl Barth's Doctrine of the Holy Spirit," in George Hunsinger, *Disruptive Grace: Studies in Theology of Karl Barth*, Grand Rapids: William B. Eerdmans Publishing Co., 2000, pp. 148-85.

———, "*Mysterium Trinitatis*: Karl Barth's Conception of Eternity," in *Disruptive Grace*, pp. 186-209.

———, *How to Read Karl Barth*, Oxford: Oxford University Press, 1991.

Jenson, R.W., "Karl Barth," in D. F. Ford (eds.), *The Modern Theologians*, Oxford: Blackwell Publishers Ltd, 1997, pp. 23-49.

———, "You Wonder Where the Spirit Went," *Pro Ecclesia* 2: 3 (1993): pp. 296-304.

———, *Cur Deus Homo? The Election of Jesus Christ in the Theology of Karl Barth*, Heidelberg: Th. D. dissertation, 1959.

———, *God after God: The God of the Past and the God of the Future, Seen in the Work of Karl Barth*, Indianapolis: Bobbs-Merrill, 1969.

———, *Systematic Theology*, Volume 2, New York: Oxford University Press, 1999.

Jüngel, E., *God's Being is in Becoming*, trans. John Webster, Edinburgh: T & T Clark, 2004.

———, "'...keine Menschenlosigkeit Gottes...' Zur Theologie Karl Barths zwischen Theismus und Atheismus, " *Evangelische Theologie* 31 (1971): pp. 376-90.

———, "The Emergence of the New," in J. B. Webster (eds.), *Eberhard Jüngel: Theological Essays II*, trans. Arnold Neufeldt-Fast and J. B. Webster, Edinburgh: T&T Clark, 1995, pp. 35-58.

Kant, I., *Immanuel Kant's Critique of Pure Reason*, trans. Norman Kemp Smith, Houndmills: Macmillan Education LTD, 1933.

Khamara, E.J., "Eternity and Omniscience," *Philosophical Quarterly* 24: 96 (Jul 1974): pp. 204-19.

Kiauka, T., *Zeit und Theologie: Philosophisch-theologische Studien zum Problem "Zeit" Untersucht an Wolfhart Pannenbergs Theologie*, Heldelberg: Ph. D. Dissertation, 2005.

Kierkegaard, S., *The Concept of Anxiety*, trans. Reidar Thomte, Princeton: Princeton University Press, 1980.

———, *The Sickness unto Death*, trans. Howard V. Hong and Edna H. Hong, Princeton: Princeton University Press, 1980.

———, *The Concluding Unscientific Postscript*, trans. David F. Swenson Princeton: Princeton University Press, 1941.

Kirwan, C., *Augustine*, London & New York: Routledge, 1989.

Knight, D.H., *The Theology of John Zizioulas: Personhood and the Church*, Aldershot and Burlington: Ashgate Publishing House, 2007.

Knuuttila, S., "Time and Creation in Augustine," in Eleonore Stump and Norman Kretzmann (eds.), *The Cambridge Companion to Augustine*, Cambridge: Cambridge University Press, 2001, pp. 103-15.

Koester, C., *Hebrews: A New Translation with Introduction and Commentary*, New York: Doubleday, 2001.

Kooi, C.V.D., *As in a Mirror: Calvin and Barth on Knowing God: A Diptych*, trans. Donald Mader, Leiden: Brill, 2005.

Kuhn, T., *The Structure of Scientific Revolutions*, Chicago: The University of Chicago Press, 1962.

Küng, H., *Justification: The Doctrine of Karl Barth and a Catholic Reflection*, trans. Thomas Collins, Edmund E. Tolk and David Granskou, London: Burns & Oates, 1964.

Lameter, C., *Divine Action in the Framework of Scientific Thinking: From Quantum Theory to Divine Action*, Newark: Christianity in 21st Century, 2005.

Lancel, S., *St Augustine*, trans. Antonia Nevill, London: SCM Press, 2002.

Larson, D.H., *Times of the Trinity*, New York: Peter Lang Publishing Inc., 1995.

Leftow, B., "Boethius on Eternity," *History of Philosophy Quarterly* 7: 2 (Apr 1990): pp. 123-42.

―――, *Time and Eternity*, Ithaca and London: Cornell University Press, 1991.

Leibniz, G.W., *The Leibniz-Clarke Correspondence*, eds. H. G. Alexander, Manchester: Manchester University Press, 1956.

Lewis, N., "Space and Time," in Thomas Williams (eds.), *The Cambridge Companion to Duns Scotus*, Cambridge: Cambridge University Press, 2003, pp. 69-99.

Lloyd, G., "Augustine and the 'Problem' of Time," in Gareth B. Matthews (eds.), *The Augustinian Tradition*, Berkeley and Los Angeles: University of California Press, 1999, pp. 39-60.

Lockwood, M., *The Labyrinth of Time: Introducing the Universe*, Oxford: Oxford University Press, 2005.

Lohse, B., *Martin Luther's Theology: Its Historical and Systematic Development*, trans. and eds. Roy A. Harrisville, Minneapolis: Fortress Press, 1999.

Lovin, R.W., "Foreword," in Karl Barth, *The Holy Spirit and the Christian Life*, pp. ix-xx.

Lucas, J.R., *A Treatise on Time and Space*, London: Methuen & Co., 1973.

―――, "A Century of Time," in Jeremy Butterfield (eds.), *The Arguments of Time*, New York: Oxford University Press, 1999, pp. 1-20.

―――, "The Special Theory and Absolute Simultaneity," in William Lane Craig and Quentin Smith (eds.), *Einstein, Relativity and Absolute Simultaneity*, London and New York: Routledge, 2008, pp. 279-90.

Luscombe, P., *Groundwork of Science & Religion*, Peterborough: Epworth Press, 2000.

Macchia, F.D., "The Spirit of God and the Spirit of Life: An Evangelical Respond to Karl Barth's Pneumatology," in Sung Wook Chung (eds.), *Karl Barth and Evangelical Theology: Convergences and Divergences*, Grand Rapids: Baker Academic, 2006, pp.149-71.

Macken, J., *The Autonomy Theme in the Church Dogmatics: Karl Barth and His Critics*, Cambridge: Cambridge University Press, 1990.

Mackintosh, H.R., *Doctrine of the Person of Jesus*, Edinburgh: T & T Clark, 1913.

Malantschuk, G., *Kierkegaard's Thought*, Princeton: Princeton University Press, 1971.

Massie, P., "Time and Contingency in Duns Scotus," *The Saint Anselm Journal* 3: 2 (Spring 2006): pp. 17-31.

Matczak, S.A., *Karl Barth on God: The Knowledge of the Divine Existence*, New York: St. Paul Publications, 1962.

McCormack, B., "Seek God where he may be found: a response to Edwin Chr. van Driel," *SJT* 60: 1 (2007): pp. 62-79.

———, "Grace and Being: The Role of God's Gracious Election in Karl Barth's Theological Ontology," in *The Cambridge Companion to Karl Barth*, pp. 92-110.

———, "Barth's grundsätzliche Chalkedonismus?" *Zeitschrift für Dialektische Theologie* 18 (2002): pp. 138-73.

———, "The Ontological Presuppositions of Barth's Doctrine of the Atonement," in Charles Hill and Frank James III (eds.), *The Glory of the Atonement: Biblical, Theological, and Practical Perspectives*, Downers Grove: InterVarsity Press, 2004, pp. 346-66.

———, *Karl Barth's Critically Realistic Dialectical Theology*, Oxford: Clarendon Press, 1995.

———, "Christ and the Decree: An Unsettled Question for the Reformed Churches Today," in L. Quigley (eds.), *Reformed Theology in Contemporary Perspective*, Edinburgh: Rutherford House, 2006, pp. 124-42.

McCready, D., *He Came down from Heaven*, Downers Grove: InterVarsity Press, 2005.

McIntyre, J., *The Shape of Pneumatology: Studies in the Doctrine of the Holy Spirit* Edinburgh: T&T Clark, 1997.

McGrath, A.E., *Science & Religion: An Introduction*, Oxford: Blackwell Publishers Ltd, 1999.

McTaggart, J.E., "The Unreality of Time," *Mind* 17 (1908): pp. 457-74.

Mellor, D.H., *Real Time*, Cambridge: Cambridge University Press, 1981.

Melnick, A., *Space, Time, and Thought in Kant*, Dordrecht: Kluwer Academic Publishers, 1989.

Molnar, P., "The Trinity and the Freedom of God," *Journal for Christian Theological Research* 8 (2003): pp. 59-66.

———, *Divine Freedom and the Doctrine of the Immanent Trinity*, London and New York: T & T Clark, 2002.

———, *Incarnation and Resurrection: Toward a Contemporary Understanding*, Grand Rapids: Wm. B. Eerdmans, 2007.

Moltmann, J., *Theology of Hope: On the Ground and the Implications of a Christian Eschatology*, trans. James W. Leith, Minneapolis: Fortress Press, 1993.

———, "Theology as Eschatology," in Frederick Herzog (eds.), *The Future of Hope: Theology as Eschatology*, New York: Herder and Herder, 1970, pp. 1-50.

———, *The Coming of God: Christian Eschatology*, trans. Margaret Kohl, Minneapolis: Fortress Press, 1996.

Mosersky, J.M., "Time, Tense and Special Relativity," *International Studies in the Philosophy of Science* 14: 3 (2000): pp. 221-36.

Mostert, C., *God and the Future: Wolfhart Pannenberg's Eschatological Doctrine of God*, London: T & T Clark, 2002.

Mouroux, J., *The Mystery of Time*, trans. John Drury, New York-Tournai-Paris-Rome: Desclee Company, 1964.

Newton, I., *The Principia: Mathematical Principles of Natural Philosophy*, trans. I. Bernard Cohen and Anne Whitman, Berkeley and Los Angeles: University of California Press, 1999.

Norris, C., "Should Philosophers Take Lessons from Quantum Theory?" *Inquiry* 42: 3 (Oct 1999): pp. 311-42.

Oaklander, L.N., *The Ontology of Time*, Amherst: Prometheus Books, 2004.

Oblau, G., *Gotteszeit und Menschenzeit: Eschatologie in der Kirchlichen Dogmatik von Karl Barth*, Düsseldorf: Neukircher Verlag, 1988.

O' Connell, R.J., *St. Augustine's Confessions: the Odyssey of Soul*, New York: Fordham University Press, 1989.

Oh, P.S., *Karl Barth's Trinitarian Theology: A Study in Karl Barth's Analogical Use of the Trinitarian Relation*, London and New York: T & T Clark, 2006.

Osborn, L., "Theology and the New Physics," in Christopher Southgate (eds.), *God, Humanity and the Cosmos*, London & Now York: T & T Clark International, 2005, pp. 119-28.

Padgett, A.G., "Eternity as Relative Timelessness," in *God & Time: Four Views*, pp. 92-110.

Pais, A., *Subtle Is the Lord: The Science and the Life of Albert Einstein*, New York: Oxford University Press, 2005.

Pannenberg, W., "Eternity, Time and Trinitarian God," *Dialog: A Journal of Theology* 39:1 (Spring 2000): pp. 9-14.

———, *Jesus—God and Man*, trans. Lewis L. Wilkins and Duane A. Priebe, Philadelphia: The Westminster Press, 1977.

———, *Systematic Theology*, volume 1, trans. Geoffrey W. Bromiley, Grand Rapids: William B. Eerdmans Publishing Co., 1991.

———, *Systematic Theology*, volume 2, trans. Geoffrey W. Bromiley, Edinburgh: T&T Clark, 1991.

Parsons, C., "The Transcendental Aesthetic," in *The Cambridge Companion to Kant*, pp.62-100.

Parsons, J., "A-Theory for B-Theorists," *The Philosophical Quarterly* 52: 206 (January 2002): pp. 1-20.

Pattison, G., *Kierkegaard and the Crisis of Faith*, London: SPCK, 1997.

Peirce, C.S., "Hypothesis of Space and Time: A Response to Kant," *Transaction of Charles S. Peirce Society* 29:4 (Fall 1993): pp. 637-73.

Peters, T., *God as Trinity: Relationality and Temporality in Divine Life*, Louisville: Westminster/John Knox Press, 1993.

Pike, N., *God and Timelessness*, London: Routledge and Kegan Paul, 1970.

Poidevin, R.L., "Relationism and Temporal Topology: Physics or Metaphysics?" in Robin Le Poidevin and Murray MacBeath (eds.), *The Philosophy of Time*, Oxford: Oxford University Press, 1993, pp. 149-61.

Pranger, M.B., "Time and Narrative in Augustine's Confessions," *Journal of Religion* 81: 3 (Jul 2001): pp. 377-94.

Prior, A.N., *Papers on Time and Tense*, Oxford: Clarendon Press, 1968.

Rahner, K., *The Trinity*, trans. J. Donceel, New York: Crossroad, 1997.

Rea, M.C., "Four-Dimensionalism," in Michael J. Loux and Dean W. Zimmerman (eds.), *The Oxford Handbook of Metaphysics*, New York: Oxford University Press, 2003, pp. 174-6.

Roberts, R.H., "Barth's Doctrine of Time: Its nature and Implications," in S. W. Sykes (eds.), *Karl Barth: Studies of His Theological Method*, Oxford: Clarendon Press, 1979, pp. 88-146.

Rogers, E.F., *After the Spirit: A Constructive Pneumatology from Resources outside the Modern West*, Grand Rapids: William B. Eerdmans Publishing Co., 2005.

———, "The Eclipse of the Spirit in Karl Barth," in John McDowell and Michael Higton (eds.), *Conversing with Barth*, Aldershot: Ashgate, 2002, pp. 173-90.

Rosato, P.J., *The Spirit as Lord: The Pneumatology of Karl Barth*, Edinburgh: T & T Clark, 1981.

Rothenberg, J.F., "Kant and the Problem of Simultaneous Causation," *International Journal of Philosophical Studies* 6: 2 (1998): pp. 167-88.

Rudolph, E., "Gibt es eine Theologie der Zeit?" *Zeitschrift für dialektische Theologie* 16 (2000): pp. 126-33.

Russell, R.J., "Time in Eternity: Special Relativity & Eschatology," *Dialogue: A Journal of Theology* 39: 1 (Spring 2000): pp. 46-55.

———, "Is Nature Creation? Philosophical and Theological Implications of Physics and Cosmology from a Trinitarian Perspective," in Niels Henrik Gregersen, Michael W. S. Parsons and Christoph Wassermann (eds.), *The Concept of Nature in Science and Theology*, Geneva: Labor et Fides, 1997, pp. 94-124.

Sanders, J., *The God Who Risks: A Theology of Divine Providence*, Downers Grove: InterVarsity press, 2007.

Sauter, G., "Why is Karl Barth's Church Dogmatics not a 'Theology of Hope'? Some Observations on Barth's Understanding of Eschatology," trans. Arnold Neufelde-Fast, *SJT* 52: 4 (2000): pp. 407-29.

———, *What Dare We Hope?: Reconsidering Eschatology*, Harrisburg: Trinity Press, 1999.

Schleiermacher, F., *The Christian Faith*, trans. and eds. H. R. Mackintosh and J. S. Stewart, Edinburgh: T. & T. Clark, 1976.

———, *On Religion*, trans. Terrence N. Tice, Richmond: John Knox Press, 1969.

Schlesinger, G.N., *Aspects of Time*, Indianapolis: Hakett, 1980.

Schrödinger, E., "The Present Situation in Quantum Mechanics: A Translation of Schrödinger's 'Cat Paradox' Paper," trans. John D. Trimmer, in John Archibald Wheeler and Kenneth Zurek (eds.), *Quantum Theory and Measurement*, Princeton: Princeton University Press, 1983, pp. 152-67.

Schwöbel, C., *God: Action and Revelation*, Kampen: Kok Pharos, 1992.

———, "Wolfhart Pannenberg," in D. F. Ford (eds.), *The Modern Theologians*, Oxford: Blackwell Publishers Ltd, 1997, pp. 257-92.

———, "Christology and Trinitarian Thought," in Christoph Schwöbel (eds.), *Trinitarian Theology Today*, Edinburgh: T & T Clark, 1995, pp. 113-46.

Scotus, D., *God and Creatures: The Quodlibetal Questions*, trans. F. Alluntis and A. B. Wolter, Princeton: Princeton University Press, 1975.

Scruton, R., *Kant*, Oxford: Oxford University Press, 1982.

Seager, W., "The reality of Now," *International Studies in Philosophy of Science* 13: 1 (1999): pp. 69-82.

Sedgwick, S., "Hegel on Kant's Antinomies and Distinction between General and Transcendental Logic," *Monist* 74: 3 (Jul 91): pp. 403-21.

Shakespeare, S., *Kierkegaard, Language and the Reality of God*, Aldershot: Ashgate, 2001.

Sherman, R., *The Shift to Modernity*, New York: T & T Clark, 2005.

Sherover, C.M., *Heidegger, Kant and Time*, Lanham: University Press of America, 1988.

Shults, F.L., *Reforming the Doctrine of God*, Grand Rapids: William B. Eerdmans Publishing Co., 2005.

Shults, F.L. and Hollingsworth, A., *The Holy Spirit*, Grand Rapids: William B. Eerdmans Publishing Co., 2008.

Slaatte, H.A., *Time and Its End*, New York: Vantage Press, 1962.

———, *A Re-Appraisal of Kierkegaard*, Lanham: University Press of America, 1995.

Sorabji, R., *Time, Creation and the Continuum*, London: Gerald Duckworth & Co. Ltd., 1983.

Stump, E., and Kretzmann, N., "Eternity," *The Journal of Philosophy* 78: 8 (August 1981): pp. 429-58.

Swinburne, R., "Cosmic Simultaneity," in *Einstein, Relativity and Absolute Simultaneity*, pp. 244-61.

Sylwanowicz, M., *Contingent Causality & the Foundations of Duns Scotus' Metaphysics*, Leiden: E. J. Brill, 1996.

Tanner, K., "Creation and Providence," in *The Cambridge Companion to Karl Barth*, pp. 111-26.

Taylor, M., *Kierkegaard's Pseudonymous Authorship: A Study of Time and the Self*, Princeton: Princeton University Press, 1975.

Teller, P., "The Ins and Outs of Counterfactual Switching," *Nous* 35: 3 (Sep 2001): pp. 365-93.

Thompson, J., "Jüngel on Barth," in John Webster (eds.), *The Possibilities of Theology: Studies in the Theology of Eberhard Jüngel*, Edinburgh: T & T Clark, 1994, pp. 143-89.

———, *The Holy Spirit in the Theology of Karl Barth*, Allison Park: Pickwick Publication, 1991.

———, *Christ in Perspective: Christological Perspectives in the Theology of Karl Barth*, Edinburgh: The Saint Andrew Press, 1978.

Thomson, J.J., "McTaggart on Time," *Philosophical Perspectives* 15 (2001), pp. 229-52.
Tooley, M., "A Defense of Absolute Simultaneity," in *Einstein, Relativity and Absolute Simultaneity*, pp. 229-43.
Torrance, A.J., *Persons in Communion: An Essay on Trinitarian Description and Human Participation*, Edinburgh: T & T Clark, 1996.
Torrance, T.F., *Space, Time and Incarnation*, London: Oxford University Press, 1969.
———, *Space, Time and Resurrection*, Edinburgh: T & T Clark, 1976.
———, *Karl Barth: An Introduction to His Early Theology, 1910-1931*, London: S. C. M., 1962.
———, "The Ground and Grammar of Theology," in Alister McGrath (eds.), *The Christian Theology Reader*, Oxford: Blackwell, 1995, pp. 85-8.
Torretti, R., "On Relativity, Time Reckoning and the Topology of Time Series," in *The Arguments of Time*, pp. 65-82.
Trowitzsch, M., *Karl Barth heute*, Göttingen: Vandenhoeck & Ruprecht, 2007.
———, "Die Zeit Jesu Christi. Bemerkungen zum Zeitverständnis Karl Barth, " *Zeitschrift für dialektische Theologie* 16 (2000): pp. 134-51.
Vondey, W., "The Holy Spirit and Time in Contemporary Catholic and Protestant Theology," *SJT* 58: 4 (2005): pp. 393-409.
Watkin, J., *Kierkegaard*, London: Geoffrey Chapman, 1997.
Watts, G.J., *Revelation and the Spirit: A Comparative Study of the Relationship between the Doctrine of Revelation and Pneumatology in the Theology of Eberhard Jüngel and of Wolfhart Pannenberg*, Milton Keynes: Paternoster, 2005.
Weber, O., *Karl Barth's Church Dogmatics*, trans. Arthur C. Cochrane, London: Lutterworth Press, 1953.
Webster, J., *Eberhard Jüngel: An Introduction to His Theology*, Cambridge: Cambridge University Press, 1986.
———, *Barth's Ethics of Reconciliation*, Cambridge: Cambridge University Press, 1995.
———, "Introducing Barth," in *The Cambridge Companion to Karl Barth*, pp. 1-16.
———, "Trinity and Creation," *IJST* 12: 1 (Jan 2010): pp. 4-19.
Weinrich, M., *Kirche glauben*, Wuppertal: Foedus, 1998.
Welker, M., "God's Eternity, God's Temporality, and Trinitarian Theology," *Theology Today* 55 (1998): pp. 317-28.

Westphal, J., "The Retrenchability of 'the Present'," *Analysis* 62: 1 (Jan 2002): pp. 4-10.
Weyl, H., *Philosophy of Mathematics and Natural Science*, Princeton: Princeton University Press, 1949.
Whitehouse, W.A., "Karl Barth on 'The Work of Creation': A Reading of *Church Dogmatics*, III/1," in Niger Biggar (eds.), *Reckoning with Barth: Essays in Commemoration of the Centenary of Karl Barth's Birth*, London: Mowbrays, 1988, pp. 43-57.
Williams, G.J., "Karl Barth and the Doctrine of the Atonement," in *Engaging with Barth*, pp. 232-72.
Williams, R.D., "Barth on the Triune God," in *Karl Barth: Studies of His Theological Method*, pp. 147-93.
Williams, R.R., *Schleiermacher the Theologian*, Philadelphia: Fortress Press, 1978.
Willis, R.E., *The Ethics of Karl Barth*, Leiden: E. J. Brill, 1971.
Wolterstorff, N., "Unqualified Divine Temporality," in *God & Time: Four Views*, pp. 187-213.
Wyschogrod, M., *Kierkegaard and Heidegger: The Ontology of Existence*, London: Routledge & Kegan Paul LTD, 1954.
Zizioulas, J.D., *Being as Communion: Studies in Personhood and the Church*, Crestwood: St. Vladimir's Seminary Press, 1985.

Langham Literature and its imprints are a ministry of Langham Partnership.

Langham Partnership is a global fellowship working in pursuit of the vision God entrusted to its founder John Stott –

> *to facilitate the growth of the church in maturity and Christ-likeness through raising the standards of biblical preaching and teaching.*

Our vision is to see churches equipped for mission and growing to maturity in Christ through the ministry of pastors and leaders who believe, teach and live by the Word of God.

Our mission is to strengthen the ministry of the Word of God through:
- nurturing national movements for training in biblical preaching
- multiplying the creation and distribution of evangelical literature
- strengthening the theological training of pastors and leaders by qualified evangelical teachers

Our ministry

Langham Preaching partners with national leaders to nurture indigenous biblical preaching movements for pastors and lay preachers all around the world. With the support of a team of trainers from many countries, a multi-level programme of seminars provides practical training, and is followed by a programme for training local facilitators. Local preachers' groups and national and regional networks ensure continuity and ongoing development, seeking to build vigorous movements committed to Bible exposition.

Langham Literature provides majority world pastors, scholars and seminary libraries with evangelical books and electronic resources through grants, discounts and distribution. The programme also fosters the creation of indigenous evangelical books for pastors in many languages, through training workshops for writers and editors, sponsored writing, translation, strengthening local evangelical publishing houses, and investment in major regional literature projects, such as one volume Bible commentaries like *The Africa Bible Commentary*.

Langham Scholars provides financial support for evangelical doctoral students from the majority world so that, when they return home, they may train pastors and other Christian leaders with sound, biblical and theological teaching. This programme equips those who equip others. Langham Scholars also works in partnership with majority world seminaries in strengthening evangelical theological education. A growing number of Langham Scholars study in high quality doctoral programmes in the majority world itself. As well as teaching the next generation of pastors, graduated Langham Scholars exercise significant influence through their writing and leadership.

To learn more about Langham Partnership and the work we do visit **langham.org**

www.ingramcontent.com/pod-product-compliance
Lightning Source LLC
Chambersburg PA
CBHW051540230426
43669CB00015B/2667